ON COMPUTER SYSTEMS AND TELECOMMUNICATIONS

Video training courses are available on the subjects of these books in the
James Martin ADVANCED TECHNOLOGY LIBRARY from Deltak Inc.,
1220 Kensington Road, Oak Brook, Ill. 60521 (Tel: 312-920-0700).

TEX	PRINCIPLES OF DISTRIBUTED PROCESSING	INTRODUCTION TO TELEPROCESSING	TELEMATIC SOCIETY
N OF PUTER UES	COMPUTER NETWORKS AND DISTRIBUTED PROCESSING	INTRODUCTION TO COMPUTER NETWORKS	TELE-COMMUNICATIONS AND THE COMPUTER (second edition)
MING IME YSTEMS	DESIGN AND STRATEGY FOR DISTRIBUTED PROCESSING	TELEPROCESSING NETWORK ORGANIZATION	COMMUNICATIONS SATELLITE SYSTEMS
OF IME SYSTEMS	DISTRIBUTED FILE AND DATA-BASE DESIGN	SYSTEMS ANALYSIS FOR DATA TRANSMISSION	FUTURE DEVELOPMENTS IN TELE-COMMUNICATIONS (second edition)
On Systems	Books On Distributed Processing	Books On Teleprocessing	Books On Telecommunications

AN INFORMATION
SYSTEMS
MANIFESTO

A *James Martin* BOOK

AN INFO
SY
MAN

Library of Congress Cataloging in Publication Data

Martin, James
  An information systems manifesto.

  Includes bibliographical references and index.
  1. Electronic data processing. 2. Management
information systems.   I. Title.
QA76.M327   1984   658.4′0388   83-17730
ISBN 0-13-464769-6

An Information Systems Manifesto
James Martin

Editorial/production supervision by Linda Mihatov
Front matter design by Judith A. Matz
Jacket design by Diane Saxe
Manufacturing buyer: Gordon Osbourne

Printed in the United States of America

10 9 8 7 6 5 4 3 2 1

ISBN 0-13-464769-6

PRENTICE-HALL INTERNATIONAL, INC., *London*
PRENTICE-HALL OF AUSTRALIA PTY. LIMITED, *Sydney*
EDITORA PRENTICE-HALL DO BRASIL, LTDA., *Rio de Janeiro*
PRENTICE-HALL CANADA INC., *Toronto*
PRENTICE-HALL OF INDIA PRIVATE LIMITED, *New Delhi*
PRENTICE-HALL OF JAPAN, INC., *Tokyo*
PRENTICE-HALL OF SOUTHEAST ASIA PTE. LTD., *Singapore*
WHITEHALL BOOKS LIMITED, *Wellington, New Zealand*

85 004308

TO CORINTHIA

MANIFESTO: A public declaration of intentions, objectives, opinions, or motives

Random House Dictionary

BOOK STRUCTURE

PART I   **THE PRESENT**

Chapters 1-13
This main part of the book describes
actions that should be taken *now* to
improve the use of computers in an
organization.

PART II   **THE FUTURE**

Chapters 14-17
This second part of the book describes
entrepreneurial opportunities, the threat
of Japanese advanced development, and
government strategies.

APPENDICES

CONTENTS

Table of boxes

PREFACE

An Information Systems Manifesto is designed to provide end users, DP staff, and senior and top management with a strategy and direction on how to change and manage the dramatically changing environment of information systems and data processing.

The revolution described in information systems is already in progress. Yet many corporations ignore it or fail to recognize the impact it will have on their organizations. The intent of this book is to provide people with the information they need to direct and implement these changes successfully.

The first part of the book describes the actions that should be taken to improve the use of computers, for example, by placing the end user firmly in the driver's seat and automating the process of automation.

The second part of the book examines the future, particularly the Japanese and the essential need for entrepreneurs.

This book was designed for a wide cross-section of people and is uncluttered with technical details.

It should be mandatory reading for *everyone* concerned with information systems and data processing.

James Martin

ACKNOWLEDGMENTS

The author wishes to thank the consultants of James Martin Associates for their contributions to this book and their ongoing work in implementing the methodologies it describes.

A steam engine built 44½ feet high, weighing 600 tons. Today an electric motor delivering the same power is 11 inches in diameter.

PART I THE PRESENT

1 THE CRISIS IN DATA PROCESSING

PROBLEMS WITH DATA PROCESSING   The power of today's computing technology is not being used as it should be in most enterprises. Data processing is bogged down in problems. Managers are not receiving the information they require from their systems. Many decisions that should be made with the aid of computers are in fact being made with hand methods or inadequate information. Systems are so difficult to change that they often inhibit the implementation of new and important procedures that managers require. Computer users are increasingly hostile to DP but feel powerless to prevent the problems.

Among top-level managers there is often a sense of anger that they are spending so much on computing and yet seem unable to change procedures or obtain the information they need. In one corporation with an expensive and elegant worldwide computer network the chief executive complained bitterly to the author that for years he had been asking for daily or even weekly figures and cash balances but seemed no closer to obtaining these or other information he needed.

Box 1.1 lists the problems of computing as seen by users and management.

Failure to use computers effectively is serious on a national scale because it affects most aspects of productivity. This affects inflation and the ability to compete overseas.

The computer is the most flexible machine invented, capable of a staggering diversity of applications. It is rapidly dropping in cost and its power needs to be used as fully as possible for improving the efficiency of organizations. The problem lies not in the machine itself, but in the methods we use for creating applications. The traditional "application development life cycle" is slow and rigid. Its methods have been cast into concrete in many organizations with standards and procedures. But in many ways the procedures are not working.

BOX 1.1 Problems of computing as seen by users and management

- Users cannot obtain applications when they want them. There is often a delay of years.
- It is difficult or impossible to obtain changes that managers need in a reasonable amount of time.
- The programs have errors in them or sometimes do not work.
- Systems delivered often do not match the true user requirements.
- It is difficult to understand DP and communicate precise requirements.
- Specifications, on which users have to sign off, are difficult to check and are usually full of inconsistencies, omissions, and errors.
- Systems cost much more to develop and to maintain than anticipated.
- Because of the long time required to obtain results, the most important decision-support systems are never implemented. The support is needed more quickly than the time needed to create the programs.

This inability to use computers effectively should be regarded as a major organizational problem to which solutions *must* be found. The problem has reached crisis proportions. The solutions now exist but many organizations are not using them except in isolated pockets. They require new software, new procedures, and new management structures.

As we look at the history of technology we can observe certain times when a major break with the past methods had to occur. In computing, a set of application development methods has been accepted and slowly refined for more than two decades. We have now reached a point when these are inhibiting the most effective uses of computers. Fundamentally different methods are needed and are coming into use. Unfortunately, many data-processing (DP) organizations are not adopting the new methods rapidly enough.

Steam engines made earlier this century were beautifully intricate machines. They had many polished brass sliding rods, levers, and cams. Engineers had invented elaborate mechanisms for extracting a fraction of a percent of extra performance. They lovingly tuned the mechanisms and held technical symposia on steam engines long after the electric motor was in use.

Comparing relational data-base facilities with some of the old data-base management systems, or comparing new-architecture small computers with the old large operating systems, seems like comparing an electric motor with steam engines. The architects and maintainers of the old software are making elaborate additions which give only minor improvements, when a switch to fundamentally better mechanisms is needed.

The difference between COBOL development and the creation of applications with the new application generators is even more dramatic. Many powerful new techniques exist today for creating software and building applications, but a million programmers and analysts around the world have not heard about them. Amazingly, in Europe steam engine designers were still refining these machines 50 years after the electric motor had been invented.

In Victorian factories with steam engines there were overhead shafts 100 feet long with large pulleys and belts going down to each machine tool. With electric power each machine tool could have its own motor. But the shafts remained in many factories long after their usefulness had ended. New tools often need fundamentally new methodologies. The procedures manuals in DP are often referred to as the "Bible" of DP development and it is heresy to disobey the Bible even when new software and techniques render it hopelessly obsolete. The old DP procedures, like the steam-driven shaft and pulleys, can preclude the freedom that is necessary to move flexibly with the new methods.

The *Random House Dictionary* defines a *manifesto* as "a public declaration of intentions, objectives, opinions or motives." In organizations everywhere a manifesto is needed from top management giving their policy for information systems. This can be translated into manifestos concerning the fundamental changes in DP techniques and productivity and how they should be handled by DP executives, systems analysts, and programmers.

APPLICATION
BACKLOG

In most well-managed corporations the demand for new applications is rising faster than DP can supply them. The imbalance between demand and supply is steadily becoming worse.

Because of this, the backlog of needed applications is growing. Most corporations now have a backlog of from two to four years. One bank executive informed us that the bank's backlog was seven years. This situation is likely to become worse as machines drop in cost, unless better methods of creating applications are found.

The long backlog and inability of computer departments to respond to end users' needs quickly is very frustrating for the users. In many cases the users have felt that they cannot wait and have obtained their own departmental minicomputer or desktop computers.

INVISIBLE
BACKLOG

Even though today's application backlogs are so long, they reveal only part of the story. When the documented backlog is several years (as it is in most installations), the end users do not even consider making requests for many of the applications they need. There is thus an *invisible backlog*.

The invisible backlog cannot easily be measured. Its size is indicated in those installations where end users have acquired a capability to develop their own application quickly. Such examples indicate that the *invisible* backlog is often larger than the *documented* backlog.

The Sloan Business School set out to measure the invisible application backlog in typical Fortune 500 corporations [1]. It concluded that in the organizations it studied the invisible backlog was about 168% of the formal measured backlog. In other words, many users need applications that would be valuable to them, but do not ask for them because of the DP overload.

THE NEED FOR VASTLY IMPROVED PRODUCTIVITY

At the same time that computers are rapidly dropping in cost, end users are becoming much more knowledgeable about how they could use computers. The more computers drop in cost, the more end users are challenged to put them to work to improve their decision-making capabilities and power, eliminate time-wasting paperwork, improve productivity, and build more advanced facilities.

End users from scientists to clerks are improving their ideas about how computers could help them. The problem is that until recently most of these ideas could not be implemented because the processes of systems analysis and programming were too slow. Most application programs are individually designed and hand coded with very slow methods. Imagine the automobile industry if cars were still built by craftsmen with hand tools. Most organizations have not yet reached the era of the Model T Ford in application creation.

Application programming is one of the most labor-intensive jobs known. We are now beginning to perceive how to automate much of it. To do so we need better software, which is becoming available. We also need new approaches to the analysis and design of information systems. To change the building of cars from individual hand tooling to mass production needed a substantial infrastructure to be put into place. The same is true with the move to information system automation. The necessary infrastructure takes some time to build and costs money (although not much compared with the maintenance and hand crafting of earlier systems).

MAINTENANCE

The problems of DP and software development are made worse by the maintenance problem. The term "maintenance" is used to refer to the rewriting of old programs to make them accommodate new requirements or make them work with changed system resources. Reprogramming is often needed because separately developed programs do not fit together, or interface problems exist when data are passed from one system to another. A needed change in one program sets off a whole chain reaction of changes that have to be made to other programs.

Maintenance, if not consciously minimized, tends to rise as the numbers of programs grow. The interactions among programs grow roughly as the square of the number of programs, unless deliberately controlled.

The growing maintenance burden greatly worsens the application backlog. In many organizations, and often those moving fastest into on-line and interactive systems, the ratio of maintenance activity to new application development has reached 80%. Large corporations often have some systems or application areas where 100% of the programmer effort is spent on maintenance.

The U.S. Department of Defense is now spending $2 billion per year on maintenance of software and has estimated that this will rise to $16 billion by the end of the 1980s. The United States as a whole is spending about $20 billion per year on maintenance. It would be catastrophic if this rose by the same ratio. There are tools and techniques with which much of the maintenance cost can be avoided [2].

It is often thought by systems analysts that existing programs that work well can be left alone. In reality, the data such programs create or use are needed by other applications and are almost always needed in a slightly different form, unless thorough logical data-base analysis has been performed.

The maintenance mess has become a nightmare in some large corporations. It is alarming to reflect what it would be like 20 years from now if more and more applications and systems were added with conventional methodologies.

Under appropriate conditions, microbes can multiply exponentially like today's computers. But if they multiply when shut in an enclosed laboratory dish, they eventually drown in their own excrement. One top DP executive compared this to his maintenance problems. New growth, he said, was being stifled by the use of old COBOL and PL/1 systems. If new techniques were not widely accepted and used, the programming team would eventually drown in its own maintenance.

STRATEGIC INFORMATION

One of the most important aspects of computing is getting the right information to the right people at the right time. Information is increasingly being regarded as a *strategic* resource, not merely a resource for routine data processing. Strategic uses of information are greatly affecting the profits of corporations and increasingly will become a key to corporate survival. Box 1.2 lists examples of corporations achieving major financial advantage from *strategic* uses of computerized data.

In spite of the fact that computerized data exists, many executives are *not* obtaining the information from computers that could help them most. To achieve this requires tools and techniques for information resource management which are better than those in common use. Chapter 6 describes them.

BOX 1.2   Examples of corporations achieving major financial advantage from strategic (as opposed to routine) uses of computerized data

- *American Airlines* gained major competitive advantage by using a detailed data base of their customer travel information to restructure fares after deregulation. They and United gained market share by allowing travel agents to obtain information at terminals from their automated reservation systems.

- *Fidelity Brokerage Services Inc.* moved up to the number 2 position in the discount brokerage business, passing several much larger rivals, by using information which allowed a broker with a terminal to execute stock trades less expensively (and more quickly) than from most competing firms.

- *Sears* employs computerized information on its 40 million retail customers to reach targeted groups such as appliance buyers, gardeners, mothers-to-be, and to provide marketing for its insurance, brokerage, and real-estate subsidiaries.

- *Deere & Co.* built a data base showing dimensions and characteristics of its 300,000 parts. This enables engineers to search for existing parts rather than design or buy new ones, and shaved $9 million in two years off the cost of new parts and processes [3].

- *Xerox* cut manufacturing costs in its copier division by 18% in three years by strategic uses of information which changed materials handling and inventory control practices. Xerox exchanges quality control information with suppliers to eliminate the expensive inspection of incoming parts. It gives suppliers its master manufacturing schedule so that they can ship parts at precisely the time Xerox needs them to keep inventories lean [3].

- *Equitable Life* created a computer-assisted underwriting system for use at client sites permitting annual renewal analysis for policies based on historical data. The system recommended changes in premium rates based on underwriting objectives and experience. Nearly 100 underwriters used the system daily. Its objective was to provide them with the decision-making skills of a top actuary [4].

- *Massachusetts Mutual* lured many new clients by offering a money-saving payment plan based on calculating rates for large customers on a daily, rather than monthly, basis. This helped turn a loss of $32 million in two years into a profit of $6 million [3].

- *A manufacturer of small armaments* implemented a control system that enabled it to adapt production to a volatile marketplace by using information engineering methods. Production and inventory costs were cut by 21%.

BOX 1.2 *(Continued)*

- *The Santa Fe railroad* improved revenue ton miles/employee hour (a basic measure of railroad productivity) by 28% in four years with the help of a new relational data-base system with extensive user involvement.

- *Owens–Corning Fiberglass* used information from research and development to generate data on the energy efficiency of a wide variety of house designs. It uses energy-efficiency ratings of new building designs as a sales tool for builders who buy Owens–Corning insulation, like car salespeople use miles-per-gallon ratings.

DECISION SUPPORT SYSTEMS   There are all manner of decisions being made every day in an organization by managers high and low. Most of these decisions need information—the best information possible. Often, complex data need techniques which clarify them for the user. Calculations need to be done with the data. These are often repetitive calculations exploring what would happen if certain circumstances occur.

A large chemical company conducted a survey to identify its most critical decision makers, those whose decisions cause the largest financial swing. In some cases the difference between good and bad decision making of *one person* resulted in several million dollars per year profit or loss: for example, the transfer of funds among the world currencies, or the purchase of massively used chemicals. The company identified 100 of its biggest-money decision makers and studied their methods. It concluded that *none* of them were using computers to assist with their decisions. All would be likely to have made better decisions with computer assistance.

In many cases a complex decision is unpredictable and needs to be made urgently. Often unpredictable, urgent decisions need a vast amount of computing. The question may arise, for example, whether a complex purchase should be made, or a new production facility designed, or what strategy should be adopted in a takeover bid. For this important type of computing it is totally impractical to wait because of the application backlog. Immediate programming is needed. It is completely impractical to employ the traditional procedures for application development because these would require a delay of many months while specifications were written and approved, and then slow programming and testing.

Because of the slowness of the traditional development cycle, computers are not being used for many of their most important potential applications. Many such applications have a short life—a decision has to be made *now* and the need for it will be gone in a few weeks' time.

It is the view of some computer manufacturers that in five years' time more than half of the computer expenditures in efficient corporations will be for decision-support systems (in the broadest sense of this term). Such systems will need a substantial infrastructure of data bases and computer networks, which, in turn, need careful planning.

The portfolio of applications awaiting development has changed with time. In the 1960s most applications were routine batch processing such as payroll and invoicing runs. In the 1970s most applications were also routine but often on-line transaction-driven systems. In the late 1980s the most important class of application will probably be decision-support systems. Most of the routine processing will have been done (although it will usually require maintenance).

TYPES OF MANAGEMENT SYSTEMS

The Sloan School study breaks down the applications requested by user management into four types [1] :

- **Monitor**: Routine systems that monitor daily transactions and produce standard reports on a fixed schedule
- **Exception**: Systems that produce predefined reports about predefined exception conditions
- **Inquiry**: Systems that provide flexible inquiry capability, enabling users to design and change their own reports when they wish
- **Analysis**: Systems that provide powerful means of analyzing the data in data bases in order to support decision making (e.g. optimization, modeling, "what-if?" questions, simulation, and statistics)

The study indicated that the ratios of these applications was approximately the same in the invisible backlog as it was in the declared backlog, but substantially different from the installed mix of applications. User management are asking for *six* times as many *analysis* systems, *three* times as many *query* systems, and *twice* as many *exception* systems as are currently installed. Professor Alloway, who conducted the study, projects the future demand as:

- 12 times as many *analysis* systems as currently installed
- 4 times as many *query* systems
- 1.5 times as many *exception systems*
- $\frac{1}{4}$ the number of *monitor* systems

The analysis and query categories are *demand* systems, which cannot generally be prespecified. They need to satisfy the need for information *when it arises,* and when the users see the information they are likely to change their requirements.

In these categories it is vital to bypass the traditional systems analysis stages of writing specification documents. The application needs to be created by methods that are much quicker and more flexible.

Finding or analyzing the requisite information is usually an iterative process. It is common to hear an executive say, "I don't know what I want, but I'll recognize it when I see it." The data in different records may be associated in different ways, often on a trial-and-error basis. The decision maker says: "Let's try a different cut at the data." The decision makers often want the data immediately, including the ones who say, "I don't know what I want but. . . ."

When managers are provided with preplanned listings of data it is a common sight to see them scanning the data and using a pocket calculator, trying, often with inadequate success, to make estimates or create information not provided. Such users should be able to browse in large data systems, extract the information they need, put it into palatable forms, do calculations on it, plot the results, and create charts and reports. Languages with which end users can perform these activities are now excellent.

THE FALLACY OF PROGRESSIVE SUMMARIZATION

Data processing often tries to serve the needs of managers with summaries of data. The higher the level of management, the greater the degree of aggregation or summary. In fact, high-level managers often have questions more subtle or complex than those which can be answered by the preplanned summaries. It is because managers' needs are different that they are seen inadequately manipulating with pocket calculators the data they are given.

What they really need is the ability to have questions relating to the data answered *when they arise.* They need to be able to access, or have assistants who can access, all of the relevant data, summarize it, do calculations with it, ask "what-if?" questions, and so on.

High-level managers certainly need summaries. They need an essence distilling from the unwieldy mass of data, but that essence is likely to be different as different problems and needs arise, and sometimes these needs require a detailed examination of portions of the data.

These different patterns of user needs require a different approach to the DP development. The attempt to meet such needs with structured analysis and structured COBOL is doomed to failure. Instead, corporations need appropriate data systems establishing, often much more flexible than traditional data-base systems. The raw data in an enterprise can be identified independently of specific applications and can be made available for analysis in unanticipated ways with the powerful new languages. The user query and analysis process will often be ad hoc and trial-and-error.

Box 1.3 describes typical characteristics of decision support systems.

BOX 1.3 Characteristics of decision-support systems

Immediacy

The information is often needed quickly to support an urgent management decision. There is no time for the traditional systems analysis specification cycle.

Often Unanticipatable

While some decision needs can be anticipated, many arise which are unforeseen crisis decisions: "What is the effect of a sudden vendor strike?" "How will the price increase affect the cash flow?"

Existing Data Types

While the decision need may be unanticipatable, the data types have usually existed long before and can be stored in data systems for future extraction and analysis.

Unstructured Processes

Whereas processes for routine operations can be highly structured, processes for decision support often cannot be. One question often leads the decision maker to another in an iterative fashion.

Structured Data

The data have properties independent of how they are used, which enable them to be structured ready for use in unanticipated ways.

BOX 1.3 *(Continued)*

Flexible Data Use

The decision maker sometimes says: "I don't know what I want, but I'll recognize it when I see it." He is often investigating complex situations with multiple interrelated factors. A flexible data system is needed so that different data from different normalized records can be freely associated (as in a relational data base).

Short Life

Many applications are once-only, or have a short life. Some applications may be found useful enough to be cataloged for repetitive use.

Speed

Speed may be more important than completeness. Approximate results before a decision is made are more valuable than exact results after it has been made.

Personal

Decision makers often have personal styles and needs. A program created for one person is often not usable by a different decision maker.

Non-DP-Trained Users

The users are usually not trained in DP. They often do not use a keyboard for any other purpose.

Busy Users

The users are often busy, handling a wide diversity of situations in a day. They are usually too short of time to learn complex languages and would rapidly forget mnemonics. Highly user-friendly dialogue structures are needed.

Noncurrent Data

Most decision support does not need data that are current up-to-the-second. Usually, an extraction of yesterday's or last week's data suffice. Many decisions need historical or time-series data so that trends and changing data relationships can be examined. Man-

(Continued)

BOX 1.3 *(Continued)*

agement often learn from the past and relate it to the current situation.

Calculations

Decision makers need an easy means of expressing calculations which they can apply to the data. Often they modify the calculations in an iterative fashion.

Spreadsheets

Intelligent spreadsheets form a valuable tool, permitting calculations to be automatically performed numerous times.

"What-If?" Questions

Many decisions are better made if multiple "what-if?" questions are posed. This can often be done simply by changing certain data values and calculating the effects with intelligent spreadsheets (like Visicale, Lotus 1-2-3, etc.). Users may create their own versions of the data with "what-if?" modifications made to the data.

Tools

Various tools are needed for analyzing data, such as regression analysis, time-series analysis, linear programming, or algorithms for minimizing cost, time, or other variables. Such tools need to be packaged for convenient use.

Graphics

Graphics displays provide useful ways of understanding data, using tools, and exploring the potential effects of decisions.

Off-Line Study

Some managers need to print reports of data or analyses for off-line study, for example at home.

Easy Access

The system must be easy to access and constantly available. Any obstacle or inhibitor tends to frustrate and put off the potential user.

BOX 1.3 *(Continued)*

Response Time

Fairly fast on-line response time is needed, so that data can be searched and alternative analyses developed, modified, and compared.

Justification

Tangible numeric justification for decision-support systems is often missing. Cost-benefit studies are often not done. However, the value of better informed decisions is often high, and management's complaints usually relate to the insufficiency of systems rather than to their cost.

All Levels of Management

Decision support systems are needed at all levels of management:

- *Operations management* for tracking and analyzing operational alternatives
- *Tactical management* for developing alternative plans, comparing actual to planned performance, and evaluating sudden opportunities or crises
- *Strategic management* for evaluating strategies in a simulated rather than a real environment

---

SOLUTIONS It is important for general management to understand that solutions exist to the problems discussed above, and that they have been implemented in some corporations. This report discusses them and gives references to more detailed reading matter. The solutions and how they can be implemented is the subject of the author's World Seminars.

The solutions come from several directions. Most of them involve fundamental changes in the software for application development. Instead of programming applications in traditional programming languages, such as

COBOL, FORTRAN, PL/1 or Pascal, we need to move to a higher level of automation. We must automate the job of the programmer so that it can be done much faster. Chapter 2 discusses this.

New types of computer languages are in use which enable developers to achieve results *much* faster than with traditional languages. These are sometimes referred to as fourth-generation languages. With them it is often possible to create a program with a tenth of the number of instructions that COBOL would require, and in less than a tenth of the time. Chapter 8 discusses what an ideal development language requires.

We need much better languages for expressing users' requirements and specifications. These languages need to be as user-friendly as possible and need to be designed so that program code can be generated from them automatically. These are discussed in Chapter 5.

After years of unsuccessful attempts to apply mathematics to programming to create provably correct code, a technique has now emerged that makes this practical and simple for the system creator. Employing techniques that generate guaranteed bug-free code will change much of the future of computing. This is discussed in Chapter 9.

Traditional computer applications have been created by a data processing department. Now, more powerful user-oriented software is permitting users to employ computers directly as a more flexible decision-making tool. It becomes necessary to separate user-driven computing from traditional computing. Different standards and management procedures need to apply to user-driven computing. Chapter 3 discusses this.

The concept of the *information center* is important in managing user-driven computing. This provides a framework for encouraging, training, and helping users to employ computers directly and obtain the information they need for doing their jobs. It also helps to prevent the many problems that arise with uncontrolled user computing. The information center is discussed in Chapter 7.

User-driven computing, automation of programming, provably correct code, decision-support software, and low-cost hardware are powerful DP developments, but they are not enough to provide the information systems necessary for running large organizations unless they are linked to detailed planning of the information resources. A set of disciplines called *information engineering* have evolved to provide the tools and procedures for designing and implementing the information resources that a corporation needs. Information engineering needs the support and understanding of top management. It is discussed in Chapter 6.

The enterprise of the future will have many small computers as well as large data processing centers. Data will reside in many distributed machines. These computers will be connected to networks which will service workstations in most locations. The evolution of these distributed resources needs careful strategic planning, as discussed in Chapter 12.

CULTURAL CHANGES

The solutions to information system problems discussed in Chapters 2 to 13 require major changes in the management of corporate computing. They change the historical life cycle of DP development. This is discussed in Chapter 11.

The manual of standards and procedures in most organizations is obsolete and does not reflect the powerful new directions in computing. It is the cause of, rather than the solution to, DP problems.

The DP methodologies that were appropriate for the 1970 time frame are crippling in the present environment. These methodologies have become bureaucratized. Some DP organizations seem incapable of breaking away from them.

Some organizations that did not develop their own "Bible" of data processing are purchasing "methodologies" from outside vendors. Some of these externally purchased DP standards manuals are hopelessly obsolete. Adherence to them prevents adoption of the new solutions and cripples DP evolution. New methodologies are needed as described in Chapters 2 to 13.

Appendix I lists the many different approaches to improving DP productivity.

A MANIFESTO FOR TOP MANAGEMENT

Most top-level managers in the next 10 years will be in charge of building an electronic enterprise. They need to understand how technology can change their procedures, services, and products. They should ask: who could take their business away from them by using technology more aggressively in new directions?

How can they ensure that the tools exist in their organization for the best decision making, and that computers, networks, and data bases are used in the most effective way? Box 1.4 gives a manifesto for senior management.

There is a revolution taking place in the methodologies of DP. Everybody perceives the revolutionary changes in hardware (personal computers, powerful microchips, distributed systems), but many DP staff have not adapted their organization to the change in methodologies. *Now is the time to change.*

Appendix II gives manifestos for DP executives, systems analysts, and programmers.

BOX 1.4   A Manifesto for senior management

Understand how your organization ought to change as it becomes a fully electronic enterprise. Electronics are changing products, services, fabrication techniques, selling techniques, decision making, flows of information, mechanisms of control, and management structures.

Understand that a revolution is taking place in DP but that many DP departments are not moving fast enough to the higher-productivity techniques. There is often psychological or political resistance to the new methods, which management needs to overcome. Ensure that *your* organization is migrating away from slow methods and can respond rapidly to information needs by using fourth-generation languages, information center techniques, flexible data bases, and the maximum automation of the DP function as described in this book.

Ensure that decision makers at all levels have the tools they need for making the best possible decisions. Ensure that the necessary information resources are available to them. To achieve this, ensure that information engineering has been done throughout the enterprise.

Information engineering needs top-down management of information resources, thorough data modeling and strategic planning of networks. These essential aspects of managing a computerized corporation have often failed because of organizational and political factors. They have been managed at too low a level. Top management must understand the need for them and ensure that an appropriate information infrastructure is built.

2 THE AUTOMATION OF AUTOMATION

INTRODUCTION As computers continue to drop in cost, increase in power, and spread in vast quantities, it is essential to be able to develop applications with far less manpower. We need vast increases in the productivity of application creation. This will be achieved by the use of application packages and by automating, where possible, the jobs of the programmer and systems analyst—the automation of automation.

DP staff and computer users need to be searching for automated tools and techniques with which manual design can be speeded up and programming can be avoided. Much software of this type exists, but too often it is not being used where it should be. DP staff are often unaware of the software that could help them. Programmers and analysts have automated many people's jobs but are remarkably reluctant to automate their own!

MEAT MACHINES Our human brain is good at some tasks and bad at others. The computer is good at certain tasks that the brain does badly. The challenge of computing is to forge a creative partnership using the best of both.

The electronic machine is fast and absolutely precise. It executes its instructions unerringly. Our meat machine of a brain is slow and usually is not precise. It cannot do long, meticulous logic operations without making mistakes. Fortunately, it has some remarkable properties. It can invent, conceptualize, demand improvements, create visions. The human being can write music, start wars, build cities, create art, fall in love, go to the moon, colonize the solar system, but cannot write COBOL or Ada code that is guaranteed to be bug-free.

Many of the tasks that DP professionals do are tasks that are unsuited to our meat-machine brain. They need the precision of an electronic machine. Human beings create program specifications that are full of inconsistencies and vagueness. A computer should be helping people to create specifications and checking them at each step for consistency. It should not be a human job to write programs from the specifications because people cannot do that well. A computer should generate the code needed. When people want to make changes, as they frequently do, they have real problems if they attempt to change the code. A seemingly innocent change has ramifications that a person may not perceive, which can cause a chain reaction of errors.

If the programs needed are large, we are in even more trouble because we need many people to work together on them. When human beings try to interact at the level of meticulous detail needed, there are all manner of communication errors. When one person makes a change it affects the work of the others, but often the subtle interconnection is not perceived. Meat machines do not communicate with precision.

The end user perceives the meat machines in the DP department to be a problem but does not know what to do about it. A major part of the problem is that they are so slow; they often take two years to produce results and they do not start for a long time because of the backlog. It is rather like communicating with a development team on another solar system, where the signals take years to get there and back.

Today there is much that can be automated in the creating of specifications and the generating of programs. We have report generators, application generators, tools for creating data bases, tools for using data bases, computer-aided design of specifications, and software for creating code from specifications. Chapter 8 describes features needed in DP development facilities. Chapter 9 describes a tool for building precise and rigorous specifications and automatically converting them into code that is guaranteed bug-free.

Tools exist for the automation of all programming, not just commercial DP systems. The tools differ greatly in their nature.

It is a subtle blow to the dignity of a professional to hear that a major part of what he is paid for can be automated. Subconsciously, he wants to disbelieve it and finds all manner of arguments for opposing the automation. Because of this we find new graduates adopting the new techniques faster than experienced professionals.

It is the job of management, including non-DP management, to understand that more automated tools exist, to make a buyer's judgment of them, and to make sure that they are put to work rapidly and effectively wherever they can solve problems and improve the bottom line.

QUANTUM LEAPS   Computing hardware has progressed through a number of steps which dramatically changed its capability—the coming of magnetic tape in the 1950s, the coming of discs in the 1960s, the coming of terminals and data transmission, the spread of distributed processing, and the arrival of the microcomputer. Computer industry observers have sometimes lamented that there have not been revolutions of equivalent power in software. We are now beginning to see dramatic changes in software, equivalent in their importance to the coming of discs or terminals.

One might dread to reflect what the computer world might be like in 10 years' time if we did *not* have dramatic breakthroughs in software. Computing power is plunging down in cost. Big machines are becoming bigger. Small machines are springing up like mushrooms. Numerous machines are being interconnected into computer networks.

IBM has commented that in a few years there will be one computer for every 10 employees in the United States. There cannot be one professional programmer for every 10 employees. Today there is one programmer for about every 300 employees.

The VHSIC program of the U.S. Department of Defense is creating a microprocessor on a chip the power of a large mainframe of ten years ago. Such chips will become mass-producible like newsprint. Future computers need to be fundamentally re-architected so that they can take advantage of such microelectronics. They will have large numbers of microprocessors operating in parallel. Amdahl is creating chips the size of wafers with 100 times the circuitry of conventional chips.

The Japanese have described a fifth generation of computers with which they hope to wrest computer industry dominance away from the United States. They have described a highly parallel mainframe with 10,000 processors capable of executing a combined instruction rate of 10 billion instructions per second, and operating with fundamentally different software.

Any way that we assess the future of the computer industry, computing power will vastly outstrip that of today. But the number of professional programmers will increase only slowly. Somehow or other one programmer must support a vast increase in processor power.

In the next 10 years, computers, on average, will increase in speed by a factor of 10 or more. If the most advanced goals of the Japanese and others are realized, the increase could be 1000 or so, this large number being made possible by highly parallel architectures incorporating many processors which are cheaply mass-produced. As computers plunge in cost, many more will be sold. The number of applications in today's data processing centers is growing by 45% per year, according to an IBM survey. Ten years' growth at 45% multiplies the number of applications by 41. At the same time the number of installations is growing greatly because of small cheap mainframes, minicomputers, and desktop machines.

Most estimates of future computing power indicate that the *productivity of application development needs to increase by two orders of magnitude* in the next 10 years.

There is no shadow of doubt that we are going to see a spectacular growth in the quantity and power of computers. We *must* achieve a quantum leap in software creation in order to be able to use the hardware we can mass-produce.

INSUFFICIENT IMPROVEMENTS FROM STRUCTURED TECHNIQUES The main hope for improving programming productivity in the 1970s was *structured techniques.* We now can survey extensive experience with the techniques advocated by Yourdon, Constantine, Gane and Sarson, Michael Jackson, and others. Research into the impact of these techniques shows that there are few installations where the move to structured programming *by itself* has given an overall programming productivity increase of greater than 25% [1]. Usually, it is less. Structured analysis as commonly practiced usually takes longer than conventional systems analysis (albeit for good reason). It is clear that much better techniques are both possible and essential as computers continue to plunge in cost.

The effectiveness of the move to conventional structured techniques is addressed in extensive research done by T. C. Jones [1]. He divides programming productivity improvements into four ranges and discusses what techniques have achieved improvements within these ranges.

1. Methods that may yield up to a 25% improvement

2. Methods that may yield a 25 to 50% improvement

3. Methods that may yield a 50 to 75% improvement

4. Methods that may yield more than a 75% improvement

1. Improving Productivity up to 25%

Most of the success stories and firm evidence of productivity improvement with conventional languages lie in this range.

Often the baseline for comparison is programs that are unstructured, designed in a bottom-up fashion, with no formal reviews or inspections prior to testing, and no use of interactive methods. If this is the starting point, almost any step toward structured techniques or interactive development will give results. These results are rarely more than a 25% improvement (if there is no change in language and no move to programmers of greater talent).

Small programs written by individual programmers benefit from interactive methods [2]. Large programs needing multiple programmers benefit from the better discipline of structured methods [3,4] and from inspections [5].

In one installation the author studied, a much heralded move to interactive programming actually lowered the overall programmer productivity because the programmers made more mistakes. They seemed to be less able to contemplate their code carefully when entering it on a screen than when using off-line coding sheets.

2. Improving Productivity by 25 to 50%

Achieving more than a 25% improvement is more difficult because programming is so labor-intensive. Real people in real life, Jones concludes, cannot move a great deal faster than they already do. To achieve more than 25% improvement requires techniques that replace human effort in some way.

Jones concludes: "It can almost definitely be stated that no *single technique* by itself can improve productivity at the 50% level for programs larger than trivial ones," except for a change in programming language.

Jones states that there are a few success stories at the 35 to 40% improvement level. Sometimes these related to an unusually backward installation, so that the improvement looked better than it perhaps should have.

3. Improving Productivity by 50 to 75%

Jones concludes that there are only two general ways to achieve programming productivity gains that approach 75%:

(*a*) Search out those programmers and analysts who have exceptionally high personal achievement. There are a few isolated stories of abnormally high productivity, such as the programming of the *New York Times* information system (87,000 instructions in one year by three people: Harlan Mills, Terry Baker, and an assistant who checked the code). This is a productivity four or five times higher than the norm. It is sometimes quoted as a triumph of structured programming, which it is, but it is more a triumph of selecting brilliant individuals and giving them the fullest support. An IBM executive with the project in his area said: "Baker was supported in a way similar to a great surgeon in an operating room" [6].

The best programmers need to be paid more than average ones. But the increase in results can far exceed the increase in pay. The salary histogram is not nearly as elongated as the productivity histogram, so it pays to seek out programmers of exceptional productivity and avoid the others.

(*b*) Use program generators, very-high-level languages, shared systems, or other forms of program *acquisition* in place of program *development.*

4. High Productivity Gains

In stark contrast to the surveys of programmer productivity improvement are the results that have been achieved with data-base user languages, report generators, graphics packages, and application generators. With these, productivity improvements of over 1000% are not uncommon [7].

Some of them can generate only certain well-defined classes of applications. Code generators are needed that generate much broader ranges of software. The technique described in Chapter 9 can generate any type of software. It is particularly useful with highly complex logic which conventional application generators cannot handle.

AVOIDANCE OF MANUAL TECHNIQUES
There is a major imbalance of supply and demand in computer applications. The way to change productivity is to *avoid* hand coding in languages such as COBOL, FORTRAN, and Ada. DP organizations should be seeking every opportunity to avoid writing such programs. Not only do the so-called structured techniques have too small an effect on productivity, they also have too small an effect on the numbers of errors made.

As long as systems analysts and programmers use *manual* methods they will be restricted to methodologies with which a humble human being can cope. More powerful methodologies will remain academic. They will remain too tedious to be practical unless automated.

It is sometimes a shock for analysts and programmers to automate their own jobs. But only when that is done can computing take off beyond the confines of the human sitting at a pad of paper.

Daniel McCracken tells a parable about a man with an old car who wanted to go from New York to California in a day. He souped up the engine, changed the transmission, and modified the car any way he could to make it faster. He fitted it with superb police radar detectors, but the attempt to make it sufficiently fast was doomed before it began. When told that he could use a different technology to get to California—take a jet—he said "Oh those things! They'll never fly!" Many programmers have the same attitude to application generators.

RIGOROUS SPECIFICATION
The problem with structured techniques as practiced in most installations is that they are still manual techniques. They are refinements of the manual methods that programmers and analysts have always used. As such they improve productivity by a small amount only. We can teach a swimmer to swim faster by improving his technique, but the increase in speed is small compared with giving him a motorboat.

Structured techniques have an important part to play in one type of automation of programming, but in order to do that another problem has to be solved. *Most* structured techniques as currently practiced are not rigorous. Their designs are not computable; in other words, they cannot be converted automatically into executable code. We do now have techniques with which we can draw structured specifications which *are* computable and rigorous. When we employ rigorous techniques to examine the data flow diagrams and structure charts that most analysts use, this reveals how sloppy conventional structured design is. Often the diagrams and structure charts are simply *wrong*. They are clearly not an adequate basis for the automation of programming.

CATEGORIZATION OF DEVELOPMENT SOFTWARE

Automating the job of the programmer depends on having appropriate software tools. New types of software for creating applications have come into existence recently. Figure 2.1 categorizes software which creates applications without conventional programming. Many of the facilities available cover multiple parts of this diagram.

The categorization includes the following:

1. Simple-Query Facilities

These have existed since the earliest disc storage devices. They enable stored records to be printed or displayed in a suitable format.

2. Complex-Query-and-Update Languages

These are data-base user languages which permit the formulation of queries that may relate to multiple records. The queries sometimes invoke complex data-base searching or the *joining* of multiple records. For example "LIST ALL U.S. SHIPS WITHIN 500 MILES OF THE STRAITS OF HOR-

	Suitable for End Users	Suitable for Systems Analysts	Suitable for Professional Programmers
Simple-Query Facilities			
Complex-Query-and-Update Languages			
Report Generators			
Graphics Languages			
Decision-Support Languages			
Application Generators			
Specification Languages			
Very High-Level Programming Languages			
Parameterized Application Packages			
Application Languages			

Figure 2.1 Categorization of facilities for application creation without conventional programming. Many software packages include facilities in more than one of the above categories.

MUZ CARRYING CREWMEMBERS WITH EXPERIENCE IN DESERT COMBAT." Because of the searching and joining, only certain data-base systems are appropriate for on-line use of such languages.

Many data-base user languages now exist. They differ greatly in their syntax and structure. Some are marketed by the vendors of their host database management systems; others are marketed by independent software houses.

Many query languages permit the users to enter and update data as well as query it. With some, users can create their own files.

3. Report Generators

These are facilities for extracting data from a file or data base and formatting it into reports. Good report generators allow substantial arithmetic or logic to be performed on the data before they are displayed or printed.

Some report generators are independent of data-base or query facilities. Others are an extension of data-base query languages. Some are extremely easy and fast to use.

4. Graphics Languages

Graphics terminals are dropping in cost and give a particularly attractive way for certain types of end users to display and manipulate data. Software for interactive graphics is steadily improving. It can enable users to ask for data and specify how they want it charted. They can search files or data bases and chart information according to different criteria. Like report generators, some graphics packages allow considerable arithmetical and logical manipulation of the data.

5. Decision-Support Tools

A very valuable type of language is that designed to help in making decisions. These languages make it easy for a user to build decision-support data bases and perform calculations automatically on data when they are entered. Again the user can explore "what-if?" questions. He can enter formulas for manipulating data, and perform statistical, time-series, and trend analyses. Some decision-support languages are designed for financial or investment analysis, or for business planning. They perform rate-of-return calculations, discounted cash flows, currency conversions, etc. Some are linked to graphics tools.

Languages for ferreting truth from complex data have become a valuable resource in some enterprises. Occasionally the name of such languages is used as a verb. When data need investigating one may hear people say, "Let's RAMIS it." Some languages allow complex models to be built.

Much business decision making can be tackled with relatively simple tools designed for manipulating two-dimensional arrays of data as with VISICALC or LOTUS 1-2-3. Some tools facilitate multidimensional computing on data. Some use a three-dimensional array showing for various "what-if?" propositions a two-dimensional chart such as variables mapped against time periods, thus:

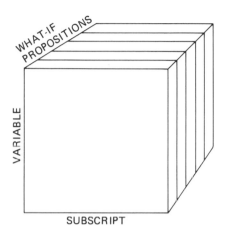

Some decision-support tools, such as EXPRESS, allow multiple subscripts and provide many facilities for manipulating and examining the data. Multiple regression analysis, linear programming, and many types of time-series, marketing, or financial analysis are packaged in these tools, along with graphics facilities for charting, comparing, and setting into perspective complex data.

6. Application Generators

These contain modules that permit an entire application to be generated. The input can be specified, its validation, what action it causes to happen, details of that action, what arithmetic/logic is performed, and what output is created. Most application generators operate with data bases. They can greatly speed up application development.

Some applications can be generated only partially. They require certain operations which the application generator cannot create. It is still useful to employ the generator provided that it has a mechanism which permits the inclusion of routines written in a program language.

Some application generators are designed to create heavy-duty applications in which efficient coding and data accesses are needed because of the high transaction volumes.

7. Computable Specification Languages

We have traditionally written specifications for programs in English. This is generally imprecise, and much human interpretation by the programmer is needed to create the code. Formal ways of representing specifications with high precision now exist. These are called *specification languages*. A few specification languages are *computable* and code can be generated directly from them. Chapter 5 discusses specification languages.

A computable specification language linked to a code generator is, in effect, an application generator (category 5 above). Most application generator software, however, can only generate applications of a certain type. It might generate transaction-based data-base-update applications, for example. A specification language should be broader, with the ability to specify all types of applications. Some notations can specify highly complex logic. A particularly interesting specification language discussed in Chapters 9 and 10, which has the ability to prove mathematically the correctness of the specification, permits its users to correct any faults easily, and to generate bug-free code.

8. Very-High-Level Programming Languages

New programming languages started to emerge in the late 1970s which permit data processing applications to be created much faster. These languages include FOCUS [8], RAMIS [9], NOMAD [10], MANTIS [11], NATURAL [12], IDEAL [13], SAS [14], and many others. Most such languages employ a data-base management system (sometimes their own unique data management system). Many of them employ a report generator, graphics generator, and other generators.

With high-level languages such as NOMAD, the user can say LIST, PLOT, TITLE, INSERT, AVERAGE, SORT, SUM, and so on. He need not describe in code the format of a report. The software selects a reasonable format and the user can adjust it if he wishes.

Most of these languages are relatively easy to use, so that a programmer writes a larger number of lines of code per day than he would with COBOL. The code generally contains far fewer bugs and is easier to debug. In addition, a program can often be written in a tenth of the number of lines of code that COBOL requires. These factors together make it possible to obtain results much faster than the traditional DP programming.

9. Parameterized Application Packages

Packages can be purchased for running certain applications. These pre-programmed packages are increasing in number, diversity, and quality. They often require a considerable amount of tailoring to fit the organization that installs them and are designed with parameters that can be chosen to modify their operation. This parameterization is the key to success in many cases. As the marketplace for packages grows, they tend to be built with a richer set of parameters so that they have wider applicability.

Some application packages are marketed directly to end users so that they can avoid involvement with their DP department. Some are designed to operate on end-user minicomputers.

Figure 2.1 divides these development facilities into those suitable for end users, systems analysts, and professional programmers. To be in the first category the language needs to be very user-friendly. Some corporations today have excellent experience of end users creating their own applications, or at least generating their own reports from data bases set up by DP. Some of the query-and-update languages and report generators are extremely easy for users to employ.

INTEGRATION OF FEATURES

Application generators are not capable of generating all applications. Sometimes they lack the capability to generate particular logic or algorithms which are needed. Too often a generator is rejected for this reason. An important feature of a generator is the capability to associate with it modules of logic written in programming languages. This is sometimes called an *escape* feature. Where possible it is desirable that the user of the generator can also use the language to which the escape is made.

In some cases a programmer is required to handle the *escape* language, but if the programmer is part of the DP department doing conventional coding, the problems with programming backlog affect the use of the generator. Ideally, then, the products in Fig. 2.1 should be integrated as much as possible. The query language should support the creation of reports and graphics, and be the basis of an application generator. A high-level programming language should be available both for use in its own right and for *escape* from the application generator. Many products in existence today do not yet have this degree of integration. Some computer manufacturers and software houses have created *separate* languages for data-base query, report generation, graphics, application generation, and high-level programming. Decision-support tools are often separate from the data-base access facilities, which they ought to be integrated with.

Several query languages and report generators today are suitable for end users, but many application generators at the time of writing are not. Application generators *can* be designed for end users and some good ones exist.

There is *much* software of these types on the market.

PROCEDURAL AND NONPROCEDURAL LANGUAGES

We can classify computer languages as *procedural* and *nonprocedural.* A procedural language tells the computer exactly *how* to do something. A nonprocedural language does not tell it *how,* but tells it *what* is to be accomplished; the compiler or interpreter must then determine *how* to do what is asked for.

Traditional programming languages such as COBOL or PL/1 are *procedural.* Their programmers give precisely detailed instructions for how each action is accomplished. An application generator, whose users fill in forms to tell it what to do, is nonprocedural. The user merely says *what* is to be done and is not concerned with the detailed procedure for *how* it is done.

Most query languages, report generators, graphics packages, and application generators are nonprocedural. Some high-level programming languages are now acquiring nonprocedural capabilities. NOMAD, for example, is a high-level language with which some end users obtain fast results from a computer. Most professionals would call it a programming language because it has IF statements and DO loops. However, results can be obtained with brief nonprocedural statements such as

LIST BY CUSTOMER AVERAGE (INVOICE TOTAL).

This is a complete "program." It leaves the software to decide how the list should be formatted, when to skip pages, number pages, how to sort into CUSTOMER sequence, and how to compute an average.

Some nonprocedural languages employ graphics. The user sees displays on a screen and can fill them in, point to them, and manipulate them. The result is a statement of requirements that the software can translate into executable code. A picture can be worth a thousand words and graphics representations of requirements or logic can be made easy to use and manipulate.

Many nonprocedural languages can handle only limited classes of applications, such as query languages or report generators. A few, however, can handle general applications with highly complex logic.

We can use the analogy of giving instructions to a taxi driver. With a procedural language you have to tell him exactly *how* to proceed: "Drive 500 yards. Turn left. Drive 380 yards. Turn right. Drive to the traffic lights. If the lights are green. . . ." With a nonprocedural language you tell him what you want: "Take me to the Criterion Cinema in Market Street."

We will see nonprocedural languages of greater power emerge. A more powerful semantics for instructing the taxi driver would be: "Take me to 'Star Wars'." The taxi driver has to solve the problem stated. He has to find out where "Star Wars" is playing and take you there.

We would like to have the greatest power we can in computer languages. However, with more powerful semantics there is a danger that the computer might set out to do something more expensive or time consuming than we want. It is possible that "Star Wars" is not playing nearby. The nearest theater showing it is a thousand miles away. The taxi sets off on a long journey. When you eventually say that that was not what you wanted, he says, "I was only obeying orders." Computers obey orders, so we had better make sure that the orders are correct. With powerful languages we need some feedback about the cost or consequences because we tell the machine to proceed.

Nonprocedural languages represent a higher level of automation of the application creation process. It is possible to make them user-friendly so that end users can express their requirements in a simple fashion and a computer can execute them.

Whereas many languages are purely procedural or purely nonprocedural, others combine both of these types of statement. This is generally desirable because nonprocedural operation speeds up and simplifies the use of the language, whereas procedural code extends the range of applications that can be tackled, giving more flexibility of logical manipulation.

Powerful languages of the future will combine procedural code and nonprocedural code or screen interaction.

FOURTH-GENERATION LANGUAGES   The languages in Fig. 2.1 are sometimes called "fourth-generation languages." [15]

The first generation of computer languages was *machine language,* which came into use in the 1940s and 1950s. It used no compilers, assemblers, or interpreters.

The second generation was various forms of *assembler language,* which came into use in the late 1950s. The early assembler languages would optimize the position of program instructions on a drum that stored the programs. Later attempts were made to create machine-independent assembler languages.

The third generation came into use in the 1960s and was called *high-level languages.* Some of these were for scientific work, such as ALGOL and FORTRAN; some were for commercial work, such as COBOL. COBOL became by far the most commonly used computer language. Some languages, such as PL/1, encompassed both scientific and commercial computing. Manufacturer-independent standards were created for these languages, but portability was still sometimes a problem.

Fourth-generation languages were created for two main reasons, first so that nonprogrammers could obtain results from computers, and second in order to greatly speed up the programming process. Some fourth-generation languages are nonprocedural. Some are procedural but results can be obtained with an order-of-magnitude fewer lines of code than with COBOL or ·PL/1. Many contain both procedural and nonprocedural statements. A proliferation of such languages has emerged differing widely in syntax and capability.

There are no standards yet. New language ideas are emerging too rapidly. Most fourth-generation languages link into a data-base system. Some allow users to create their own personal data base. Some create and employ relational data bases because these provide more powerful and flexible user commands then do traditional data bases. Some fourth-generation languages are very user-friendly and users become competent at obtaining useful results after a two-day training course.

With most fourth-generation languages a user does not have to specify how to do everything. Instead, the compiler or interpreter makes intelligent assumptions about what it thinks the user needs. For example, it may automatically select a useful format for a report, put page numbers on it, select chart types for graphics display, put labels on the axes or on column headings, and ask the user in a friendly, understandable fashion when it needs more information. Where a language makes intelligent default assumptions, these assumptions are likely to become steadily *more* intelligent as the language evolves and improves. An assumption behind such languages is that a relatively large amount of computer power can be used for compiling or interpreting.

Now that we have the term "fourth-generation language" it is likely that every new language will be called "fourth generation" by its advertising copywriter. Some new languages, however, have the characteristics more of third-generation languages. For a language to be worth calling "fourth generation," it should have the following characteristics:

1. It is user -friendly.

2. A nonprofessional programmer can obtain results with it.

3. It employs a data-base management system directly.

4. Procedural code requires an order-of-magnitude fewer instructions than COBOL.

5. Nonprocedural code is used where possible.

6. It makes intelligent default assumptions about what the user wants, where possible.

7. It is designed for on-line operation.

8. It enforces or encourages structured code.

9. It is easy to understand and maintain another person's code.

10. Non-DP users can learn a subset of the language in a two-day training course.

11. It is designed for easy debugging.

12. Results can be obtained in an order-of-magnitude less time than with COBOL or PL/1.

Many new languages have these properties, but many also have the characteristic that they cannot create all types of applications. They are not general-purpose. That is a price we may have to pay for the great productivity improvements that fourth-generation languages bring. In this case we have to *select the language to fit the application*. This is repugnant to some programmers and purists. But it is a vitally important fact that languages of limited scope are enabling users to obtain the results they need *fast,* whereas the traditional programming process in COBOL or PL/1 was not.

Figure 2.2 gives examples of fourth-generation languages and categories into which they fall. Their use is discussed further in later chapters.

Fourth-generation languages need data bases, and often make it easy for end users to create their own data bases. If this happens in an uncontrolled fashion, it will be a formula for chaos in data. As the powerful new languages come into widespread use, it is essential to link them into the information engineering or data administration processes discussed in Chapter 6. This linkage may be accomplished with a form of management called *information center* management, discussed in Chapter 7. Chapter 8 describes the properties that an ideal facility for the development of data processing might have.

Given the full costs of specification, coding, debugging, documenting, and maintenance in COBOL or PL/1, management ought to conduct an inquiry whenever a proposal is made to use these to see whether any higher-productivity alternative can be found. COBOL-level blow-by-blow coding should be avoided wherever possible.

SOLVING THE WRONG PROBLEM

Much of today's research into the development process is oriented toward improving the existing methods. Improve programming with the move to structured programming. Improve systems analysis with the move to structured analysis. Formalize the conventional development life cycle and provide tools within it for documentation and review. Add yet more reserved words and instruction types to COBOL. Adapt languages and compilers for better structured programming. Develop the Ada language. And so on.

In a sense these activities (although valuable because such conventional programming will remain) are solving the wrong problem. The important problem is how to migrate from conventional programming and the old development life cycle to development methodologies which are fast, flexible, interactive, and create provably correct code; methodologies in which interactive prototyping replaces formal, voluminous specifications which must be frozen; methodologies which are automated; methodologies with which end users, managers, specifiers, implementers, and maintainers can interact without mismatches.

If a hammer is not achieving much success in fixing screws, the solution is not to obtain a better hammer. The problem is that the wrong methodology is being used. More appropriate tools are now available for software development. In some cases computer executives still want to use the old development life cycle even with the new tools. This is rather like the old hammer enthusiasts driving in screws by hitting them hard with the handle of the screwdriver.

	SUITABLE FOR END USERS* OR DP PROFESSIONALS	VENDOR	SUITABLE FOR DP PROFESSIONALS	VENDOR
DATA-BASE QUERY LANGUAGES	QUERY-BY-EXAMPLE INTELLECT QWICK QWERY EASYTRIEVE ASI/INQUIRY SQL	IBM ARTIFICIAL INTELLIGENCE CACI PANSOPHIC ASI IBM	GIS MARK IV DATATRIEVE	IBM INFORMATICS DEC
INFORMATION RETRIEVAL SYSTEMS	STAIRS CAFS	IBM ICL		
REPORT GENERATORS	NOMAD ADRS II	NCSS IBM	GIS IBM SYSTEM 38 UTILITIES RPG II RPG III MARK IV/REPORTER	IBM IBM VARIOUS IBM INFORMATICS
DECISION-SUPPORT TOOLS	VISICALC MULTIPLAN LOTUS 1-2-3 SYSTEM W EXPRESS	VISICORP MICROSOFT LOTUS COMPUSERVE MANAGEMENT DECISIONS INC.		
APPLICATION GENERATORS	MAPPER RAMIS II FOCUS LINC	UNIVAC MATHEMATICA INC. INFORMATION BUILDERS INC. BURROUGHS	ADF DMS ADMINS 11 USER 11 ADS	IBM IBM ADMINS NORTHCOUNTY CULLINET
VERY HIGH-LEVEL PROGRAMMING LANGUAGES	APL/DI NOMAD AME	IBM NCSS IBM	APL FOCUS MANTIS NATURAL IDEAL ADMINS	IBM INFORMATION BUILDERS INC. CINCOM SOFTWARE AG. ADR ADMIN INC.

Figure 2.2 Examples of the types of fourth-generation languages discussed in this chapter and elsewhere in the book. There are *many* other examples. Note that what is "suitable for end users" and what is not is not always open to debate.

* Items are in this column if end users can learn to use them after a two-day training course.

34

CAUTION　　　　　　　　The success stories with the new languages are spectacular. There is no question that they will change the entire future of DP development. However, there have also been some serious *failures* in attempts to use these languages.

The failures have had multiple causes: lack of training, lack of commitment, lack of controls, the new language not being suited to the application, lack of understanding of how to achieve adequate machine performance.

It requires considerable skill to select fourth-generation languages, ensure that they are suited to a complex application, and ensure that they are used so as to give adequate machine performance. In general a high level of professionalism is needed in guiding the use of the languages. The developers may have a low level of skill in employing a user-friendly language but a high level of skill is needed in controlling the operation.

When we refer to application development without programmers we do not mean application development without professionalism. Much professionalism is needed to raise DP productivity to the levels needed (Appendix I).

Unfortunately, if a new facility is used and the effort fails, the whole subject will have a bad name for years to come. People say "Application generators" or "Product X," "We tried that and it was a dead loss." They do not allow the use of such a facility again as long as they can avoid it.

In the eighteenth century a Swedish engineer, Marten Triewald, installed a steam engine for pumping out a mine in Sweden. This technology had been successful in England. Triewald had trouble with it. The machine, which he called a "fire and air" machine, jerked violently because of an improved seal between the piston and cylinder. The pumps, rods, and bearings were not strong enough for its convulsive hiccups. The engine worked for only two days at a time between repairs. It took two years to pump the mine reasonably dry. By then the machine was a wreck and so was everybody associated with it. The outraged mine owners sued Triewald. Triewald improved his machine, but it was 40 years before anyone in Sweden would try another steam engine, even though many such machines were in successful use in England.

OBSOLETE STANDARDS MANUALS　　　A major reason for resistance is that DP organizations have struggled to achieve discipline in the DP development process. This process used to be an unruly free-for-all until standards and guidelines were established relatively recently. The standards and methods have assumed the force of law, have been taught to all DP staff in an organization, and are regarded as a vital necessity in the crusade against unmet requirements, unmaintainable code, and nonportable programs. The installation standards, religiously adhered to, have frozen the methodologies of large installations at a time when the technology is plunging into new forms.

One typical corporation with many computer installations in many countries spent much effort in the 1970s perfecting a project management system. This incorporates installation standards, guidelines, and some software for project control. It is referred to as the installation "Bible." No DP manager will admit that he does not use it; to do so would be detrimental to his career.

If the Bible is followed literally, it prevents DP managers and analysts from using most of the methods we advocate in this book. It insists that specifications for all applications be created with techniques that are entirely nonrigorous. These are typically 1 inch thick or more, are usually difficult to read, impossible to verify, and full of ambiguities, inconsistencies, errors, and omissions.

The last act of a dying organization is often to write an all-encompassing rule book.

One methodology sold and used in many installations consists of 32 2-inch-thick binders which spell out in detail how to create requirements and specifications. They expand the methods of the 1970s, which are so inadequate, into a bureaucracy that is immensely time consuming, entirely nonrigorous, prevents automation of code generation, and is unchangeable.

Many government departments are still issuing application development directives which lock their vast organizations into conventional procedural techniques which prevent productivity, nonprocedural languages, and rigorous methods.

Most of this bureaucratization of inadequate techniques is accompanied by high-sounding phrases. A paper about the Department of Defense programming directives states, typically, "The theme pervading all of these steps is to elevate software policy, practices, procedure and technology from an artistic discipline to a true engineering discipline." The directives referred to *prevent* the use of rigorous engineering-like methods.

ON ENGINEERING

C. A. R. Hoare, Professor of Computing at Oxford, describes the term "engineering" in connection with such practices as a startling contradiction: "*The attempt to build a discipline of software engineering on such shoddy foundations must surely be doomed, like trying to base chemical engineering on phlogiston theory, or astronomy on the assumption of a flat earth*" [16]. He compares the characteristics of engineering as a profession with "software engineering" as currently practiced.

An engineer has a range of trusted and proven techniques which give a precise result at minimum cost. He recommends these to his customers and insists that only proven techniques be used. He often understands the true needs of his client better than the client himself. A "software engineer" more often concocts his own programs. "How many of them are ignorant of, or prefer to ignore, the known techniques used successfully by others, and embark on some spatchcocked implementation of their own defective invention" [16].

Second, an engineer is vigilant in seeking to reduce the costs and increase the reliability of his product. He realizes that these conflicting objectives require a search for the utmost simplicity. Great engineering is simple engineering. Some programmers, by contrast, revel in complexity, finding excitement in projects of a complexity slightly beyond their comprehension. Hoare comments: "Among manufacturers' software one can find what must be the worst engineering products of the computer age. No wonder it was given away free—and what a very expensive gift it was to the recipient" [16].

Third, an engineer uses designs based on sound mathematical theories and computational techniques. These designs are represented in manuals, textbooks, and codes of practice. The typical programmer makes up new program structures for each problem, with no mathematical basis.

An engineer respects his tools and demands from them the highest precision, convenience, quality, reliability, and the minimum cost. He has developed an intuitive ingrained mastery of his tools so that his mental effort and creativity focuses entirely on the customer's problem. A fatal attraction to the programmer, however, is the complexity of software which would "revolt the instincts of any engineer, but which to the clever programmer masquerades as power and sophistication" [16]. The programmer's use of unreliable operating systems, etc., excuses the unreliability of his own code; their inefficiency excuses the inefficiency of his own programs; their complexity protects his work from close scrutiny by his client or manager.

We might add that an engineer builds prototypes designed to help him understand a problem better. He observes his prototypes in pilot operation and obtains much design feedback which enables him to improve the final product.

We now have tools and techniques that enable us to do true software engineering. We have prototyping tools, tools for generating mathematically precise specifications, tools for generating control structures of minimal complexity which are provably correct, tools for rigorous data-base design, tools for generating code automatically.

SOFTWARE FACTORIES

With these tools we can build software factories. We can give the software specifiers powerful tools which force them to produce rigorous computable specifications, and we can then automate the generation of program code. We can enable developers to obtain and employ the proven mechanisms of other developers. We can interlink mechanisms to build large powerful constructs. We can build user-friendly interfaces to complex systems. We have, working today, the basis for grand-scale engineering of software.

CLINGING TO THE PAST

The big problem that remains is how to convert a multibillion-dollar industry with vast vested interests in earlier techniques. Conventional programming in conventional languages has the momentum of a giant freight train. It will not be deflected from its course quickly.

One of the tragedies of the computer industry today is that while true engineering techniques do *exist* for avoiding slow, ad hoc, error-prone programming, most DP executives are sending their staff to courses that teach variants of the messy, nonrigorous, manual methods. Most textbooks and packaged courses were created in an era before the new power tools were understood. Most industry seminars are disastrously obsolete.

While some DP executives welcome the new era, many are clinging to the past. The author has recently been consulting in a large government agency in which personal computers are completely banned. In one large aerospace corporation, new graduates entering DP have to spend two years as COBOL programmers—that is their path to promotion! All new graduates, eager to learn new techniques, should be made to put the new power tools to work. They should be motivated for maximum productivity. They should be taught to build systems with the fastest, most powerful techniques.

3 THE USER IN THE DRIVER'S SEAT

INTRODUCTION   In the early days of the U.S. car industry production volumes were growing fast and a well-known sociologist was asked to predict the total number of automobiles that would ever be manufactured. After a great deal of study the sociologist reported that no more than 2 million would be manufactured in the life cycle of the car. If the car lasted 10 years on average, the maximum annual production would never exceed 200,000. This conclusion was based on the much-researched figure that no more than 2 million people would be willing to serve as chauffeurs.

Today we might conclude that no more than 2 million people in the United States would be likely to become professional programmers—six times as many programmers as there are today. Computers will increase in speed by a factor of 10 in less than a decade and require, say, six times as much programming. At that time, the sociologist might calculate there could be no more computers than there are today because of lack of programmers.

Henry Ford created not only a mass-production line, but also simplified the controls of his Model T so that most people could drive it. The computer industry will have Model-T-like computers mass-produced with microelectronics. *They will sell in the vast quantities possible only if they can be put to work without professional programmers.* This is now beginning to happen. Application development without programmers is the most important revolution in computing since the invention of the transistor.

ALTERNATIVES TO   There are two types of alternatives to the use of
PROGRAMMERS   professional programmers. First, *systems analysts* can use tools that generate code automatically. A much broader range of tools exists than most analysts realize. Even highly

complex systems can be generated from specifications. Second, *end users* can create the facilities they need directly with easy-to-use software. They can extract the information they need from data bases, generate reports, design spreadsheets for automatic manipulation, create procedures, build their own data bases, perform complex calculations, and analyze complex data.

In the long run it is certain that much computing will be user-driven. Just as technology improved the motor car so that a chauffeur became unnecessary, so technology will improve the user interface to computers so that for many applications the users will not need a computer chauffeur.

In some cases today the user works with an analyst employing the software we described in Chapter 2. The analyst creates a prototype of what the user asks for and together they refine it in a step-by-step fashion to adapt it to the user's needs as well as possible. A characteristic of good application generators and other fourth-generation software is that *the analyst can create a working application faster than he could write a detailed specification for it.* Conventional specification writing therefore disappears for certain types of applications. The program or input from which it is generated *is* the specification.

VARIETIES OF END USERS

Society has endless varieties of people, with enormously differing interests and skills. It is desirable that they should have available a wide variety of techniques for using the computing power that is now spreading to users. A type of dialogue structure that is good for one user is not necessarily good for another. Some end users will learn to program; most will not. Some end users will learn mnemonics; most will not. Some end users will be happy with simple menu selection dialogues; others will find these slow and restricting. For all end user systems human factoring should be a prime consideration. Value in obtaining results is usually more important than machine performance; machine performance is important with high-volume computing.

We sometimes make the mistake of talking about "end users" as though they were all the same. In fact, they are as diverse as all of Shakespeare. While the new software gives one class of users terminal dialogues of extreme simplicity, other software offers the capability to use sophisticated languages. The brightest end users build themselves highly sophisticated tools. Other users are too busy to learn computer techniques and need help at every stage.

We have often made the mistake in the past of assuming that certain classes of users will never operate a terminal or computer. We said "The President will never touch a boob-tube." Now in some cases he is using videotex regularly or employs Lotus 1-2-3 at home and brings the spread sheets, charts, or cash flows he generates to meetings. The difference is made by several factors. First, the tool is extremely easy to use. We use the term "user-friendly"; "user-seductive" is an even better goal. Second, genuinely useful results are obtained quickly. Third, there may be an urgent problem that needs a computer solution.

The role of the end user is being changed by a variety of technologies: microelectronics, desktop computers, minicomputers, cheap terminals, distributed processing, better terminal dialogues, and powerful software.

The personal computer, along with the excellent software packages created for it, is making a huge difference to users' perceptions of computing. Good uses of personal computer tools need to be spread much faster in most organizations.

Today, because of the backlog with low-level application development techniques, many DP managers perceive the pressure from end users for applications as being excessive. *In reality, however, most end users have barely begun to realize the potential of computing for improving how they do their job.*

In Bank America, at the time of writing, nearly 100,000 mainframe applications have been created by end users employing the language NOMAD. Most companies that bring such methods into successful operation find that there is a huge pent-up demand for computer solutions that was unrealized and often unsuspected.

DEVELOPMENT THAT DOES NOT WORK

The growing demand for applications and the shortage of programmers would be a powerful reason for user-created computing. There is, however, another reason that is often more powerful: in many situations the conventional development process *does not work*.

Time and time again one finds stories of a system being cut over after years of development effort and the end users saying it is not what they want, or trying it for a while and then giving up. Frequently, after using a system, laboriously created, for a few weeks the users say they want something different.

A common reaction to this unfortunate situation is to say that the requirements were not specified sufficiently thoroughly. So more elaborate procedures have been devised for requirements specification, sometimes resulting in voluminous documentation. But still the system has been unsatisfactory.

The fact is that many of the most important potential users of DP do not know what they want until they *experience* using the system. When they first experience it, many changes are needed to make them comfortable with it and to meet their *basic* requirements. Once comfortable with it, their imaginations go to work and they think of all manner of different functions and variations on the theme that would be useful to them. And they want these changes *immediately*.

MORE RIGOROUS SPECIFICATIONS Many DP organizations have realized that their application creation process is not working to the satisfaction of the users, and have taken steps to correct this. Unfortunately, the steps they take often make the situation worse.

Steps are often taken to enforce more formal procedures. Application creation, it is said, must be converted from a sloppy ad hoc operation to one that follows rules like an engineering discipline.

The U.S. Department of Defense recognized that it had software problems and *mandated* certain actions in response to them, in DoD Directive 5000.29. A major concern in creating this directive was that the programs created did not meet the user's requirements. The directive specified more formal requirements documentation prior to the design, coding, and testing. A Computer Resource Life Cycle Management Plan was specified. This formalized the stages of development and depicted certain milestones that are to be attained and documented. The milestones are to be used to "ensure the proper sequence of analysis, design, implementation, integration, test, deployment and maintenance" [1].

This formal approach can work well *if and only if* the end-users' requirements can be specified in fine detail before design and coding begins. With some systems they can, and with others they cannot. The requirements for missile control can and must be specified completely beforehand. The requirements for management information systems cannot be specified beforehand and almost every attempt to do so has failed. The requirements change as soon as an executive starts to use his terminal.

Most commercial organizations exist in an environment of constant, dynamic, unpredictable change. The requirements for computerized procedures cannot be predicted with accuracy. Predefined specifications for some systems are about as realistic as trying to call all the plays before a football game starts.

The classical development life cycle succeeds for certain types of systems. For other types of systems it does not work and the attempt to enforce it makes it impossible to attain the results that are needed. The types of systems for which it does not work are becoming more common and more important in running corporations.

A more ad hoc approach is replacing the classical life cycle for certain types of computer usage. It is characterized by quick and easy building of prototypes or applications which can be quickly modified. It employs user-friendly languages and avoids third-generation languages such as COBOL and PL/1. It relies on interactive application building at a terminal screen and step-by-step refinement of the results.

Although these methods work well for most ordinary data processing, they are not appropriate for highly complex, technical systems such as those for refinery operation, satellite image processing, air traffic control, or moon launches. With these, a very precise requirements specification and formal development life cycle with tight controls are needed.

It is, then, necessary to distinguish between systems that need dynamic user-driven modification of requirements after the system is initially implemented and systems that need complete, formal, requirements analysis and specification before implementation. Much commercial and administrative data processing and systems oriented to human needs fall into the former category. Their development requires a technique that facilitates trial and error. Step-by-step adjustment of a prototype is desirable.

USER-DRIVEN VERSUS PRESPECIFIED COMPUTING

We will use the terms *user-driven computing* and *prespecified computing.* Box 3.1 shows characteristics of these two types of computing. All application development ought to be categorized as one or the other. One needs entirely different techniques and management from the other.

Most computing that ought to be *user-driven* is being developed today as *prespecified* computing. A drastic change in the management of application development is needed, together with the introduction of the new software and techniques. When the power and efficiency of application generators increases substantially, and thorough data modeling has been done, it is likely that user-driven methods will be employable for most (but not all) commercial data processing, rather than the long life cycle of traditional DP. The data should be analyzed, modeled, and documented. After that, there is scope for argument about what ought to be prespecified.

Both user-driven and prespecified computing need changes in the classical development life cycle. The problem with prespecified computing is that the classical life cycle is *too slow and expensive,* and the specification techniques are *insufficiently rigorous.* The problem with user-driven computing is that the old methods are insufficiently flexible. With most user-driven computing the classical life cycle is hopelessly slow. Results are often needed in a day, not a year, and changes must be made quickly.

THE UNCERTAINTY PRINCIPLE

The uncertainty principle in physics says that the act of observing subatomic events *changes* those events. There is an uncertainty principle with data processing. The act of providing what an end user says he needs *changes* his perception of those needs. The mere act of implementing a user-driven system changes the requirements for that system. The solution to a problem changes the problem.

BOX 3.1 **Distinction between prespecified computing and user-driven computing. Much of what has been** *prespecified* **ought to be** *user-driven* **with today's software.**

Prespecified Computing

- A formal requirements analysis is performed.

- Detailed, precise specifications are created.

- The traditional development life cycle is used, or a variant of it related to higher levels of automation.

- Programs are formally documented.

- The application development time is many months or years.

- Maintenance is formal and carefully specified.

Examples: Compiler writing, airline reservations, air traffic control, missile guidance, software development.

User-Driven Computing

- Users do not know in detail what they want until they use a version of it and then they modify it quickly and often frequently. Consequently, formal requirement specification linked to slow application programming is doomed to failure.

- Applications are created with a generator or other software in Fig. 2.1, more quickly than the time to write specifications.

- The system is self-documenting, or interactive documentation is created when the application is created.

- Users create their own applications or work with an analyst who does this in cooperation with them. A separate programming department is not used.

- The application development time is days or at most weeks.

- Maintenance is continuous. Incremental changes are made constantly to the applications by the users or the analyst who assists them.

- The process may employ data models and data systems which are centrally created with the information engineering processes (Chapter 6).

- Control is imposed via the data models, dictionary, and authorization procedures.

Examples: Information systems, decision-support systems, paperwork avoidance, administrative procedures, shop floor control.

End users have a long learning curve to climb in assessing how they should use today's data processing. They cannot climb far on this curve as long as it remains at the talking stage. It is only when they have a terminal and use it on their own work that they begin to understand the reality of the computer's challenge and limitations. Their imagination slowly begins to realize what they *could* do with that screen. After implementation the users have a common basis for discussion of the system. They argue at lunch about what it does well and badly, what it ought to do better, and how it could benefit them in different ways from what it is doing now. They would like to modify its behavior *quickly*.

As a system becomes live it affects the rest of a department in a variety of unforeseen ways. It suddenly becomes possible to move work from one person's screen to another. Salesmen can suddenly provide a service that was previously so difficult that they ignored it, and demands for that service boom. A manager suddenly sees information that was previously hidden from him, so he makes changes in the department. Some users do not like the system and insist on using their previous methods. Others want new types of reports or want the computer to do calculations not in the system requirements.

The system has many unforeseen psychological effects. It may make some employees feel unwanted and resentful. Some become prima donnas with the new terminals. It changes the organizational interaction and power patterns.

In many cases the functions of a user-driven system when first installed are a fraction of those the users feel they need a few months after installation. These new functions are more valuable because they are based on experience. But the rigid development cycle prevents them from making the changes they want.

The system makes it possible to have more finely structured inventory reorder points. The reordering rules can now be changed easily to better adapt to seasonal peaks. It becomes possible to deal with problems on the shop floor that were quietly ignored before, but to do so needs additions to the data base, or different patterns of data entry.

It is often the case that the end user does not know what he wants until he gets it. When he gets it, he wants something different.

MANAGEMENT INFORMATION

Perhaps the most notorious class of systems-that-don't-work is management information systems. In spite of repeated failures, these remain one of the most important classes of data processing.

Using the traditional development approach, the MIS designer would go to managers and ask them what information they would like to have. It took long and painful experience to discover that most managers do not really know. To know what information he needs an executive must be aware of each type of decision he will (or should) make, and how he will make it. Some executives play it safe and ask for everything. Some designers have tried to provide everything on bulky reports that tend to hide rather than reveal the few pieces of information that are pertinent.

In some cases an executive with a strong personality makes firm statements about the information he or his department wants. A systems analyst at last sees a clear directive and an unambiguous statement of requirements is created. The project life cycle then rolls on, but by the time the programming and testing are finally done the executive in question has moved on. His replacement does not like the system. Systems that are highly personalized almost never survive the departure of the user they were created for.

A NEW TYPE OF DP IMPLEMENTATION

What is needed to deal with these problems can now be seen in operation in a small fraction of installations. It represents a new type of DP implementation. At its best it is very impressive compared with the traditional DP development cycle.

Its characteristics are as follows:

- It uses the types of software shown in Fig. 2.1.
- Application creation is *fast*.
- Applications can be modified *quickly*.
- Where possible, users create their own applications. Often a systems analyst creates the application working at a terminal with the end user much of the time.
- Where possible, users modify their own applications; again a systems analyst working with the end user may do this.
- Where conventional programs are written, this is not done without prototyping. Prototypes largely replace the use of lengthy written requirements documents. Where possible the prototype is converted directly into the application.
- The process is incremental and interactive, as opposed to the single great-leap-forward associated with requirements documentation and a specification freeze.
- The process usually uses data-base facilities and needs tight data administration controls with computerized tools.

PROTOTYPING

The concept of prototyping is particularly important.

With most complex engineering a prototype is created before the final product is *built*. This is done to test the principles, ensure that the system works, and obtain design feedback which enables the design to be adjusted before the big money is spent. A chemical plant is built in a laboratory form before the plant is finally designed. The hull shape of a boat is tested. A new airplane is simulated in a variety of ways before it is built.

Complex data-processing systems need prototyping more than most engineering systems because there is much to learn from a pilot operation and many changes are likely to be made. Prototypes would help to solve the problems we have discussed of systems not working in the way the end users really need.

The reason DP prototypes were not generally used until the 1980s was that the cost of programming a prototype was about as high as the cost of programming the live working system. Fourth-generation languages enable prototypes to be created cheaply and quickly.

A systems analyst working with an end user can create and demonstrate dialogues for data-base queries, report generation, and manipulation of screen information. The analyst discusses an end user's needs with him and then creates a specimen dialogue on a terminal. This might take him an hour or a week, depending on the complexity and the language that is being used. Initially, he ignores questions of transaction volumes and machine performance.

The end user is shown the dialogue and trained quickly to use it. Usually, he has some suggestions for changes he would like and the analyst makes these. The user may add subtotals or extra columns. He may want to perform certain calculations. The analyst may show him the different types of charts that could be created: scatter plots, bar charts, charts with regression lines, linear versus log scales, and so on. The user remembers a different type of customer, or some union rule that was forgotten, or other factors that only the user would be likely to know.

As the analyst and user continue their discussion of what is needed, the running prototype is now a focus of the debate, which helps to ensure that they are both talking about the same thing. The screens are printed and the end user takes them home to think about them. The analyst works further, improving the screen interaction, adding new features, and improving the displays.

Finally, the user is satisfied, excited, and says "When can I get it?" In some cases he can have it very quickly. The data base exists and the prototype can become the final application. In other cases he cannot have it yet because design work is needed to achieve machine efficiency, security, auditability, telecommunications networking, or to create the data base. In the latter case the prototype becomes, in effect, the requirements document for application programming.

In a sense the system created by the traditional two-year DP life cycle is a prototype. It is not *meant* to be a prototype and is not regarded as such, but it has all the imperfections of a prototype. These imperfections are expensive to correct and so often remain in the system.

THE CHANGE NEEDED IN DP MANAGEMENT

The mature DP executive should *welcome* end users creating their own applications and not fight it. He should regard it as his job to provide them with the software tools, networks, and consultant analysts that they need. But particularly important, he should link their activities to the data modeling and data systems created by information engineering (Chapter 6).

There are many advantages in application development without professional programmers. However, the idea encounters great emotional resistance in many installations. There are several reasons for this. First, to many DP people the whole idea of application creation without programmers still seems strange and alien to the God-given order. Second, programmers, not surprisingly, resist the idea and concoct scornful arguments against it. Higher DP executives can be alarmed by it also and sometimes envision their empires dwindling if end-user departments learn to create their own applications.

A major reason for resistance is that DP organizations have struggled to achieve discipline in the DP development process. This process used to be an unruly free-for-all until standards and guidelines were established relatively recently. The standards and methods have assumed the force of law, have been taught to all DP staff in an organization, and are regarded as a vital necessity in the crusade against unstructured methods, unmaintainable code, nonportable programs, and lack of scientific discipline. The installation standards, religiously adhered to, have frozen the methodologies of large installations at a time when the technology is plunging into new forms.

Discipline is certainly needed. However, this can come from formal information engineering techniques (Chapter 6), firm data administration, and information center management (Chapter 7).

The old installation standards, so laboriously created in many organizations, are full of trip-wires that prevent the productivity increases which new methods and end users are demanding. It is not easy to reverse the standards because so many people have been trained and drilled in their use.

Some experienced computer professionals have a nearly hysterical reaction to the idea of user-created applications. The chief scientists of one of America's leading electronics firms compared it to do-it-yourself brain surgery.

A WALL BETWEEN USER AND PROGRAMMER

The traditional techniques for application development tend to build a wall between the application *user* and the application *creator*. The programmer is kept away from the end user.

The formal development life cycle requires written specifications to be created. This takes much time but is rarely adequate. The specifications must be *frozen* at the start of the design and coding phase. Often they are frozen when the ideas about what the system ought to do are still fluid. The user often does not know what he wants until he sees it on a terminal and uses it. This is becoming increasingly so as we move to more complex applications. We have now done the simple, easily standardized applications—payroll, invoicing, and the like—and are faced with more subtle and valuable applications, such as decision support systems, operations control, and financial planning. With these applications a rapid rate of adjustment is needed as the end users begin to change their methods of working. With many such applications, *prototypes* should be created quickly to see if the users like them. The prototypes should be rapidly changeable.

In this environment it is vital that the application creator work hand in hand with the application users. The systems analyst who learns to understand the user's needs should himself create the application and work with the user to adjust it interactively. For most applications this can be done with the new software for generating applications, graphics, reports, and data-base queries.

Programming in languages such as COBOL or PL/1 takes a long time. The programmer must document the code. In typical installations which are well controlled with a development standards manual there are about 10 pages of program documentation to each 1000 lines of code. In some installations documentation never gets done.

Often a production line is established for use of programmers. Jobs for coding wait in a queue until a programmer is free. This maximizes the use of programmers—the scarcest resource—but adds further to the overall elapsed time.

The user sees a multiyear delay before work starts on the application he needs. When work is under way the time between specifying requirements and obtaining results is so long that during this time the requirements have changed.

Many end users, now beginning to understand what computers could do for them, do not formally notify DP of their need because of overload on DP and the multiyear backlog.

The DP creation process is slowed down further by errors that have to be corrected. Most of the errors are in requirements analysis or interpretation, specification, and design.

Errors in analysis become less of a problem when the analysts can create the applications themselves, quickly, and show them to the end users. Relatively fast end-user feedback enables the analysts to make adjustments while they are still familiar with what they created. This fast cycle of application creation and feedback, using the new application generation software, makes prototyping and adjustment a natural procedure.

Program bugs are reduced by the move to higher-level application creation facilities. Errors are also reduced by removing, where possible, the traditional interaction between systems analyst and programmer. Too often the analysts' program specifications are misinterpreted. When the analyst *creates* the application directly, this cause of errors is removed.

To build this wall between application user and application creator is the worst thing we could do. It is becoming more serious as we evolve to more user-driven applications. New methods of application creation are vital to the future of the computer industry. This future lies with vendors, who make possible application creation without the wall.

SPECTACULAR END-USER SYSTEMS   There are now many case histories of end users having created comprehensive systems with multiple applications which are by any standards spectacular [2]. The moral of such case histories is that *we have grossly underestimated end users.*

Some end users are amazingly bright people. They need only the right tools and encouragement. Many end users want to create their own facilities but have not been given the tools to do it; the vast majority have not yet glimpsed the possibilities. In showing a user-created system to one typical end user the comment was made, "If I had something like that I could save 40 to 60 hours a month." This realization needs to spread among white-collar workers everywhere (and some blue-collar ones).

The system and software architects of the computer industry understand the need for improving DP productivity, but most of them think that this must come via DP experts. Highly influential staff in the development laboratories commonly talk about end users as though they are idiots, and tell one story after another to reinforce this view. Because of this the facilities that change users' employment of computers often come not from the old-established computer firms but from entirely different sources. This was true, for example, of the first personal computers, Visicalc, Microsoft, Lotus, Lisa, videotex, Telidon, etc.

There is a vast world of end users with important needs for computing. They need the right tools and encouragement.

Box 3.2 lists reasons why end users should use computers. Box 3.3 lists the technical and human facilities needed to make this work well.

THE INFORMATION CENTER CONCEPT   The installation bible is not going to be abandoned overnight, nor should it. What is happening instead is that *alternative means* of creating applications are coming into existence, and coexist with the traditional methods.

In *some* cases the end users have created the alternative method, without DP approval. User departments acquire their own minicomputer or use software that permits fast application creation. Sometimes they use time-sharing services with languages such as NOMAD, sometimes a partition of a mainframe, and often personal computers. DP executives in some organizations have tried to stop the uncontrolled spread of minicomputers and lan-

BOX 3.2   Reasons why end users should "do their own thing" with computers

- Only the end users truly understand the subtleties of their own applications (especially if they are complex).

- The end users should be made responsible for how they employ computers.

- End users can obtain the applications they want earlier, thereby relieving the extreme frustration with DP that some end users feel.

- Spontaneous demands for information may be satisfied quickly.

- End users should be encouraged to use their imagination about what computers can do for them.

- The total number of people working on application development can be much larger.

- The understanding of what is needed comes slowly with experience of using the system. A facility is needed with which users can make many rapid modifications to their system.

- Complex administrative procedures tend to evolve a step at a time, each step being a reaction to current problems and pressures. Computerized procedures should evolve in the same way.

- End users are much brighter than many DP professionals admit; the best of them can be highly inventive in their use of computers.

- End users often invent uses of computers that would not be created by a typical systems analyst. They think about computers differently and live with the business problems.

- The traditional development life cycle does not work for user-driven systems.

guages. In other cases they have allowed it to happen, only too glad to get some of the end users off their back. *Uncontrolled* spread of user computers and data bases, however, stores up trouble for the future because multiple versions of incompatible data come into existence, as well as multiple machines that cannot be linked into networks.

A valuable approach is the *information center* concept. The information center is a group within the DP organization designed to serve the end users directly and speedily. The group is aware of which data bases exist and sometimes sets up other data bases. It makes this information available to end users, employing user-friendly languages. Information center consultants

BOX 3.3   Facilities needed for user-driven computing

TECHNICAL FACILITIES

- User-seductive software.
- Well human-factored computer screens and interaction devices.
- Self-teaching software and HELP functions that encourage the user to experiment.
- Software which is subsetted so that it appears simple to a beginner, and expands to a rich and powerful set of functions.
- Linkage to appropriate on-line data systems and data-base support facilities.
- Tools built into the software for managing and controlling its use.
- Good security, authorization, recovery, and auditing facilities.
- A complete absence of DP jargon. There is no need for difficult words or acronyms.

HUMAN FACILITIES

- General management that motivates end users to invent and acquire the facilities they need.
- Excellent training.
- Demonstrations designed to reflect strong user needs.
- Encouragement, hand holding, and sympathy.
- A management approach that seeks out early adaptors and motivates them to encourage their less adventurous colleagues.
- Cooperation and encouragement from DP, not competition with and isolation from DP.
- Thorough data administration linked to the user-driven computing.
- Data in data systems which have been planned with sound data modeling techniques, computerized tools, and the techniques of information engineering.
- Information center management as described in Chapter 7.

work with the end users and create, where possible, the applications they want. The consultants help to create the decision support systems, personal computing facilities, information retrieval systems, and organizational support systems. They help users with personal computers to find and employ the best software for their needs. A major reason for establishing this mode of operation has been the extreme dissatisfaction expressed by end users about the way DP has responded to their information needs.

The consultants encourage the users to employ the information facilities that already exist. They sit at terminals with users helping them to create query procedures, report-generation routines, or graphics-generation routines. They train the users to employ the facilities.

Where more complex applications are needed the information center consultants decide how they can be created, selecting where possible an application generator or language that avoids the formal programming development cycle.

Prototyping allows new frontiers to be explored. Sometimes a system is created that users will never employ. This can be done quickly with application generators, and not too much time is wasted. The lessons learned enable better design next time.

PERSONAL COMPUTERS FOR TOP MANAGEMENT

Many executives have never used computers on-line for decision-making; they have used computer listings but not work stations. It is often said that such-and-such an executive "will never touch a boob tube!" In fact these executives would find the decision-support tools, spreadsheets, and graphics of personal computers extremely valuable. If they once became comfortable using them it would change the way they think about receiving vital information and doing business calculations.

Every executive who does not use a personal computer should make a firm commitment to himself to start to use one, and to ensure that his corporation gives him the help he needs. When he starts he may not like it, like when you first learn to gallop on a horse, but as with a horse he should persevere and before long it will seem more natural; eventually he will become confident enough to go places. He should make a personal commitment to learn every detail of the software tool he is employing. This should be a user-friendly tool which gives valuable results with no requirement for programming.

It is interesting to observe three types of corporate experience in giving personal computers to executives. In the first, a large insurance company gave all of its top executives IBM personal computers at their homes. Most did not use the machine, and many eventually asked that it be removed. In the second, a manufacturing company, observing this negative experience, ensured that the executives had valuable easy-to-use software. They employed Multiplan software for spreadsheet manipulation. Again the results were poor. In the third case, a corporate information center carefully selected data which was of particular interest and urgency to each executive. They used this data with the spreadsheets and color graphics of Lotus 1-2-3. Now the executives could see directly the value and importance of the tool, and all learned how to manipulate the data, explore cash flows, "what-if?" questions, etc.

The moral of the story is that time and human care are needed to make it clear to executives that they can do their job better with the tool. Once over this hurdle their natural inventiveness goes to work on what the software should be used for.

CAUTION

Although the success stories of end-user computing are spectacular, there have also been many serious problems.

Reports have been generated with incorrect data. Excessive machine utilization has occurred. Thirty-hour runs have been written without checkpoints. Chaos has grown up in the representation of data. Systems have been built which are unauditable. New types of structured techniques are important in the use of fourth-generation languages. One information center executive in New York lamented: "I can list 200 types of mistakes that end users have made." We need professionalism in the control and management of user computing. A vital function of the information center is to put the professionalism into place.

End users need much training and hand holding in adapting to new systems. The information center consultant can work closely with the users, showing them how to employ the facilities. In some cases substantial use is made of computer-based training and video tapes, for example, the tapes and computer-based courses created by the author and Deltak, Inc. [3] .

Chapter 7 discusses information center management.

4 PROBLEMS WITH SPECIFICATIONS

PROBLEMS WITH THE SPECIFICATION PROCESS
When the traditional systems analyst and potential end users first come face to face, they come from widely different cultures. It is rather like a Victorian missionary first entering an African village. However, they have to produce a very precise document—the specification of requirements.

The missionary is steeped in computer terminology and analysis methods. The villagers' culture is accounting, chemical engineering, or production control—cultures with a complex folklore. They use different languages. Somehow they are supposed to communicate with no ambiguities or misunderstandings. If the missionary is skillful at communicating and can offer the villagers a promise of better things, they can begin to learn each other's conceptual framework. However there is no way that either can understand the nuances and subtleties of the other's way of thinking.

In an attempt to clarify and formalize the process, specifications are written for the applications that must be programmed. This can take person-years to complete, and results in a set of documents that are several inches thick. For his own protection the missionary needs the villagers to sign this document.

The specification document is extremely important in the traditional system development life cycle. It guides programmers and is supposed to answer numerous questions that arise about the system. In practice there are serious problems with it.

- It is often so long and boring that key managers do not read it. They read the summary.
- It lacks precision. It cannot be converted into computer code without many assumptions and interpretations.

- It is often ambiguous, inconsistent, and incomplete.

- It is often misinterpreted by both sides. Often its readers *think* they understand it but in fact do not.

- Sometimes much trivia and motherhood is added to the document. Both sides understand this. It increases the comfort level, but has zero value.

- The specification document is not designed for successive refinement as the problems become better understood. It is intended to be a complete document that users sign.

USER SIGN-OFF   The users are coerced to sign off on the specification document. They know that until they do that the detailed design and programming will not begin. DP hopes that the need to sign off will encourage the users to check the document very carefully and find any errors before programming starts.

The sign-off is invariably a moment of apprehension on both sides. The users are not sure whether it is really what they want. They often feel that their views on the system are changing as they learn and think more about it. Halfway up a learning curve the specifications are *frozen*. It is important in the traditional development cycle to *freeze* the specifications when programming begins. DP is apprehensive because they are not sure that they understand all the users' needs. They are about to put much effort into the implementation and any imperfections in the specifications will prove expensive.

BUGS   Not surprisingly, the specification document contains errors.
In most installations there are more bugs in specifications than in program coding. In one typical case a large corporation found that 64% of its bugs were in requirements analysis and design—in spite of a formal sign-off by the user departments. Even worse, *45% of these bugs were discovered after the acceptance tests for the finished applications were completed.*

This corporation had a formal development life cycle and was following its installation standards meticulously. It was using a formal method of structured analysis in creating the specifications.

Figure 4.1 shows the distribution of bugs in a large bank, of the total, 56% were in the requirements document and 27% were in design (and most of these were related to misinterpretation of the requirements document).

The bugs in the requirements specification are much more time consuming and expensive to correct than those in coding. Figure 4.1 illustrates this. Of the cost of correcting bugs in this bank, 95% was for the bugs in requirements and design. The ratios shown in Fig. 4.1 are typical of many installations.

Time and time again one finds stories of a system being cut over after

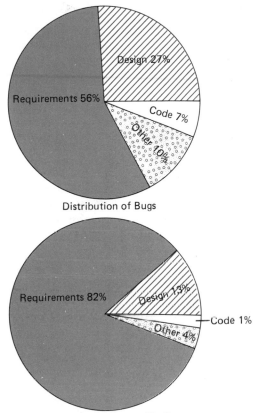

Distribution of Bugs

Figure 4.1 In a typical installation with a traditional development methodology, more bugs occur in requirements specification and design than in coding. The bugs in requirements specification are much the most expensive ones to correct. (From Ref. 1.)

Distribution of Effort to Fix Bugs

years of development effort and the end users saying that it is not what they want, or trying it for a while and then giving up.

The requirements were not specified sufficiently thoroughly, so more elaborate procedures have been devised for requirements specification, sometimes resulting in voluminous documentation. But still the system has been unsatisfactory.

Many DP organizations have realized that their application creation process is not working to the satisfaction of the users, and have taken steps to correct this. Steps are often taken to enforce more formal procedures. Application creation, it is said, must be converted from a sloppy ad hoc operation to one that follows rules like an engineering discipline. Unfortunately, the steps they take often make the situation worse.

FAILURES

In one large insurance company a system was developed for claim processing which would put terminals in all branch offices. It took about three years to develop at a cost of about $4 million. To ensure that the end users were well understood, an end-user manager was moved into a high position in the development process. When the first terminals were cut over, to everybody's horror the users gave up using them after a short period. They perceived the system as unsatisfactory compared with their previous method. The system was eventually abandoned.

A Department of Defense study was conducted of 10 major automated systems. It concluded that all 10 had *unstable and changing* requirements, indicating the need for techniques that could adapt much more quickly to such changes.

IBM designed a system to automate two Japanese newspapers, *Asaki* and *Nikei.* What do editors of newspapers really want at their terminals? They did not know. When the system was first installed it was not useful to the editors and IBM lost about $2 million on the software development effort [2]. Undaunted, newspaper automation continued. Years later, after a great effort, a requirements document of *2400 pages* was produced. It was created to automate several U.S. newspapers. It was so thorough that management thought *nothing* could go wrong. But unfortunately, when the document was used to settle questions, the developers and their customers interpreted it differently! Both worked in good faith, but the difficulty of specifying the requirement so that both parties understood the subtleties (needed for programming) was too great [2].

The difficulty of writing adequate requirements specifications has resulted in some spectacular court cases. In the early 1970s two major airlines sued computer suppliers who were to provide application programs, after $40 million had been spent, because the application programs were not about to work. At the time of writing, a European bank is in court for a $70 million claim over application software. The U.S. Air Force spent more than $300 million in a futile attempt to automate an Advanced Logistics System (ALS) [2].

The public record is replete with examples of inadequate specifications of military systems causing enormous cost escalations, or redevelopment because systems did not work as expected [3-5].

If a software engineer has unclear or ambiguous specifications, as is often the case, he tends to fill in the gaps with his own initiative. Often he is entranced with his own invention. He creates some ingenious subsystem and the rest of the system is built around this device.

A contractor or programming manager without clear specifications often has to redo parts of systems. He can then justify time slippages, cost overruns, and system failures.

For every big failure that hits the headlines there are a thousand small ones where ordinary end users abandon their terminal or complain that it does not do what they want. This can become a disaster when it results in the inability of organizations to respond to changing economic or competitive environments.

Once developed, conventional computer programs are difficult to change to respond to a changing external environment. We are locked in a thickening morass of maintenance complexity—a morass that is turning to concrete.

SOLUTIONS

There are two types of solutions to the problem with specifications.

The first is to *employ a specification language which is sufficiently rigorous that programs can be generated from it automatically.* The language permits successive refinement so that as users change their minds or the details of the requirements become better understood, the programs can be regenerated. Ideally, the specification language should be sufficiently easy to understand that users can employ it, or at least study the specifications and be involved in valuable discussions about them with the analysts.

The second type of solution is to *do away with the formal specification process* and have users interacting directly with the computer—often with the help of DP professionals, as discussed in Chapter 3. This works only with certain classes of applications.

Chapter 5 discusses specification languages. The word "language", however, might be misleading. The specification may be a drawing, or succession of drawings, just as the specification for an engineering mechanism is a succession of drawings. The engineer's drawings are very precise and are drawn with formal rules. They are, in effect, a language with which specifications are stated.

Today's computers have powerful graphics capability. We can create and manipulate drawings on a screen. We do not need to create a work of art or a drawing with the elegance of, say, Victorian architects' drawings of cathedrals. We need clear diagrams of the logic of computer applications that can be refined and automatically checked for accuracy and consistency, so that program code can be generated from them.

SYSTEM SKETCHES

Complex design processes begin with *sketches* and progress into representations that have greater detail. Eventually, a level of detail is reached from which a system is implemented. A house architect, for example, begins with sketches of what a home may look like. He converts these a stage at a time into detailed drawings from which the builders work. A computer application designer starts with sketches of the application and these are broken down into more detail until programs are created.

An extremely important property of the sketch is that it can be readily understood by the end users. The would-be homeowners want to think about the architect's first sketches before he goes into too much detail. We need to have ways of representing what a system will do that the would-be users can readily understand and think about. The more they think and argue about the sketches, the more likely they are to be pleased with the final result.

We have a variety of different ways of sketching what a system will do. Different forms of sketches may be needed to represent different aspects of a system's behavior. Some of them are necessarily more abstract than an architect's sketch of a house. The user must learn how to read them, and the form of sketch must be designed so that this is easy for him.

Among the types of sketches used are the following [6]:

- Prototyping
- Data flow diagrams
- HIPO diagrams
- Warnier diagrams
- Nasi-Schneiderman diagrams
- Action diagrams
- Data access maps
- HOS notation

Prototyping is by far the most effective for giving the user a clear, realistic representation of the system that is to be built. The analyst employs a prototyping tool to generate screens, data, terminal dialogues, and logic. Various users employ the prototype and determine whether it deals effectively with their problems. They usually discover omissions, inconsistencies, and misunderstandings. Often the need for improved human factoring is revealed. The analysts successively refine the prototype until it meets the users' needs as effectively as possible.

A prototype is tangible and real, and enables the users to make contributions to the design that would otherwise never be made. Prototyping is often the only way to be *sure* that the would-be users will like the system. It may not, however, reveal all the logic of the system or complex interactions between subsystems. Other forms of the sketch are needed showing these.

Nasi-Schneiderman diagrams show logic. Data-base action diagrams show logic and its relation to data base structures. Data flow diagrams show the interactions among separate processes.

Some of the types of sketch that systems analysts have employed are difficult for end users to learn and argue about. A major emphasis is needed on finding the most user-friendly form of sketch. The sketch needs one other property: it should be translatable into a system design *as directly as possible*.

Figure 4.2 indicates these two properties of the form of sketch.

COMPUTABLE DESIGNS

The system design that fills in detail from the sketch has one very important property. It should be *computable*. By "computable" we mean that

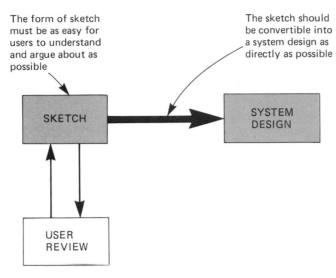

Figure 4.2 Properties of system sketches.

the design can be converted directly into executable code. It must be unambiguous and rigorous. If the design technique has this property, a program generator can be written that creates the code automatically. This saves much time and also produces code that is free from the types of errors made by human coders. The program testing time is therefore greatly reduced, and applications are created much faster.

Figure 4.3 shows what is needed for coding automation. The design is

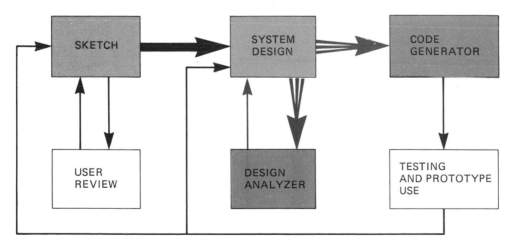

Figure 4.3 The system design should (ideally) be done in a form which is computable, that is, can be automatically analyzed and converted into program code. The striped arrows show linkages that should be automated.

checked by a design *analyzer*. This checks for syntax errors and as far as possible for semantics errors. It reveals any inconsistencies or incompleteness that would prevent code generation. When the analyzer indicates that the design is correct and complete enough to generate code, the design is passed to a program generator. The red arrows of Fig. 4.3 show that the linkage between the design representation and the analyzer and code generator are automatic.

When the code is generated it is tested to ensure that it does what was intended. The testing may cause modifications to be made to the system design or possibly to the sketch. With the best software of this type the testing process is brief because most errors have already been detected by the analyzer. Human program-coding errors do not exist.

The code generator may produce a portion of a system rather than the complete system. This portion may be tested in a simulation mode with the parts of the system not yet coded being manually simulated or bridged.

Where possible the link between the sketch and the system design should also be automatic. The sketch is an approximate overview design which needs to be refined into more detail until it is computable. The sketch may be representable on a computer screen in such a way that the designer can decompose it into the greater levels of detail needed for code generation.

It is usually the case that system sketches are changed many times as refinements are made and modifications explored. A neat drawing of each modification by hand is very time consuming. Computer-aided editing of the sketch and computer graphics for drawing it (even if crudely) increase the productivity of the design process and encourage the developers to explore the alternatives more comprehensively. A design workbench is needed, as illustrated in Fig. 4.4, for automating the design process and the generation of code as fully as possible.

A certain stage in the evolution of the specification sketch may be regarded as detailed design which is handed over to a different team. This team can feed back refinements to the chart, which are then checked by the original specifiers.

There is often argument about what should be in the requirements statement, what should be in the specification, and what should be in the design documents. This is an artificial distinction. Requirements, specification, and design are all the same process carried to greater levels of detail. It is possible to have one diagramming technique and language that handles all of these.

Different languages and techniques have been developed for different aspects of the development life cycle. Sometimes one language is used for the requirements statement (often English); a different language or technique is used for the specification, for example, data flow diagrams, and yet a different one for detailed program design; and then a programming language is used for coding. The specification writers commonly misinterpret the requirements. The program designers commonly misinterpret the specifi-

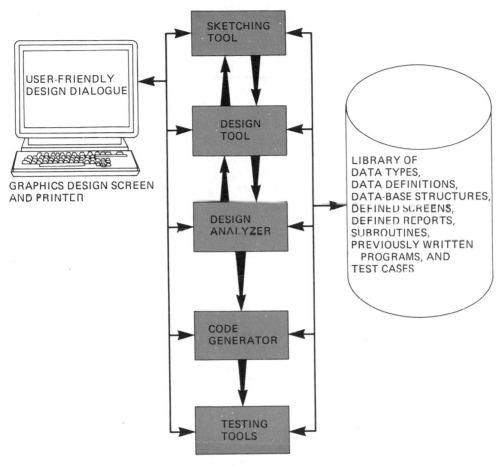

Figure 4.4 A designer's workbench is needed for automating the design process as fully as possible.

cations. The coders make errors in coding from the design diagrams. There are many opportunities to introduce manual processes during and between the phases of the life cycle. At each of these, new errors arise.

A computable specification technique that can be extended from a high-level overview to specifications detailed enough for code generation avoids these problems.

IMMEDIATE ERROR FEEDBACK Various statistics exist about the rate at which human beings make mistakes in programming and complex logic design. If a powerful language permits them to write a program in one-tenth of the number of lines of code, they can do it one-tenth of the time and make about one-tenth of the number of mistakes.

However, they can create ten times as many applications and their number of mistakes *per day* is not much changed. One might propose a law of conservation of screw-ups, saying that the same number of programmers working for the same amount of time will produce the same number of errors, regardless of the power of the language they use [7].

One factor, however, can greatly change this. If the software can check the programmer's syntax and semantics, detect errors, and notify him quickly after making the error, this fast feedback greatly lessens his error rate. Some of the new power tools for system builders have this capability. Immediate detection and feedback of error information has been shown by psychologists to be extremely valuable in teaching, in managing people, and in controlling system design. Our computerized tools need to have this capability.

THE STRUCTURED REVOLUTION   Much has been written about the "revolution" in application design represented by structured techniques. Most of the structured techniques that have been much sold and advertized, however, do not produce *computable* designs. They are insufficiently rigorous to be a basis for automatic generation of code.

We believe that the *real* revolution is not the refinement of hand methods used with hand coding, but rather the use of design techniques that automate the process.

We have commented that our human brain is good at some tasks and bad at others. Fortunately, the computer is good at certain tasks that the brain does badly. Our brain cannot do long meticulous logic operations without making errors. It needs automated tools to help it.

System design, then, needs to start with ways that make it easy for users to conceptualize what computers will do for them, to easily modify and refine these statements of requirements, and then to translate them automatically into bug-free code. It is important for all persons involved with computing to understand that this is possible and that software exists that does it for even the most complex of systems. There is, however, much scope for improving the sketching and conceptualization techniques, and the code generation and machine-efficient execution.

5 SPECIFICATION LANGUAGES

INTRODUCTION It is desirable to have high-level languages, unlike programming languages, with which we can express requirements and specifications. The early versions of such languages were useful documentation tools but were not *computable*. (By "computable", as explained in Chapter 4, we mean that executable code can be generated automatically from the specification.)

SUCCESSIVE REFINEMENT To generate code automatically, a specification must be rigorous. A rigorous specification cannot be created in one shot. There will be much successive refinement. Each step in this refinement needs to be rigorous.

A specification process designed for automation is likely to produce a succession of formal representations of the system which can steadily be broken down into more detail. Different individuals are likely to be involved at different levels of detail. It helps if all use the same type of chart.

At the highest level the chart has a few blocks that represent the broad requirements of the system. At the lowest level the chart has enough detail for automatic generation of program code. Separate portions of the chart will be developed separately. The technique must be designed so that they can be linked together without interface problems. When changes are made, as they often are, at a lower level in the chart, these are automatically reflected upward so that the high-level representations of the system can be checked.

TWO TYPES OF LANGUAGES   In the early days of the computer industry, computer languages were thought of only as programming languages. Initially, they were close in syntax to the instruction set of the machine. Human language is very different from machine language and so attempts were made to humanize the programming languages by employing English words.

The standardization of languages such as COBOL, FORTRAN, and Ada presented programmers with what in effect were virtual computers hiding the physical details of actual computers, which differed from machine to machine. The programming language, however, remained a statement of *how* to execute a set of operations in terms of computer resources.

Understanding the requirements of a complex system and writing specifications for it needs a very different type of language. In the early days (and often still today) requirements and specifications were expressed in English. Human language, however, is ambiguous and imprecise. Specifications written in English were usually incomplete and almost always open to misinterpretation. The effort to make them more thorough led to documents more voluminous than Victorian novels and far more boring. It became clear that many of the problems with systems were not the programmers' fault but the fault of the specifiers.

Because of this, a variety of techniques grew up for designing and specifying systems. A new type of language began to emerge—specification languages. These languages had little or no resemblance to programming languages. They took a variety of forms. Sometimes a formal language was used, sometimes a diagramming technique. They included SADT (Structured Analysis and Design Technique) [1], SREM (Software Requirements Engineering Methodology) [2], data flow diagramming techniques [3], HIPO (Hierarchical Input-Process-Output) [4], PSL/PSA (Problem Statement Language/Problem Statement Analyzer) [5], and IDEF (ICAM Definition Method) [6].

These were all generalized languages intended to specify any type of program. There were also specialized languages, narrow in scope, most of which were not referred to as "specification" languages. These included report definition languages, data-base query and update languages, languages that could generate certain patterns of commercial DP application [7], and languages for special functions such as financial analysis, circuit design, and coordinate geometry.

We have stressed the difference between procedural and nonprocedural languages. A *procedural* language describes precisely, step by step, how something is accomplished. A *nonprocedural* language describes *what* is to be done, not *how*.

Specification languages are nonprocedural. They describe *what* is to be done, not the step-by-step coding. This chapter describes properties that good specification languages ought to have.

COMPUTABLE SPECIFICATIONS

The computer industry thus acquired two breeds of languages, one for requirements analysis, problem description, and system specification, and one for programming.

It was generally considered to be desirable that the specification languages should be independent of machine resources or programming because the specifications were a fundamental statement about requirements and these requirements could be met with a variety of types of hardware and software. Furthermore, the hardware and software would change while the requirements remained the same.

Programming languages had to be computable. This guaranteed rigor and sufficiency in these languages. Most of the *specification* languages and techniques that grew up were not rigorous and did not enforce logical consistency. They were not computable.

It was generally assumed that the output of the specification language was meant to be used by a programmer, who then coded the programs in a different language. This led to the problems associated with conventional programming. *We believe that this assumption is wrong* for the future of computing. The specification language should be processible so that program code can be *automatically generated,* as with today's report generators and application generators. This means that the specification language requires more rigor than was available using early specification techniques. It must be *computable.* The specification should contain enough detail and be precise enough to be automatically converted into program code (whether or not the conversion software exists). This does not necessarily mean that it expresses every detail, because certain types of default options are possible. A report-generation statement can be computable, for example, even when it does not express the format of the report.

Most techniques for specifying systems are very sloppy and certainly not computable. There is often a pretense of rigor when it does not exist. Much bad design is perpetrated with the name "structured techniques." When programs so designed are finally debugged and systems delivered, it is often found that they were not what the users wanted exactly. Even when specification languages are used, much falls through the cracks. This is expensive because it means reprogramming. The lack of rigor in the specification techniques often causes ambiguity, incompleteness, and misunderstanding. Most such techniques should generally be regarded as useful for documentation or initial conceptualization, but not thought of as the rigorous disciplines that computing requires.

Although programming languages have the desirable property of computability, they are not suitable for stating system specifications because of their semantics. What is needed is a specification language that is computable with semantics appropriate for high-level conceptualization of systems. The property of computability will then permit resources to be allocated and programs created automatically (and hence without the errors that programmers make).

AUTOMATION OF DESIGN

Many specification techniques were designed to be used by hand. It is only when computers are used that rigorous methods are practical. Human beings make too many errors and find rigorous techniques too tedious to use rapidly and thoroughly by hand. When we create design techniques to be run with computerized tools, this enormously expands the scope of what is practical. Today the hardware for running computerized tools is inexpensive, so future techniques should be designed to employ computers.

Design will never be completely automated. Human inventiveness and creativity is its most important aspect. Human beings will always want to argue at a blackboard and draw sketches on paper, so the technique should provide ways to make simple drawings of concepts.

Figure 5.1 shows the essentials of computerized system design. There should be a specification language which is rigorous but which has an interactive user-friendly dialogue. Most people think and design with pictures, so an interactive graphics facility is desirable. The design so created should be capable of being analyzed to check its accuracy and consistency. The design *should be based on rules with which correctness can be enforced wherever possible.* The analyzer should check that the rules have been obeyed.

Once it has been checked, the software should generate program code. Some tools generate code in conventional programming languages. This provides programs that are *portable* among different machines (insofar as the languages are portable). It is, however, more efficient to generate machine code and avoid the additional step of compilation, which can degrade code efficiency.

Strictly, the need for human programming languages disappears when we use the facilities shown in Fig. 5.1. In practice, languages such as FORTRAN, COBOL, Pascal, and Ada may be retained to aid program portability. However, we do not want programmers to tinker with the program code generated because this would introduce errors and destroy its easy maintainability. Maintenance must occur by modifying the specifications and regenerating the executable code.

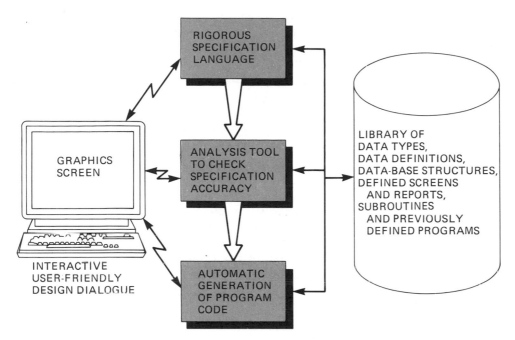

Figure 5.1 Specification languages should be user-friendly and rigorous, have tools for on-line accuracy checking, employ a library for the building of complex systems, and be capable of generating code that is bug-free.

STANDING ON THE SHOULDERS OF OTHERS

Isaac Newton wrote toward the end of his life that insofar as he had achieved anything worthwhile, he had done so by standing on the shoulders of giants. Richard Hamming comments that programmers do not tend to stand on each others' shoulders; they stand on each others' feet!

It is desirable that the tools we use should build ever-growing, ever-more-powerful libraries of subroutines and callable programs. It is desirable to be able to find out what exists in the library and be able to understand it, and use it. Most large computing installations reinvent the same routines over and over again because this capability is missing. We need to be able to link these routines into new programs without interface errors. This absence of *interface* errors is one of the major reasons for using rigorous design tools.

Figure 5.1 shows the tools employing a library. As well as the code of callable routines being stored, their descriptions in the specification language are stored, and this should make them easy to understand. A directory or thesaurus of callable modules may be used to make them easy to find.

Even relatively simple programs should be built up in blocks. These blocks need to be stored and made accessible for linking to other blocks. The library mechanism should serve this short-term need as well as the long-term need of providing an encyclopedia of existing routines and data structures.

Everything in the system is built from certain semantic primitives. The primitive mechanisms are themselves in the library. *All mechanisms added to the library, then, are defined in terms of mechanisms already in it.*

Rigorous interfacing rules throughout the library and the systems that use it should allow the library to grow in an orderly fashion, and should allow modules and systems to be interchanged among libraries.

DATA MODELS

Well-managed commercial DP installations have done strategic planning of data [8], built stable models of their data [9], and stored details of them in a dictionary. A data modeling tool is an important part of the family of tools.

The data in the data model should be automatically convertible to the representations of data needed by the tools shown in Fig. 5.1. The library contains the data dictionary and representations of data needed for building procedures and generating program code.

INTEGRATION OF DEFINITION LEVELS

We commented that with many systems the requirements definition is written in one way, usually in English; the specification is created with a different technique; and the implementation is yet again different—a programming language. When the requirements are translated into the specification there are errors, and when the specification is translated into code there are errors. It is difficult and costly to keep the requirements current once the specification is begun, or to reflect program changes back into the specifications. When the programs are maintained the documentation or higher-level systems descriptions are often not changed accordingly. They become out of date.

The specification is usually verified on a self-contained basis with only occasional ad hoc checks to the requirements documents. The programs are tested in a self-contained way with only occasional ad hoc checks to the specifications. The evolution through the development phases is usually not formally traceable.

The solution to this is to have *one language* that is formal input to a computerized design tool, with which requirements, specifications, and details can be expressed. The requirements statements are decomposed into greater detail and become the specifications. The specifications are decomposed into greater detail until sufficient detail is reached that code can be generated automatically. When changes are made at a lower level, these are automatically reflected upward. There is then structural integrity among the requirements, specifications, and detail. In fact, these words cease to have sharp demarcations. A high-level description is decomposed into successively more detailed descriptions.

The documentation does not slip out of date when successive maintenance changes are made because these changes require regeneration of program code from the specification language. The entire structure, top to bottom, reflects the change. Subsequent maintainers will then have a clear and detailed description from which to work.

A COMMON COMMUNICATION VEHICLE

A major reason for problems with systems is inadequate communication between users and developers, or between requirements definers and programmers. The most successful requirements definition projects are those where the implementers and users work on and understand the requirements together. The implementers understand better what the users need. The users understand better the constraints of implementation. Each group can trigger creativity in the other so that the combination produces something better than either group alone. A few exciting projects catch fire when there is excellent understanding between the instigators and implementers.

A good specification language should build a bridge of understanding between the users, requirements planners, specifiers, and implementers. A common language should be usable by all of these. The high-level view of the users or requirements planners should be decomposable into the detail needed by the implementers. The high-level planners or specifiers should be able to choose what level of detail they want to go in specifying the system. Changes made at lower levels should reflect back into this higher-level specification to preserve integrity of the levels.

A language that provides this communication bridge accelerates the understanding of the user requirements by the implementers, and enables the user or planner to understand his requirements better. Particularly important, it reveals misunderstanding among the users, planners, and implementers.

A developer may be better able to evaluate cost trade-off possibilities if he and the users employ a common way of looking at system specifications. This may save much money. Early feedback from the developer to the users is always beneficial.

UP-FRONT DETECTION OF ERRORS

The earlier in a project that errors are detected, the less expensive they are. Figure 5.2 illustrates this. Statistics from various organizations show that the errors detected during program testing are 10 or more times as expensive to correct as errors detected at the specification

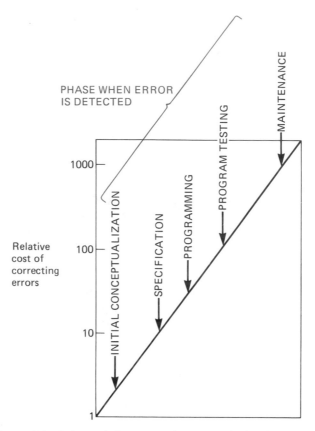

Figure 5.2   It is much less expensive to catch the error early.

stage. Correcting errors at the maintenance stage is another order of magnitude more costly.

On one avionics system the cost per line of code, including debugging and documentation, was reported to be $70. Its cost per line of code of maintenance, however was $4000 [10]. These figures were unusually high because of the complexity of the system, but would clearly have been much, much lower if the techniques described in this report had been used.

A language with rigorous verification which extends from the initial requirements definition down to the detailed phases increases the chance of catching errors at the earliest and least expensive time. A language that enables users, requirements planners, and implementers to communicate greatly decreases the chance of errors slipping through to phases where they are expensive to correct.

Traditionally, most errors are caught in the program testing or maintenance phases. As indicated earlier, many of these are specification errors which, by then, are very expensive to correct. An objective of the specification language is to find every problem as early in the development cycle as possible.

INTEGRATED TOP-DOWN AND BOTTOM-UP DESIGN
The development methodology should facilitate both top-down and bottom-up design, and should integrate them. There is a perennial argument about which is best. In practice, almost all complex systems design uses both. Pure top-down design is impractical. Pure bottom-up design would be a mess. Bottom-up design leads to interface problems, if uncontrolled. In writing a book I use a mixture of top-down and bottom-up design. Writing the details always causes me to change the table of contents. It is the same in systems design and a tool is needed which allows the changes and inventions that occur when modules are being worked out in detail to be reflected back naturally into the higher-level specifications.

A change made in one lower-level module may affect others and it is desirable that this ripple effect should be immediately traceable. The designer needs to be able to add requirements from the top or bottom. In designing systems with the technique described in this book, detailed work at a lower-level frequently causes data type references to be changed at a higher level. This continual adjustment can occur easily and could be largely automatic.

Often detailed design is done on one part of a system before another. The language should permit this to occur naturally and not cause later interface problems. On some systems one component is developed to completion while specifiers are still debating the concepts of another. Detailed design in one area should not be held up waiting for complete top-down specification of the layers above. It is normal to write one or more chapters of a book before the table of contents is complete. The top level is not *really* complete until the lower levels are done and the necessary iterations have taken place.

MATHEMATICALLY RIGOROUS LANGUAGES
To achieve the rigor that is necessary, the best specification languages will be mathematically based. Chapter 9 describes one such language in use today. Everything specified relates back to data types, functions, and control structures which are based on mathematical axioms. This enables constructs to be built which are provably correct. As separate modules are interlinked, this is done with rigorously verifiable interfaces.

Everything in the system is built from primitives which are known to be correct. The primitives are interlinked in provably correct fashions. Everything that uses them and obeys the rules is then free from bugs. The mathematically based interfacing rules distinguish this library concept from a conventional subroutine or program library. Increasingly large constructs can be built from what is in the library and then stored in the library with the knowledge that they are correct. As the library builds up the developers will have less work to do, and there will also be less to verify because it is known that everything in the library is bug-free.

The mathematical rules would be far too tedious and difficult to enforce by hand, so such a method depends on having a fully automated tool.

USER-FRIENDLINESS   Particularly important is the user-friendliness of the specification language. It may be mathematically based to enforce bug-free logic and interfaces between modules, but the mathematics should be completely hidden because most managers and analysts are terrified of mathematics. The telephone system is exceedingly complex and designed with mathematics, but most of its users know nothing about Erlang equations.

It is likely that different dialects of a specification language will be needed, and different forms of representation. All of these should be built from the same fundamental set of primitives.

If separate systems are defined from the same primitives, technical arguments can be resolved by breaking them down to the primitives to see whether there is real disagreement. With most requirements documents and specifications there are no means of analyzing them into common primitives.

Once the underlying structure of primitives exists, higher-level constructs should make the specification language as powerful as possible and as user-friendly.

SPECTRUM OF   The properties of being user-friendly and being
SPECIFICATION   rigorous often seem in conflict. Mathematical lan-
LANGUAGES   guages are not user-friendly; user-friendly languages
                         are generally not rigorous. We can rank them on a
chart like that in Fig. 5.3. Readability, or user-friendliness, is on the vertical scale. Traditional axiomatic languages appear at the right of Fig. 5.3, but at the bottom; they are difficult or impossible for ordinary analysts or users to read.

Traditional English specifications are at the extreme left of Fig. 5.3. They may be (fairly) readable but are entirely nonrigorous. Sometimes software is employed for formatting, editing, and storing specifications. This makes them easier to access, change, and manipulate, but does not make them more rigorous. Some text specification formatters have additional capabilities. They detect key words, format specification phrases, and generate tables of contents and indices. The program design language PDL [13] is an example. This improves the specification readability with clauses such as

```
IF CUSTOMER_CREDIT_CODE < 3
THEN ORDER IS REJECTED
```

It helps designers to find and cross-reference items in the specifications. It does no consistency or ambiguity checking, so there is little increase in rigor.

Another text approach advocates the use of a limited, well-defined, fairly nonambiguous subset of English [14]. This lessens the scope for misinterpretations and gives slightly more precision to the specifications. Software tools can help search for ambiguities and inconsistencies in such specifications [15].

Data flow diagramming techniques [3] give a step toward formality and are easy to understand. Clear diagramming techniques in general help analysts to conceptualize systems and clarify complex flows and interrelationships. Diagrams that are too symbolic, however, are not necessarily understood by end users. Most analysts find their diagramming techniques very useful and assume that users find them useful, too. In practice, many users are bewildered by the diagrams, thinking that they are more technical than they really are. Users sometimes complain that they understand the written specifications but not the diagrams.

Data flow diagrams are an improvement over unstructured text in terms

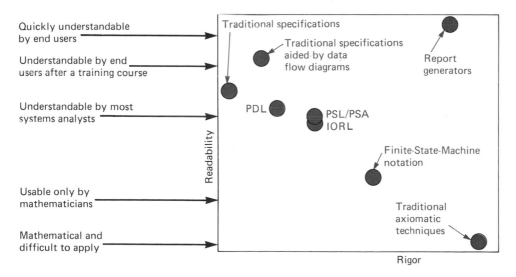

Figure 5.3 Spectrum of specification languages. (Analysts can argue about the exact positioning of the languages on the chart.) (From Ref. 12.)

of formality but are still far from being rigorous. They are far from the desired property that program code could be generated from them automatically. Much more detail is needed. Much more is needed to enforce consistency and completeness.

PSL with its associated PSA (Problem Statement Language and Problem Statement Analyzer) [5] is one of the best known specification languages. It divides system functions into subfunctions, precisely specifying the inputs and outputs of each. The analyzers perform consistency checking between functions. No function, for example, is allowed to use a data item not generated by another function. PSL is farther to the right in Fig. 5.3 but it is still far from completely rigorous or capable of automatic program generation. Beside it in Fig. 5.3 is another language for functional decomposition and input/output specification: IORL (Input/Output Requirements Language) [16]. Although these do some useful specification checking, they cannot check detailed logic or specify the order and timing constraints needed in real-time systems.

A more rigorous approach is the use of *finite-state-machine notation.* This permits complex logic to be described in terms of entities that have discrete *states.* The analyst determines what types of stimulus cause a state to change. The state of an entity is a function of the previous state and the inputs received. The output is a function of the inputs and the state when those inputs are received. State diagrams are drawn to represent the possible states and the stimuli that change them. Associated with the diagrams is a table showing all possible states and stimuli, to make sure that all combinations have been thought about.

Finite-state-machine notation has been used extensively in defining complex protocols for computer networks [17] and communications switching systems. The CCITT Standards Committee for International Telephony and Networking has a language for protocol specification based on this approach, SDL (Specification and Description Language) [18]. Other more generalized specification languages use this approach, for example, RSL (Requirements Statements Language) [19].

Finite-state-machine notation is farther to the right in Fig. 5.3. It is a major step in the direction of rigorous logic specification but not sufficiently so for automatic program generation. Some manufacturers' network software designed with finite-state-machine notation has exhibited mysterious and infuriating misbehavior! Finite-state-machine notation is extremely difficult for most end users to understand, so it is lower on Fig. 5.3. It is not normally used in general data processing or in most scientific computing, and in general has a limited class of applications. It is possible to build software that translates finite-state-machine representation into English-like constructs to aid in user checking [20].

NARROWLY FOCUSED LANGUAGES

Computable specification languages are found in narrowly focused areas. Probably the most commonly used example is report generators. A required report can be specified by users or analysts with software which often works in conjunction with a data base system. The program for creating the report is automatically generated. The circle at the top right of Fig. 5.3 is for report generators.

Report generators are not usually described as specification languages because their range of capabilities is so narrow. Broadening the scope somewhat, we have nonprocedural languages for querying, updating, and sometimes manipulating data bases. These are linked to graphics languages and decision support aids, and form the basis of most application development without programmers [7]. Very different types of specification or problem statement languages exist for certain specific applications, for example coordinate geometry, CAD/CAM, architect's drawings, and the building of telephone switching systems [21].

We really need, then, to add another dimension to Fig. 5.3 which indicates the *generality* of the language or the degree to which it can handle a comprehensive range of applications. This is done in Fig. 5.4. Given this way of looking at specification languages it is clear that the computer industry needs to progress in the direction of the arrow in Fig. 5.5.

The HOS technique which we describe in Chapter 9 appears to the author to be a major breakthrough. It is completely general and could be applied to any type of system. At its high levels it is reasonably understandable by users. English documentation can be displayed in association with any of its rigorously structured blocks. It can be linked to a variety of powerful forms of system representation for analysts or end users. Most important, it is based entirely on mathematical theorems and proofs, and so is entirely rigorous. It automatically generates program code which is provably correct.

Using the HOS technique, provably correct modules in a library are linked into new modules which are being created. The technique eliminates interface errors so that the combined construct is provably correct. Increasingly large or powerful modules can be built and stored in the library. This seems an ideal technique for operating a software factory. The HOS technique is positioned on the right hand side of Fig. 5.4.

The HOS technique is not near the top of the ease-of-use scale. New graduates learn to use it quickly and effectively. Old programmers are often bewildered by it. No mathematics is needed to use it, but it could be more user-friendly. A challenge now is to make such a technique user-friendly and anchor it to an encyclopedia designed for information resource planning and management in an organization.

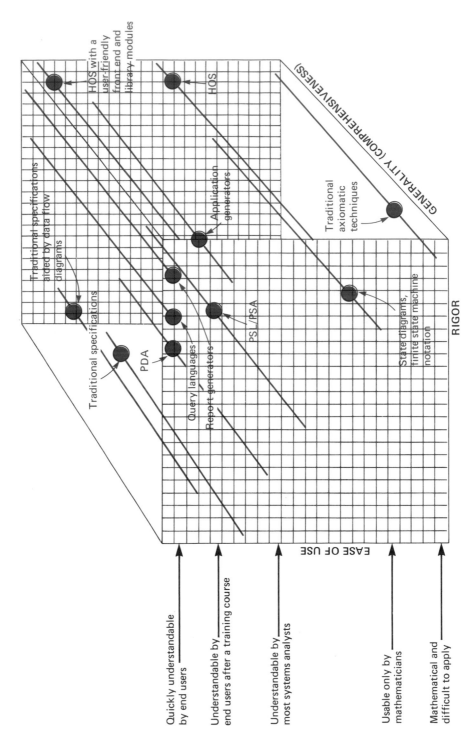

Figure 5.4 An extra dimension added to Figure 5.3.

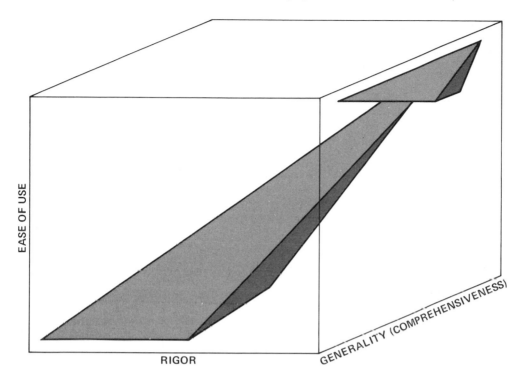

Figure 5.5 The computer industry needs to progress in the direction of
the arrow. It is now clear that there are techniques which can take us to
the head of this arrow. This portends a complete revolution in software
and application building.

SUMMARY

Box 5.1 lists the properties desirable in a specification.

Box 5.2 lists the properties desirable in a specification language. The facilities
we describe in the following chapters have almost all of the properties in
Box 5.2.

When specification languages with the properties described in Box 5.2
are used they change the whole nature of systems development. The development life cycle is different, as discussed in Chapter 11. The improvements in
correctness, maintainability, and user communication are clearly desirable,
but also the development process is speeded up and the cost reduced typically by an order of magnitude.

True software "engineering" needs the properties in Box 5.2. To build
software without provable correctness will one day seem like building a
bridge without stressing calculations.

BOX 5.1 Desirable properties of a specification [11]

A proper specification should:

- be free from errors.
- have conceptual clarity.
- be easy to understand by managers, analysts or programmers.
- be presentable in varying degrees of detail.
- be easy to create.
- be computable, i.e., have enough precision that program code can be generated automatically.
- be formal input to a program code generator.
- be easy to change.
- be complete.
- be traceable when changes are introduced.
- be independent of hardware.
- employ a data dictionary.
- employ a data model based on formal data analysis.
- employ a program module library with automatic verification of interface correctness.
- employ computerized tools which make it easy to manipulate and change.

BOX 5.2 Desirable properties of a specification language

- It should provide a way to think about systems which improves conceptual clarity.
- It should be easy to learn and use. At its higher levels it should be usable by non-DP personnel.
- It should be computable and program code should be generatable from it automatically.
- It should be designed for maximum automation of systems analysis, design, and programming.

BOX 5.2 *(Continued)*

- It should be rigorous and mathematically based so that it employs the maximum verification of the design.

- Its mathematical basis should be hidden from the average user because most users are terrified of mathematics.

- It should be versatile enough to remove the need for all manual use of programming languages. (Manual programming immediately violates the requirement of provable correctness.)

- It should extend from the highest-level conceptualization of systems down to the creation of enough detail for program generation. In other words, one language should suffice for complete system creation. The more detailed versions of a specification should be a natural extension of the more general ones. The high-level specifier should be able to decide into how much detail he wants to go before handing over to the implementer.

- It should be a common communication medium among managers, designers, implementers, verifiers, maintainers, and documentors.

- It should use graphical techniques which are easy to draw and remember.

- It should employ a user-friendly computerized graphics tool for building, changing, and inspecting the design. The language should be formal input to automated design.

- It should employ testing tools that assist in verification and permit simulation of missing modules so that partially complete designs can be tested.

- It should employ an integrated top-down or bottom-up design approach. Most complex systems come into existence through a combination of top-down and bottom-up design. The technique should allow certain elements of a system to be specified in detail while others, possibly parents or ancestors in the hierarchy, are not yet defined.

- It should indicate when a specification is complete (so that code can be generated from it).

- It should employ a hierarchy that descends into steadily increasing levels of detail. It should guarantee that each decomposition is logically valid and that each lower level completely replaces the one above it.

- When modifications are made lower in the hierarchy, these should be quickly and perhaps automatically reflectable in the higher levels.

- It should employ an evolving library of subroutines and programs, and of all the constructs the language employs. The primitive constructs will be in the library, so everything added to the library will be defined in terms of what is already there. The library becomes, in effect, an extendable requirement definition language. Everything in such a library employs the common primitives and has been verified by the software.

(Continued)

BOX 5.2 *(Continued)*

- It should link automatically to data-base tools, including a dictionary and directory that stores conceptual data-base models.

- It should guarantee interface consistency when subroutines or callable programs are used or when separate systems intercommunicate. Mathematical techniques should guarantee logical interface consistency as well as data consistency.

- The specification should be easy to change. It should be able to accommodate the unexpected. It should be easily changeable by persons who did not create it.

- All elements of a system should be traceable. All accesses and changes to data should be traceable throughout the system. This process should ensure that the inputs to each operation could only come from the correct source.

- The language may permit multiple dialects or multiple types of nonprocedural representation. These should all translate to a common set of control structures and a common set of rules for verifying correctness.

- A common set of primitives should be used to which rigorous verification techniques apply. All nonprimitive structures and semantics should then translate to the primitives. The common primitives provide definitive communication between users employing different semantics or dialects.

- Default options may be used where they simplify specification, for example with the formatting of screens or reports.

- The language should be independent of hardware or other resources which are likely to change. It should be translatable into many different resource environments.

6 INFORMATION ENGINEERING

THE MESS IN DATA LIBRARIES   In the first decades of computing, the programs in a corporation became an unruly mess, far removed from the orderliness one would normally associate with an engineering discipline. We now have techniques that can create better programs: generators, fourth-generation languages, and computable specification languages.

These tools alone, however, are not enough, because in data processing there is another mess—the data. Most large corporations' tape and disc libraries have vast numbers of volumes containing redundant, inconsistent collections of data, chaotically organized. What are, in effect, the same data are represented in numerous different incompatible ways on different tapes and discs. The grouping of data items into records is such that it leads to all manner of anomalies and maintenance problems. The use of fast and rigorous techniques for generating programs would not eliminate these problems without overall management and control of the data in an enterprise.

THE FAILURE OF DATA ADMINISTRATION   Many enterprises have disastrously failed in achieving overall coordination of data. This failure is extremely expensive in the long run in inflated DP costs, failure to implement needed procedures, and in lost business. Box 6.1 lists the reasons for failure of corporate data administration.

The Information Systems Manifesto for top management must make clear to them the financial importance of successful data administration. It is the job of management to build a computerized corporation, and the foundation stone of that is the data models that are used.

BOX 6.1   Reasons for failure of corporate data administration

Many early attempts at corporate data administration failed. The reasons for failure were as follows:

- Organizational politics prevailed, partly because of a lack of strong management with a clear perception of what was to be accomplished.
- The human problems of making different accountants or managers agree on the definitions of data items were too great.
- The magnitude of the task was underestimated.
- The data administrator was a low-paid technician.
- Methodologies for the design of stable data structures were not understood.
- The necessary data models were too complex to design and administer by hand, any appropriate computerized tools were not used.
- There was not an overall architect who could use the design methodology.
- Attempts of data modeling took too long and users could not wait.
- Data model design was confused with *implementation* and physical database design.

Many corporations have achieved successful data administration. Box 6.2 lists the requirements necessary for this to succeed.

BOX 6.2   Essentials for the overall control of data in an enterprise

Human

- Top management must understand the need for building the foundation stones of Fig. 6.4.
- Information which is strategic to the running of the enterprise should be identified [1].
- The data administrator must report at a suitably high level and be given full senior management support.
- The span of control of the data administrator needs to be selected with an understanding of what is politically pragmatic.

BOX 6.2 *(Continued)*

- The data administrator must be highly competent at using the design methodology and the methodology must be automated.

- An appropriate budget for data modeling must be set.

- Data modeling should be quite separate from physical data-base design.

- End-user teams should be established to assist in data modeling and to thoroughly review and refine the data models.

Technical

- Strategic planning should be done of the entities in an enterprise [1]. All entities should be represented in a rough entity model.

- The rough entity model should be expanded into detailed data models in stages, as appropriate.

- The detailed data model should represent all functional dependencies among the data items.

- All logical data groups should be in third normal form [2].

- Stability analysis should be applied to the detailed data model [2].

- The entity model and detailed model should be designed with an automated tool [3].

- Defined operations may be associated with the data to ensure that integrity. accuracy, and security checks are applied to the data, independent of applications.

- Submodels should be extractable from the overall computerized model when needed for specific projects.

- Ideally, the data modeling tool should provide *automatic* input to the library of the specification language, application generator, or programming language that is used.

THE COSTS OF BAD DATA ADMINISTRATION

A large commercial volume library has tens of thousands of tapes and discs, most of them containing different types of data items. One commercial application receives data from, or passes data to, many other applications. If these applications are developed without integrated planning of the data, chaos results. Higher management cannot extract data that needs to be drawn from multiple systems. Expensive conversion is needed and often important business options are lost because the data are not available in the right form.

When a corporate president angrily protests that for years he has been asking for weekly cash balances and he is no nearer to receiving them in spite of millions spent on computers and networks, the cause of this problem is that the data needed for such computation are ill-defined and incompatible. The computer world is full of horror stories about information being urgently needed by management or customers but the computers being unable to provide that information even though the requisite data were in their volume library.

When the Franklin National Bank went under, one other bank in New York compiled a set of questions that top management wanted answered urgently. They related to conditions that might apply in the bank and to answer them data from many differently written applications had to be assembled. After two days the computing executive had to admit defeat. *Yes,* the data were on discs, but *no,* the questions could not be answered.

Again in New York a bank tried to introduce an on-line cash management service. Competition had introduced this and it had great customer appeal. No new data were needed; they were all on discs, but the urgent application could not be introduced without massive data conversion, which required very time-consuming reprogramming. The competition stayed ahead.

In many organizations the lack of good data-base design and integration results in huge maintenance costs and delays. Procedures cannot be changed quickly. New procedures that are urgently needed take years to introduce.

The data-processing world is full of inspired subsystem builders who want to be left alone. Their numbers are rapidly increasing because small computers are proliferating, end users are learning to acquire their own facilities, and user-seductive software is spreading. In many cases they are doing an excellent job. However, the types of data they use overlap substantially, and this is often not recognized. The subsystems need to be connected, but often this cannot be done without conversion. Conversion, when the need for it becomes apparent, is often too expensive to accomplish, so incompatible systems live on, making it difficult or impossible to integrate the data that management need.

When good data-base administration has not been done there can be very expensive surprises late in the development phases, or during subsequent evolution.

SEPARATE DEVELOPMENTS WITH INCOMPATIBLE DATA

Traditionally, each functional area in an organization has developed its own files and procedures. There has been much redundancy in data. A medium-sized firm might have many departments each doing their own purchasing, for example. Before computers, this did not matter; it was probably the best way to operate. After computers, it did matter. There might be a dozen sets of purchasing programs to be maintained instead of one. There might be a dozen sets of incompatible purchasing files. The incompatibility prevented overall management information from being pulled together.

Earlier data-processing installations implemented one application at a time. (Many still do.) Integrating the different applications seemed too difficult. Integration grew slowly *within* departments or functional areas. To achieve integration *among* functional areas would have needed new types of management.

Each functional area had its own procedures which it understood very well. It did not understand the procedures of other areas. Each area kept its own files. The structure of these files was unique to the responsibilities of that area. Unfortunately, data had to pass among the areas, and management data needed to be extracted from multiple areas. These data were usually incompatible. Worse, individual areas frequently found the need to change their data structures, and often did so without appreciating the chain reaction of problems this would cause. Figure 6.1 shows the environment of this style of data processing.

In this nonintegrated environment, most communication of changes is done by paperwork—which is error-prone, time consuming, and highly labor intensive. Suppose, for example, that the engineering department prepares an engineering change report. It makes multiple copies, one for Production Control, one for Inventory Control, one for Accounting, and so on. Production Control concludes that the engineering change requires changes to be made to its product file. It requires a new request for materials to be sent to Inventory Control. Inventory Control must determine the effects of the change on its purchasing operations. These affect the costs of raw materials and parts. Inventory Control communicates these to Accounting. Accounting concludes that a change in sales price is necessary to retain profitability. It communicates this to Marketing. And so on.

When data for different areas are separately defined and incompatible, this passing of information among the separate systems is complex and inflexible. Manual handling of paperwork is needed. Accuracy is lost. Items slip through the cracks. Changes made to one system can play havoc with others. To prevent harmful effects of change the management procedures become rigid and change is made difficult.

In one factory more than $1 million worth of work-in-progress was unaccounted for on the shop floor due to items "slipping through the cracks" in the paperwork process. This unaccountability was a major motivation for the end-user management to create an on-line system, and that totally changed the administrative procedures of the factory [4].

The solution to the problems illustrated by Fig. 6.1 is centralized planning of the data. It is the job of a data administrator to create a *model* of the data needed to run an organization. This model spans the functional areas. When it is modularized it is broken up by data subjects rather than by departmental or organization-chart boundaries. Figure 6.2 illustrates the use of a common data model.

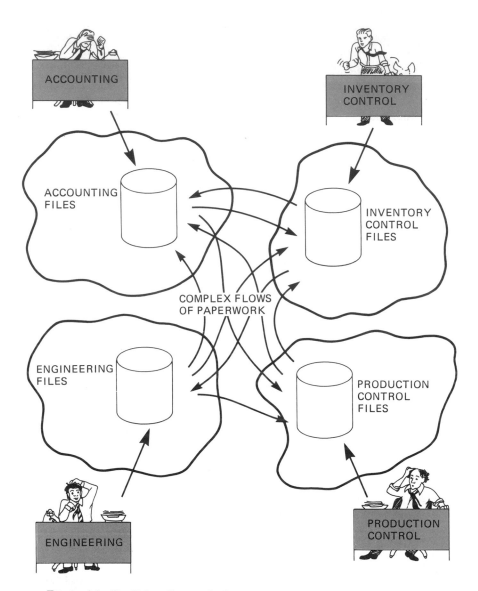

Figure 6.1 Traditionally, each functional area has its own files and procedures. Because of this, there is a complex flow of paperwork between the areas to reflect changes in all versions of the data. When this is computerized with separate files, the system is complex and inflexible. Data for different areas are separately designed and not equivalent. Accuracy is lost. Items "slip through the cracks" in the paperwork processes. Maintenance and change are difficult to accomplish, so the procedures become rigid. Management information spanning the areas cannot be extracted.

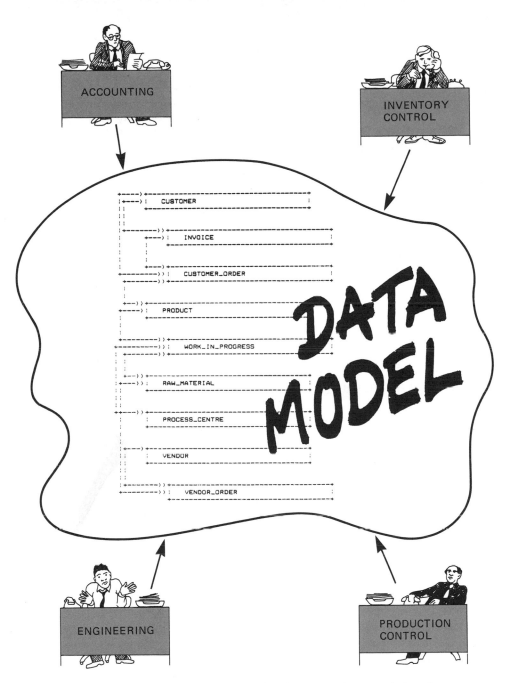

Figure 6.2 When data are consolidated into an integrated data base, data modeling is the key to success. The data structures become more complex, but the data flows are greatly simplified. The data are consistent and accurate. New forms of management information can be extracted quickly with fourth-generation languages. Changes in procedures can be made rapidly with these languages. Paperwork is greatly lessened. The administrative procedures of the organization need to be completely rethought. Fundamentally different analysis and design techniques are needed.

STABLE FOUNDATION STONE

In well-organized commercial DP the data models become a foundation stone on which the procedures are built. A basic reason why this has proven to be practical is that the types of data used in an enterprise do not change very much. Although the information requirements of executives change from month to month, the basic entities in an enterprise remain the same unless the enterprise is itself drastically changed.

An entity is anything about which data can be stored—a product, a customer, a salesman, a part. A data model shows the relationships between entities: a *salesman* is an *employee;* a *branch office* has many *salesmen,* and so on.

We store *attributes* giving data about the entities. For example, a salesman has a given address, territory, quota, salary, has sold a certain percentage of his quota, and so on. The data model shows what attributes relate to each entity.

The types of entities and attributes that are used in running a corporation usually remain the same with minor changes. They are the foundation of data processing. Their *values* change constantly. The *information* or types of reports which we extract from that collection of data may change substantially. The technology that we use for storing or updating the data will change.

When a corporation changes its administrative procedures, the entities and attributes usually remain the same. It may require a small number of new entities or some new attributes for existing entities, so the foundation data model grows somewhat over the years.

A typical medium-sized corporation has several hundred entities (when redundancies are removed). A large diversified corporation has more, and a separate data model might be created for each of its subsidiaries. There are often 10 or so attributes to each entity on average.

The author worked in a large bank when computers were first introduced. There was batch processing, many manual procedures, no terminals, and much form-filling. Today the customers use automated teller machines on-line to distant computers; there are large numbers of terminals and the administrative procedures have entirely changed. However, the raw types of data that are stored are the same as 20 years earlier. There has been a huge change in automation but if a data model had been created 20 years ago it would still be valid today, with minor changes.

Of course, if the bank decided to diversify into the whisky distillation business (appropriate for some bankers), a fundamentally different data model would have to be created and added on to the existing model.

With some data-base management software new attributes can be added without causing disruption. New entities can be added. Some types of data system software have more flexibility than others. An appropriate choice is needed.

It might be argued that some enterprises change more than banks in their types of data. That is true, so their data models need to be updated, preferably in an automated fashion.

STABLE DATA BASES

There is a huge difference between data bases that are specifically designed to be *stable,* and the files that have been used in traditional data processing. Typical file structures tend to change continually because the requirements of users change. No enterprise is static and management perceptions of what information is needed change rapidly.

We seek to isolate the programs from the changes in data structures. We use the term data independence. *Data independence* means that when the data structure changes the programs keep running because they are isolated from that change. The programs have a "view" of the data that can be preserved even though the actual, physical structure of the data changes.

Data independence is achieved by means of data-base management systems. The most important difference between a data-base management system and a file management system is that data-base management translates between the application program's view of data and the actual structure of the data. It preserves the program's view of data when the actual view changes in either a logical or physical manner. With data-base systems many application programs can have different views of the same data.

The use of a good data-base management system does not, by itself, give us the protection we need. We also need good logical design of the data structures used.

LOGICAL DESIGN OF DATA BASES

Unless controlled, systems analysts tend to design records which group together any collection of data items which they perceive as being useful. All manner of anomalies can arise because of inappropriate grouping of data items. Some of these anomalies are subtle and often not perceived.

A data base contains hundreds (and sometimes thousands) of types of data items. If the logical structures are designed badly, a large financial penalty will result. A corporation will not be able to employ the data bases as it should, so productivity will suffer. The data bases will constantly have to be modified, but they cannot be modified without much application program rewriting. The end users will not be served as they need, and because of this many try to create their own alternatives to employing the data base.

In the late 1970s it became clear that many data-base installations were not living up to the publicized advantages of data base. A few rare ones had spectacularly improved the whole data-processing function and greatly increased application development speed and productivity. Time and time again the difference lay in the design of the overall logical structure of the data.

One of the arguments for using data-base management systems is that they greatly reduce maintenance. In practice data-base techniques have often not succeeded in lowering the maintenance costs because a need is felt to create new data bases as new applications come along. The reason for this again lies in the logical structuring of the data, and the success of the data administration function.

WHAT IS INFORMATION ENGINEERING?
The methodologies for creating data-processing systems are rapidly changing. The term "engineering" is used in describing modern methodologies to imply that they use formal disciplines with precise, well-thought-out techniques rather than the invent-it-as-you-go and often sloppy methods of much conventional programming.

The term *software engineering* refers to the set of disciplines used for specifying, designing, and programming computer software. The term *information engineering* refers to the set of interrelated disciplines which are needed to build a computerized enterprise *based on data systems.* The primary focus of information engineering is on the data that are stored and maintained by computers and the information that is distilled from these data. The primary focus of software engineering is the logic that is used in computerized processes.

Software engineering techniques became formalized in the 1970s. They encompass software development methodologies such as structured programming, structured design, and structured analysis, and tools to support these. They are vital in the creation of complex software with complex logic. In much data processing, however, the design of the logic can be made relatively simple by appropriate data-base techniques, but it is complex to create the right data bases and tools for employing them effectively. Different techniques of the 1970s were rarely good enough, and many information systems were inadequate for the needs of corporate management.

Today some corporations have excellent information systems. Information engineering formalizes the techniques by which they were created. It uses different types of diagrams, tools, and methods from those used by software engineering.

The basic premise of information engineering is that data lie at the center of modern data processing. This is illustrated in Fig. 6.3. The data are stored and maintained with the aid of various types of data systems software. The processes on the left in Fig. 6.3 *create* and *modify* the data. The data must be captured and entered with appropriate accuracy controls. The data will be updated periodically. The processes on the right of Fig. 6.3 *use* the data. Routine documents such as invoices, receipts, freight bills, and work tickets are printed. Executives or professionals sometimes search for infor-

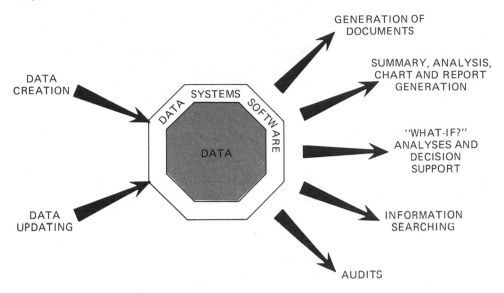

Figure 6.3 Most modern data processing is composed of actions that create and modify data, with appropriate accuracy controls, and processes that use, analyze, summarize, and manipulate data, or print documents from the data.

mation. They create summaries or analyses of the data, and produce charts and reports. They ask "what-if?" questions and use the data to help them make decisions. Auditors check the data and attempt to ensure that they are not misused.

The data in Fig. 6.3 may be multiple data systems. They may be stored in different ways. They will often be distributed. They are often updated and used by means of transmission links and terminals.

A second basic premise of information engineering is that that types of data used in an enterprise do not change very much, as we have described. The entity types do not change, except for the occasional (rare) addition of new entity types. The types of *attributes* that we store about these entities also change infrequently. The *values* of data change constantly, like the data in a flight information board at an airport, but the *structure* of the data does not change much if it was well designed to begin with.

Given a certain collection of data item types, we can find an optimal way to represent them logically. To do this is the task of the data administrator. The data administrator uses formal techniques (which have been automated [3]) to create stable models of the data. If well designed, these models change little and we can usually avoid changes that are disruptive. In information engineering these models become a foundation stone on which most computerized procedures are built.

Although the data are relatively stable, the procedures that use the data change fast and frequently. In fact, it is desirable that systems analysts and end users should be able to change them frequently. We need maximum flexibility in improving administrative procedures and adapting them to the rapidly changing needs of management. Every business changes dynamically and the views of management on how to run it change much faster.

The procedures, then, change rapidly (or should); the computer programs, processes, networks, and hardware change; but the basic types of data are relatively stable. The foundation stone of data is viable only if the data are correctly identified and structured so that they can be used with the necessary flexibility.

Because the basic data types are stable whereas procedures tend to change, *data-oriented* techniques succeed if correctly applied where *procedure-oriented* techniques have failed. Many of the procedure-oriented techniques have resulted in systems that are slow to implement and difficult to change. Information engineering seeks to fulfill rapidly management's changing needs for information. We can obtain results quickly once the necessary data infrastructure is established, by using high-level data-base languages and application generators.

THE BUILDING BLOCKS OF INFORMATION ENGINEERING

Information engineering provides an integrated set of methodologies, as shown in Fig. 6.4. In this diagram each block is dependent on the one beneath it. However, the blocks can be assembled in different ways.

① The stone on which all the others rest in Fig. 6.4 is the development of an enterprise or business model by *strategic information planning*. This attempts to determine the objectives of the enterprise and what information is needed for enabling it to accomplish its objectives.

② The next stage is the planning of information resources by *entity relationship analysis*. This is a top-down analysis of the types of data that must be kept and how they relate to one another. Entity relationship analysis is sometimes done across an entire enterprise; sometimes it is done for one division, subsidiary, factory, or portion of an enterprise.

The edifice of Fig. 6.4 can be built without the bottom two blocks, but to do so is like erecting a building on soft ground without good foundations.

③ The third stage is *data modeling*. Entity analysis surveys the types of data needed across an organization. It creates an entity model which is a broad overview but which does not contain all the details needed for database implementation. Data modeling creates the detailed logical data-base design and attempts to make it as *stable* as possible before it is implemented. Stage 3 is an extension of stage 2 which carries it into more detail and applies various checks for stability.

One of the important realizations that led to information engineering

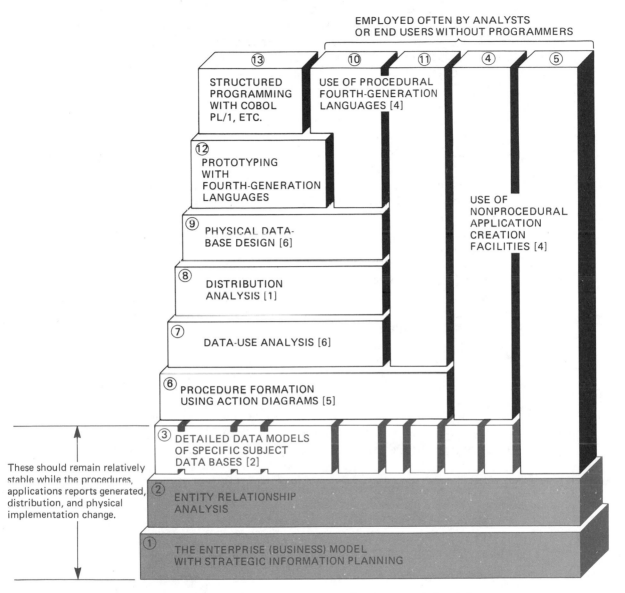

Figure 6.4 Information engineering: modern methodologies for DP management need information resource planning with sound data modeling, data administration, and the full use of fourth-generation languages.

is that data in an organization exist and can be described *independently of how those data are used.* Furthermore, the data need to be structured. We must not group any old collection of data items into a record. The data have certain *inherent* properties which lead to correct structuring. These properties are, again, *independent of how the data are used*. If we structure data in a way that violates the inherent properties, it is likely that we will have to restructure them in the future and that restructuring will be expensive because programs using the earlier structure will have to be rewritten. If we structure data in accordance with their inherent properties, the structure will be stable.

Data modeling is often done without the corporate-wide planning represented by the bottom shaded blocks of Fig. 6.4. Localized models are built which relate to a particular area or particular group of applications. Localized models are easier to create and use because they avoid arguments among separate departments or divisions. An objective of information engineering, however, is to achieve agreement on data definitions and structures across an organization, at least where that data have to be shared or used in an overall control system.

The bottom two blocks of Fig. 6.4 attempt to create commonality of data across an organization. The rough entity model is then divided into clusters which are sometimes called *subject data bases,* and these are modeled in detail (stage 3 of Fig. 6.4). Corporate-wide entity analysis cannot be achieved without top management support, and that is often lacking. To build a fully computerized corporation it is necessary to harness the perspectives of top management, and put the bottom blocks of Fig. 6.4 into place. The techniques of information engineering give top management a plan of action with which to direct the development of information resources.

④⑤   The bottom three blocks of Fig. 6.4 form a foundation on which most future data processing will be built. Once it, or part of it, exists, it is desirable that information be extractable from the data bases and reports and charts generated *as quickly as possible* with nonprocedural easy-to-use languages—blocks 4 and 5 of Fig. 6.4.

⑥   To create the procedures that employ a data base, a diagramming technique is needed to represent the actions that create data, and to retrieve, update, or delete data. These *data-base action diagrams* [5] are easy to create but are drawn in such a way that they can be converted directly into the code skeletons of fourth-generation procedural languages. This is the basis of block 4 of Fig. 6.4.

⑦⑧⑨   Analyzing how the data are used is important for heavy-duty applications (block 7). It leads to decisions about distributing the data (block 8) and physical organization of the data base (block 9). For applications with a low transaction volume, detailed use analysis is not necessary when appropriate data management systems are used. These data management systems may be quite different from the vintage data-base management systems.

(10) (11)   Fourth-generation languages and generators enable computer procedures to be created much more quickly than with third-generation languages such as COBOL or PL/1. That is a vitally needed improvement in the DP process provided that the users do not invent their own data structures. In many cases users do exactly that—glad of their newfound liberation from the DP programming organization. Where the data are shared data, rather than personal data, the use of fourth-generation languages should be linked into the data models as represented by blocks 10 and 11 in Fig. 6.4.

(12)   In many cases fourth-generation languages are used for creating prototypes. The prototypes may be adjusted many times after users interact with them.

(13)   In some cases procedures which are prototyped are reprogrammed with third-generation languages (usually COBOL) in order to obtain adequate machine performance.

The computing environment of Fig. 6.4 differs greatly from the old methods of systems analysis. When performed with automated techniques it greatly enhances the productivity associated with computer use in corporations. It enables systems to be built which can react rapidly to management's computing and information needs. It can greatly lower the costs of DP maintenance. It represents a major change in the management of DP.

Data-base usage can be further enhanced and application development speeded up by means of another layer added to the conventional data-base models, called *intelligent data base*. An intelligent data model contains logic and rules which are generally executed whenever the data are accessed.

COMPUTERIZATION OF INFORMATION ENGINEERING

Any attempt to do information engineering without computerized tools will become a mess. The data models are too complex to design, draw, and update by hand. Computerized design tools exist to create the models, help check their accuracy, link them to a data dictionary, update them, and make subsets of them available to persons who need to check or use them. These subsets become the basis of individual application building. The application creator can edit the submodel, determine a logical sequence of accesses through it, and use it in an application generator, fourth-generation language, or possibly third-generation programming.

A HOUSE UPON THE SAND

It is enormously tempting to build data systems without the foundation blocks at the bottom of Fig. 6.4. It will become much more tempting as data systems software becomes more powerful and user-seductive.

Most data in an enterprise need to pass from one department to another. Some data need to be gathered from a number of areas to form the information needed for decision making or control. There are not many data with which we can afford uncoordinated random design by local enthusiasts who wish to be left alone.

Strategic data planning, if done efficiently with a proven methodology, does not cost much compared with the hidden costs of chaotic data. It is largely a one-time expense, with only a minor cost for keeping it up to date. When done, it does not restrict the freedom of local developers. Once appropriate data systems exist, they greatly enhance the freedom to change the corporate procedures.

To build modern data processing without the foundation blocks of Fig. 6.4 is like building one's house upon the sand. Sooner or later it will be in trouble and have to be rebuilt. Absence of the foundation stones of data planning is one of the reasons why so much data-processing activity steadily bogs down in maintenance. The maintenance caused by absence of planning is enormously more expensive than the planning would have been.

Many corporations have indeed built their MIS house on sand. They have not accomplished the necessary data coordination, either because of lack of understanding of the necessity or methods, or because corporate politics has prevented it. It is up to top management to ensure that appropriate foundation stones are built.

TWO IMAGES

The reader should create in his mind two vividly contrasting images of the use of computers in an enterprise. In the *first image* all application creation is done by a hard-pressed DP group using COBOL, with detailed (but nonrigorous) systems analysis and requirements specification. Structured analysis and structured programming are used—in fact, the best of the structured software techniques. However, there is an application backlog of years, and an invisible backlog which is even greater. The users seem to be remarkably unsatisfied with the results when they get them. Top management perceives DP as a problem. End users have tried to bypass DP by obtaining their own minicomputers, but this has not been very satisfactory either.

The *second image* is one in which DP has done strategic data planning and data modeling throughout the enterprise and has made the data available on data-base systems. Users have work stations with which they can access these data. Some use a simple query language designed to be as user-friendly as possible. Others use a language with which they can manipulate the data, extract their own files, perform data entry, and ask "what-if?" questions. The shop floor supervisors, expediters, and the purchasing, marketing, and personnel departments all create computerized reporting and control procedures with a data-base-oriented application generator. This increases the productivity and efficiency of these departments, decreases the capital tied up in inventory, work-in-progress, and machine tools, and improves customer service. The financial staff, budget controllers, planners, and engineers create the programs they need with user-friendly languages, and make extensive use of decision-support tools. DP operates an information center designed to give users the maximum help in finding the information they need, processing it or reformatting it to their requirements, and generating procedures, reports, and intelligent spreadsheets.

Many DP representatives have become consultants, helpers, and instructors to the end users. Systems analysts work interactively with the end users to create their applications. Almost all data are on-line. Almost all users who need computing have access to terminals. The systems analysts almost never write specifications or draw data flow diagrams. They create prototypes of applications interactively, charting complex procedures with action diagrams which they can convert directly into code with fourth-generation languages. DP creates the data bases, networks, and the infrastructure necessary to support this activity. End users of many types throughout the corporation are inventing how they can use computers to improve their own productivity and are constantly adjusting their own applications.

The *second image* is what computing *ought* to be like. It needs support facilities creating by DP. It needs substantial coordination, which is what information engineering is all about.

Today's software makes it practical for many end users to do their own application generation. Whether they do it themselves or with help from a DP specialist, it needs to be done within a *managed* framework.

7 THE INFORMATION CENTER CONCEPT

THE PAYBACK OF AN INFORMATION CENTER

The growth of information centers is the most vigorous new trend in DP management.

An information center is a facility designed to encourage, train, and support end users who use computers directly, generating reports or creating applications. At the same time the information center should *manage* user-driven computing so as to avoid its many potential problems. Both the languages used and the types of applications differ greatly. Some users employ only data-base query languages; others do highly sophisticated computing, such as financial modeling, with languages such as APL. Some users employ decision-support tools. Many use personal computers. Some users put computers to work entirely on their own; others need substantial help from the information center consultants.

The overriding objective of information center management is to greatly speed up the creation of applications that end users require. The queue for conventional development, with its long application backlog, is *bypassed*.

One DP department was required to calculate the return on investment of all DP-developed applications. The average was 37%, with an average payback period of 30 months. This same DP department created an information center. This gave 100% return on investment [1]. A large firm in Chicago quoted a return on investment of 300% on its information center activities. The reason for these high figures is that the users are tackling problems that have a direct impact on cost or revenue, for example making better financial decisions, optimal purchases of bulk chemicals, or maximizing the goods that can be handled with given resources.

Box 7.1 lists quotes from executives in large corporations about the effects of their information centers.

BOX 7.1 Quotations from executives at companies that employ information centers

Vice-President, MacDonald's, Chicago:

The information center is our single most important productivity tool.

C. L. Dunn, Vice-President, Bank of America:

We have an *active* library right now of 83,000 NOMAD procedures written by end users with only a little assistance from our technical staff. Those procedures contain almost 4 million lines of instructions that would have taken 2120 man-years to develop using traditional tools and approaches. [2]

R. L. Crandell, President, Comshare Inc.:

At Comshare alone, we've solved 8000 or 9000 business problems over the past 16 years. We couldn't have done that—we wouldn't even have attempted it—without those tools. [2]

R. Jackson, Senior Internal Consultant, Dow Chemical Co.:

By 1987, end users at Dow will be handling 50% of their computer application needs without help from the data processing staff. [2]

S. G. Abbey, Director, Morgan Stanley & Co., New York:

Several years ago we realized that Morgan Stanley's product is really information; our goal is to provide it in the most productive manner. [2]

Dr. C. Oldenburg, General Manager, Standard Oil of California:

We were in the information center business even before we knew to call it that. We now have one of the largest in-house time-sharing services in the world—it's a way of life for a quarter of our 40,000 employees. [2]

J. W. Johnson, Vice-President, Equitable Life Assurance Society, New York:

The products we sell have much in common with other insurance companies, and we stay up nights looking for a competitive edge. Equitable found it with our information center. [2]

BOX 7.1 *(Continued)*

Dick Wood, Manager, Harris Corporation:

The most important factor in our success is direct, active involvement by end users. Our information center employs only one technician; the rest are MBA's who speak the same language as users do. You have to turn over center services to the end users if you expect to achieve the benefits you seek. [2]

A. B. Crawford, Vice-President, Digital Equipment Corporation:

The information center concept has allowed us to provide truly responsive management information systems—without the typical development backlog. It has helped our user community become actively involved in satisfying their own computing requirements. [2]

Operations Executive, Santa Fe Railroad:

The freight we carry has more than doubled. That increase has been handled without any increase in staff. We couldn't have possibly handled the increase in business with our existing staff without MAPPER.

Production Coordinator, Oil Consortium

By building an information center I was able to process selected key indicators quickly, interpret them, and present an analysis of the situation by the time of the daily operations meeting held at 7:00 a.m. About 80% of the time nothing unusual was going on, and I was able to use the information center data to debottleneck production capacity. During the critical 20% of the time, I was in a position to work with operational managers on an hour-by-hour basis to balance the flow from the fields to the refinery and the export terminal.

The management system supported by information center concepts enabled us to export *an additional million barrels a month at no additional cost.*

L. Mertes, Vice-President, Continental Bank, Chicago:

Users get reports on the day they ask for them. Before it took two months. This completely changes the way they utilize information. [3]

THE NEED FOR MANAGEMENT

End-user computing needs management. Without help, training, and controls, all manner of problems can develop. The information center is the management vehicle for user computing. The reasons we need such management are as follows:

- To help avoid the numerous types of mistakes that users can make
- To spread the culture of user computing so that it reaches its full potential
- To ensure that data entered or maintained by the users are employed to their full potential rather than being in isolated personal electronic filing cabinets
- To assist the users so that they develop applications as efficiently as possible
- To ensure that adequate accuracy controls on data are used
- To avoid unnecessary redundancy in application creation
- To avoid integrity problems caused by multiple updating of data
- To ensure that the systems built are auditable and secure where necessary
- To link the end-user activities into the data administration process

The information center concept should support a natural division of labor between the end users and DP staff. Each group provides what it is best equipped for. The end users know what information, reports, and decision support they need in order to do their jobs well, and usually they need results quickly. The DP support group knows how these results can be obtained. The two groups work together in close partnership, balancing their resources for maximum productivity. To achieve this result the end users must be trained, encouraged, and motivated, and their competence developed to a point where they can generate and manipulate the reports that they need, and perform calculations, answer "what-if?" questions, perform simulations, and so on. In some cases end users have created major operations systems.

DELIVERY VEHICLES

The information center is a management concept that can support a variety of means of delivering computing. Sometimes the delivery vehicle is a terminal connected to a time-sharing system. Sometimes it is a shared minicomputer. Increasingly in the future it will involve personal computers. The single-user computers will grow more powerful rapidly, and drop in cost. They will have user-seductive software which includes data-base management, fourth-generation languages, application generators, graphics, and a variety of decision-support tools.

Single-user computers or executive workstations will need to have network connections to data storage facilities on other machines. Often the personal computer will be connectable to a mainframe with a data base or a network of mainframes. Sometimes groups of personal computers will be connected to a local minicomputer with data storage. This, in turn, will sometimes be connected to a distant mainframe. In this way hierarchical distribution of data will occur.

Information centers differ greatly in the amount of data they make available to users. Some extract data from production systems and make these available for user manipulation and decision-support activities. Some merely support the user's own data input for his own applications. Others operate major general-purpose information retrieval systems to which new data can be added whenever it is requested.

Office automation (office-of-the-future) facilities are spreading rapidly in some organizations, providing mailbox facilities, automated in-basket processing, and other services. These ought to be linked with the information center service. The office-of-the-future and information center concepts are becoming closely integrated in some organizations.

The term *administrative workbench* or *executive workbench* has been used to describe combined office automation, data-base access, computing, and graphics facilities at a terminal.

ELECTRONIC FILING CABINETS

Most information centers have access to data bases, sometimes old-established traditional data bases, and sometimes new, more flexible, relational data bases. In some cases the data accessible by users is perceived as though it were in an electronic filing cabinet to which they have personal access.

They have several types of reports in their *virtual filing cabinet*. They can specify the type of data they want to see, what calculations should be done on the data, and how they should be sorted and presented. They may ask to see data only when the data exceed certain parameters. They can determine when "exceptions" should be brought to their notice.

In some cases the data in the users' virtual filing cabinets will be derived from the master data bases (or files) which are used for the main production processes. In some cases the users will create their own personal files. Often the users will enter and maintain data important to their area. These data, with appropriate security, audit, and accuracy checks, are moved across to the central master data bases.

The users can transmit data from their virtual filing cabinets to other users. They can generate reports that highlight important information, and have these printed if necessary.

INFORMATION CENTER SUPPORT

In some organizations DP executives have tried to stop end users developing their own applications. In other organizations they have allowed it to happen, only too glad to get some of the end users off their backs. End-user development is a force that should be harnessed, encouraged, and supported to the full, but if it happens in an *uncontrolled* fashion, it can store up trouble for the future, because multiple versions of incompatible data come into existence, and multiple machines cannot be interlinked.

The information center is often a group within the DP organization designed to serve the end users directly and speedily. The group is aware of what data bases exist and sometimes sets up other data bases. It makes this information available for end users, to access and manipulate. Information center consultants work with the end users. The consultants help users to create the decision support systems, personal computing facilities, information retrieval systems, and organizational support systems. A major reason for establishing this mode of operation has been the extreme dissatisfaction expressed by end users about the way DP has been responding to their information needs.

The consultants encourage the users to employ the information facilities that already exist. They sit at terminals with the users to create the cataloged query procedures, report-generation routines, or graphics-generation routines. They train the users to employ these facilities.

Where more complex applications are needed, the information center consultants decide how they can be created, selecting, where possible, an application generator, language, or package that avoids the formal, slow, programming development cycle.

CONNECTION TO INFORMATION ENGINEERING   Some information centers have been developed without any link to the information engineering process. This is clearly disadvantageous. It is better to regard the provision of an information center as an integral part of information engineering.

The information center needs access, potentially, to any of the information in an organization. It needs to comprehend fully the information resources and data models, and have access to the data dictionaries.

A well-run information center is in close contact with the information needs of users and management. Its knowledge of their requirements should be fed into the entity analysis and data modeling process.

Perhaps the biggest danger of information center operation, or of the spread of small computers and user-friendly software, is that multiple uncoordinated data structures will be used. The answer to this is well-controlled data administration. The data in the users' data bases must be compatible, where necessary, with the data in the production data bases.

Data are often extracted from production system data bases and moved to separate information center data bases, as shown in Fig. 7.1. Sometimes they are moved back in the opposite direction, with suitable accuracy controls. These operations require common data administration and, ideally, the same data dictionary.

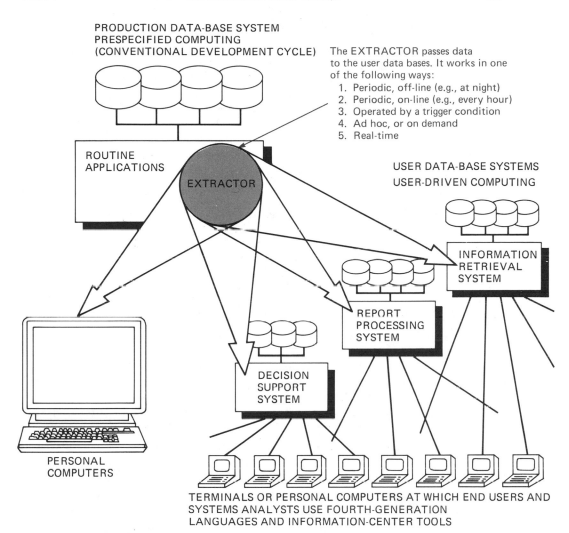

PRODUCTION DATA-BASE SYSTEM
PRESPECIFIED COMPUTING
(CONVENTIONAL DEVELOPMENT CYCLE)

The EXTRACTOR passes data
to the user data bases. It works in one
of the following ways:
1. Periodic, off-line (e.g., at night)
2. Periodic, on-line (e.g., every hour)
3. Operated by a trigger condition
4. Ad hoc, or on demand
5. Real-time

ROUTINE
APPLICATIONS

EXTRACTOR

USER DATA-BASE SYSTEMS
USER-DRIVEN COMPUTING

INFORMATION
RETRIEVAL
SYSTEM

REPORT
PROCESSING
SYSTEM

DECISION
SUPPORT
SYSTEM

PERSONAL
COMPUTERS

TERMINALS OR PERSONAL COMPUTERS AT WHICH END USERS AND
SYSTEMS ANALYSTS USE FOURTH-GENERATION
LANGUAGES AND INFORMATION-CENTER TOOLS

Figure 7.1 Certain data are extracted from the main DP systems and
transferred to the user system.

**DATA
COORDINATOR**   If end users are given the capability to create their
own files with user-friendly software, data-item
formats and definitions should be derived from a
common dictionary. Sometimes in such installations a *data coordinator* is
used. This person, sometimes a specially trained end user, ensures consistency among the users' data. This data coordinator ought to report (at least
for data administration purposes) to the official data administrator.

The data coordinator may have functions such as the following:

- Be aware of what data models exist and ensure that users' data is made consistent with such models.
- Make the dictionary definitions of data available to the users.
- Where the users' data are not yet represented in data models, coordinate with the data administrator to see if the data being created can be input to the modeling process.
- Generally liaise with the data administrator about the users' data.
- Guide and encourage the users in employing data.
- Train the users.
- Move infrequently used reports or data off-line (if this is not done automatically).
- Remove infrequently used "user views" of data.
- Establish techniques for informing users what data exist.
- Contribute to a newsletter about the systems and the available services.

CONFLICT IN SPEED OF RESULTS   There may be a conflict between the information engineering process and the information center operation.
The purpose of the information center is to obtain results as quickly as possible to end users. Information analysis and data modeling, on the other hand, takes a long time and might delay the delivery of quick results.

Once the data models are completed and implemented, results may be obtained very quickly. Until that has been done a compromise is often necessary. Data for a given application may be captured, possibly normalized by the information center analysts and converted to the form needed by the user languages. Such data may have to be retrofitted later to the detailed models as they emerge. But the modeling process should not hold up the getting of valuable results to the users quickly.

The answer to this conflict is to get the information analysis and data modeling done as soon as possible. The sooner the data models are in place, the sooner the enterprise can benefit fully from the information center methods.

To move rapidly into user-driven computing without information engineering is to risk a rapid spread of incompatible data as different users devise their own data. The mess in data will become rapidly worse.

INFORMATION CENTER ORGANIZATION   Figure 7.2 shows a type of information center organization which works well in some corporations. Data-processing development is split into two parts, conventional development and the information center. Both link to the data administration function, which has a

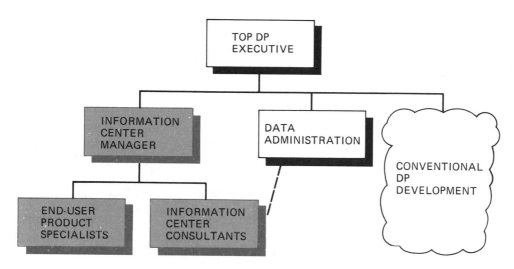

Figure 7.2   Information center organization.

vital role in standardizing the data that must pass between the two areas, and linking both areas into the information engineering processes.

The information center reports to the overall DP executive. Its staff consists of general consultants who work with the end users, and specialists who are expert on end-user products. These staff train and assist the end users, create applications for them, and where practicable encourage them to solve their own problems with the end-user languages.

An organization in the grip of traditional DP standards and methods can make a small beginning by initially having only a few staff using the information center methods. The objective should be that as the information center methods are demonstrated to work well, they should take over a rapidly increasing proportion of the DP development.

The information center must relate closely to the data administration function which is a vital part of conventional DP development (if it is well managed). The information center consultants will use the data bases, request additional data bases, and participate in all stages of the information engineering processes. The information center may design and operate its own data bases for decision support and information retrieval systems. The data in these will often be derived from conventional DP production-oriented data bases, and conform to the information engineering data models and data dictionary.

DIFFERENCES IN SCOPE Information centers in existence differ greatly in their scope.

Some are small operations within a DP department, sometimes without a full-time manager. Some are of trivial significance with a handful of users; others have changed the entire DP culture of a corporation.

Some information centers do not work on routine production systems, but only on ad hoc systems—information systems and decision support systems. Others are organized so that *all* application development without programmers goes via the information center (which may be called a different name). Some of the nonprocedural languages that a nonprogramming systems analyst can employ are appropriate for creating certain production systems as well as information systems, and produce suitably efficient machine code. IBM's DMS (Development Management System), for example, is used by nonprogramming analysts to create production systems.

Figure 7.3 splits application development into six categories. Some information centers do category 1 only. Some do categories 1 and 2. Some build decision support systems but not production systems; others have been highly successful with production systems.

Some information centers do categories 1 through 4 of Fig. 7.3 but do not use programmers. A few information centers employ programmers to create subroutines that fill a need when using an application generator. Others have created a new category of programmer trained to be very fast and efficient with a fourth-generation procedural language.

	Information Retrieval and Decision-Support Systems	Routine Processing (Production) Systems
Development by End Users Only	1	2
Development by Systems Analysts Working Hand in Hand with End Users	3	4
Development by Systems Analysts and Programmers	5	6

Figure 7.3 Some information centers support category 1 only; some support categories 1 and 2; and some support categories 1 and 3, or all application development without programmers, that is, categories 1 through 4. A few information centers employ programmers who are specialists on the new languages.

We can thus find many highly successful combinations of the categories in Fig. 7.3. The information center should not be limited to category 1. It should embrace all forms of application development without programmers.

Sometimes information centers have been set up with the blunt insistence that the staff should do no application development themselves. Some IBM courses and proposals say that a cardinal rule of the information center is that its staff not develop applications themselves. In practice, most of the information centers that are spectacular successes do have staff who build applications, but *quite differently from conventional development.* They do not write program specifications for separate programmers to code. These analysts employ application generators or fourth-generation languages which can obtain results *fast* without conventional programming. They can complete the application faster than writing programming specifications, so the traditional development cycle disappears. They work hand in hand with end users to create prototypes, constantly adjusting and expanding the prototypes.

The staff in question sometimes do not have a DP background. They might be recently hired MBAs who can understand the users' problems and who have made themselves highly skilled with an application development facility.

The information center *should* develop applications itself so that it becomes fully familiar with the problems, and thus can better support the user development, and also because the best form of development is often users and information center staff working jointly on creating applications. It should, where possible, insist that users *document* their own applications, and learn how to modify (maintain) them.

The information center should avoid the trap of having a large number of (for example, APL) programs to maintain.

TECHNIQUES ANALYST

When a demand for a new application comes up it is desirable to decide how it will be developed. Appropriate development software should be selected. It should be developed by the *fastest* method possible and with a procedure that will minimize future maintenance costs. This means that languages such as COBOL and PL/1 should be avoided where possible.

A specialist, sometimes called a *techniques analyst* (TA) may make the decision about how a new application demand should be handled. He will know the capabilities of the different software and will decide whether the application needs conventional programming and analysis, whether it can be created by a systems analyst with an application generator, or whether it is appropriate for end users development perhaps with a high-level data-base language.

The techniques analyst may act as a switch, and decide whether an application should be done by conventional development or information center development.

A major objective of the technique selection should be to avoid programming in COBOL, PL/1, FORTRAN, Pascal, BASIC, or Ada wherever it can be avoided. Not only is it expensive, but it results in programs that are very costly to maintain and which cannot be changed quickly.

FUNCTIONS OF IC STAFF

Selection of the techniques or software is one of many services that should be provided by the information center staff. They need to train, encourage, support, and assist the end users in obtaining the applications they need. Box 7.2 lists functions that should be carried out by the information center. It divides them into two groups—those performed by the analysts or consultants who work with the end users, and those performed by a technical support group or person. This follows the division shown in Fig. 7.2.

The size of the information center staff varies greatly depending on the number of users supported and whether the consultants *develop* the applications along with the users or insist that users do their own development.

Some corporations have started an information center with a low-level commitment and allowed it to grow. In some small operations the staff carries out all of the support functions in Box 7.2; there is no division into technical and consultant staff as in Fig. 7.2. The staff play a role which is similar to that of an IBM systems engineer.

One large bank started this operation with a manager, assistant manager, two professional staff, and a clerical coordinator. The manager was an enthusiast of the software used, had a technical background, and was chosen because he wanted to do the job. The assistant manager was an ex-operations shift supervisor with no programming or systems background. It was argued that he was going to guide users who also had no technical background, so it would be an advantage for him to have gone through the learning process relatively recently.

This information center (which is called by a different name) is a low-key operation with a low budget compared to the bank's overall DP budget. In other cases a much more aggressive move has been made into this form of operation with a tough executive heading it who believes that a high proportion of new application development can be done with techniques that bypass conventional DP programming and analysis.

SELLING

The more aggressive information centers regard *selling* the new capabilities to end users to be of primary importance so that advanced technology can make a more rapid penetration. In the bank mentioned above there is a department which is responsible for the services the bank provides to its customers—a payroll service, a check reconciliation service, and so on. The bank put its information center in this department, arguing that people who were good at selling and supporting computer services outside the bank could also do it inside the bank. The manager of the department had experience in dealing with dissatisfied and disgruntled customers, and these talents were useful to the information center.

RIVALRY

Sometimes harmful political rivalry has grown up between the management of the information center and the management of conventional DP development. The manager of the information center naturally wants to satisfy as many user demands as possible and remove them from the slow, conventional DP cycle. In some cases he assumes a missionary fervor about doing this. He sees conventional development as being cumbersome, expensive, and obsolete. He makes his views known about this and gains many disciples among previously frustrated end users. He advocates that instead of doing expensive maintenance on conventional programs, these should be scrapped and redeveloped with the information center methods where possible.

The manager of conventional development may feel attacked and in danger of losing his empire. His rival running the information center appears like a hero, and he does not. He may argue against the new methods. Great opposition is sometimes encountered to the setting up of, or expansion of, information center operation. Most of these are invalid compared with the major gains in productivity which can be achieved.

The solution to the rivalry lies in good overall DP management by an executive to whom both the information center manager and the manager of conventional DP report. The manager of conventional DP should be encouraged to use new software techniques also, and challenged to demonstrate how productivity can be increased and maintenance costs cut by combining the techniques of information engineering with the use of fourth-generation languages.

Often the manager of conventional development perceives that all *routine* operations are his territory and that the information center should be used only for ad hoc development such as decision support systems. The argument against this is that some case histories show successful and spectacular development of routine, transaction-driven production systems by end users.

A better division of responsibilities is to say that the information center will encourage and support all types of user-driven development that make sense (and some do not); conventional development will support all development which involves the need for DP programmers using COBOL, PL/1, and

BOX 7.2   Functions that should be carried out by
an information center

By the Consultants

- Training the users to employ the tools and create applications
- User encouragement, education, and selling
- Continual assistance in improving the effectiveness of end-user computing
- Introduction of decision-support software and hardware to all users who are making decisions
- User assistance with personal computers; finding appropriate personal computer software for the users
- Identification of all users who need decision support tools
- Generation of applications (without programmers) in conjunction with users
- Generation and modification of prototypes
- Specification of changes to prototypes that may be needed to make them into working systems
- Assistance with maintenance changes
- Consulting on user problems
- Debug support when something goes wrong
- Determining whether a proposed application is suitable for information center development, and selecting the software and methods
- Demonstrations of information center capabilities to users, including senior management
- General communication with senior management
- Communication with traditional DP development
- Ensuring that the data used conform to the corporate data models
- Close links to the data administrator(s) in defining and representing data, and evolution, if necessary, of the data models
- Providing input to the various stages of information engineering
- Maintaining a catalog of available applications and data bases
- Coordination to prevent duplicate or redundant application development
- Creating user data bases, and initiating the extraction of data into information retrieval facilities
- Assisting the user in locating the data he needs; arranging to have data converted where this is necessary

BOX 7.2 *(Continued)*

- Assisting the user in obtaining authorization to access the required data
- Conducting user-group meeting for users to interchange experience, and workshops to develop proficiency in better techniques and user self-sufficiency
- Administrative assistance to help users obtain a terminal, ID, password, workspace, and so on
- Operation of schemes for motivating users
- Tracking the benefits to the organization
- Promoting the information center facilities and benefits at all levels in the organization

By the Technical Specialists:

- System setup and support
- Dealing with technical and software problems
- Selection of fourth-generation languages and generators and the versions of those which are used
- Understanding and selection of decision-support tools
- Ongoing expertise in and evaluation of software products that might be used, and their possible applications
- Assistance in choosing techniques or software for a given application (the job of the techniques analyst)
- Acquiring information of the performance characteristics of the languages used so that realistic decisions can be made about what they can handle
- Selection of hardware where departmental minicomputers or microcomputers are used
- Communication with vendors
- Monitoring system usage, and planning future resources
- Charge-back to users
- Tuning or reorganizing an application for better machine performance
- Auditing system usage and application quality
- Ensuring that the users have the terminal they want and appropriate network access
- Providing backup, recovery, and archiving (end-user data on peripheral systems can be included in the overall backup and recovery plan)

new languages for DP programmers, such as IBM's ADF and CINCOM's MANTIS.

Because they serve the same community, often with the same data bases, it is vital that information center management, conventional development management, and maintenance management work closely together, and explore the most cost-effective trade-offs.

LANGUAGES   Information centers differ widely in their choice
SUPPORTED   and range of languages.

Some support only one software package, such as IBM's VSPC (Virtual Storage Personal Computing) or Univac's MAPPER.

Given the *widely* varying capabilities of the software it is usually preferable, when the center becomes well established, to support more than one type of software.

What makes the information center possible is the software that it uses. What can make it excellent is a good choice of software.

An information center at the Equitable Insurance Company in New York employs the following software [4]:

● **Languages to build systems:**	FOCUS RAMIS	English-like languages used by managers and professionals
● **Languages used for model building:**	APL ADRS	(A Programming Language) (An APL report generator)
● **Statistical packages:**	SAS SPSS	These contain many formulas for statistical analysis
● **Language for financial analysis:**	FPS	(Financial Planning System)
● **Language for querying, manipulating, and selecting data:**	QBE ADI FOCUS RAMIS	(An easy-to-use query language) (Giving APL programs access to data bases)
● **Packages for preparing graphs:**	SAS-graph FOCUS	

Two types of color terminals are used with this information center. FOCUS and SAS-graph are used to display a variety of types of information in graphical form.

Some of the software needed is general purpose—query languages, report generators, application generators. Some is oriented to specify types of application, such as financial planning, project management, text processing, and computer-aided design.

COMMUNICATION   A particularly important skill of the information
SKILLS   center staff is communicating with the end users.
                          Often the center is staffed by people trained as
systems analysts. Their job changes fundamentally. They no longer write
program specifications, draw data flow diagrams, and so on. They act more
as consultants, listening to the end users' problems, solving them, determining the users' needs for information, encouraging, training, and selling ideas
to the end users.

It is important to train the information center staff in the new languages and software, but this usually comes naturally to them. Sometimes
the necessary communications skills come less naturally. A particularly valuable training for some information center staff has been courses on how to
communicate well. Such courses should be followed by careful monitoring
and guidance of their activities to help them acquire the style and techniques
of a good consultant.

EARLY SUCCESS   It is generally desirable when an information center
                          is established that it should be seen to be successful
quickly. If there are no early successes, it might be regarded as an odd-ball
idea or DP plaything, rather than a facility that will revolutionize the corporation's use of computers.

The selection of the first users is particularly important. This should be
a group of users keen to develop their own query and analysis services, and
likely to cooperate well on what may be an experimental basis at first. They
should have a definite business need for the new service so that there will be
a strong payoff.

For this initial group the appropriate software products are selected,
and data bases made available, possibly with separate user data bases being
extracted from established production data bases or files and rebuilt in the
data management system of the development tool being used. A small number of users are trained and the information center staff work with them
closely.

The initial experience with the service should be evaluated carefully
both by users and DP. It may need substantial adjusting. When both parties
perceive it to be working well, it can be extended to other types of users.

SPREADING THE   Eventually, when DP staff are confident of its suc-
SUCCESS   cess and capable of giving good support, the con-
                          cept of information center operation needs to be
sold throughout the organization.

A demonstration center should be set up and demonstrations given to
all classes of users who should be employing the information center services.

Demonstrations to senior management are particularly important. These should use *real* corporate data and be designed to show *interesting* results.

The objective of the demonstrations should be to show something of direct basic value to each area manager—something that affects how well his job is done. The demonstration content should be oriented to business results, not technical wizardry. The results-oriented data should be displayed as attractively as possible, for example, on color graphics terminals.

Various operating areas should be asked to contribute data for the demonstrations. Members of the EDP steering committee might be each asked to contribute a demonstration.

The author attended a demonstration in an insurance company before senior executives. Throughout almost the entire two-hour session the discussion was about business results and finances, not about computing technology. Data had been captured relating to the current concerns of the executives in question and had been converted to the relational structures which the software could manipulate. Breakdowns of expenses were analyzed; cash flows shown in color graphics; the comparative performance of competing insurance companies was analyzed. It was essential to use *real* data to generate the interest that was shown. A substantial amount of work had gone into developing the demonstrations. The persons who created the demonstrations operated the terminals and could quickly modify their nonprocedural code to answer the executives' questions. These top executives were fascinated to see how their business concerns could be explored: "What if the prime rate goes to 19%?" "What is the effect of holding this budget down to $600,000?" "Why did the Travelers Insurance Company do so well in this area?"

Such demonstrations can constitute a powerful form of selling. They can help to improve communication between DP and top management, which is often not good enough.

AUDITORS

Some types of user computing can be a problem for the auditors. It could increase the possibility that users could commit fraud. The auditors certainly need to know what is going on in this area.

One bank finds that the following arrangement for auditors works well. Every end-user-developed application is formally authorized. The chief auditor (who is a very powerful person in the bank) receives a copy of the authorization and a copy of any documentation the end users produce. The end users are responsible for their own application documentation and standards are established for this. If the auditor wants to investigate the user system further, that is a matter between him and the users. The information center keeps out of it.

The chief auditor and his department became, themselves, major users of the information center. This mode of operation pleased them because it enabled them to make investigations and write checking programs without the DP organization or programmers knowing in detail what the auditors were doing or looking for. Previously, they went to each branch periodically and went through the books manually, looking for irregularities. Now they write programs that go through each branch's computer files in the head office. The DP manager states that the auditors created these programs *far faster* than the DP department could have [5]. The auditors can modify the programs whenever they wish, maintaining secrecy over the modifications, and this improves the thoroughness with which they can search for irregularities.

In other organizations also, the auditors ought to employ user software to improve the thoroughness of their inspections. Auditors should be one of the first customers of the information center.

WHO PAYS?

With user-driven computing in general it is desirable that the user should pay for the facilities he employs.

Some DP organizations operate as a cost center rather than a profit center. It is desirable that the information center be a profit center.

This has several advantages:

- It causes the user departments to justify their use of computing or access to information.
- It increases the incentive of the information center to *sell* and to provide a level of service worth paying for.
- It is easy for users to take actions that use excessive computer time. Making them pay for the time they use seems the best way to control this.
- Sudden excessive upswings in usage are less likely to occur, so it is easier to plan and control growth.

How should the users be charged?

Some organizations have charged for terminals, connect time, CPU hours, and disc space. When users ask for certain information to be made available on an existing information retrieval system, the main extra cost is the disc space and the charge may relate to that. Some organizations have charged a flat fee for the use of a terminal. One charged $500 per month for an information center terminal.

Another organization charged an arbitrary 75% of the user's 'current outside time-sharing rate. This encouraged the users to lessen their use of outside time sharing and move across to the internal facilities.

It is almost impossible to find a completely fair and rational charging formula. Attempts to do so with complex formulas have generally bewildered the users. It is better to have a simple, clear set of charges so that the users know how to budget and do not receive unpleasant surprises.

It is generally desirable to make the use of the information center free when it first starts, or possibly free to departments in their first year of usage. This is to encourage new users to whom the idea often seems alien. When the use of the center has truly caught hold, the users will be charged.

BUSINESSPEOPLE IN CONTROL   In commercial DP the object of the information center should be to put the businesspeople in control of how computing is used.

INFORMATION CENTER MANAGER:

Our motto is "Put computing into the businessmen's hands." We are in business to support the business.

DP EXECUTIVE:

We tried to solve our age-old problem of turning programmers into bankers by instead turning bankers into programmers.

OPERATIONS EXECUTIVE:

An interesting by-product of the information system is that I have more feeling of control but my managers have more feeling of responsibility.

We have all the information on the projects we manage in the organization. Managers at the first level use that information to do their job; they use it as a guide on how to manage. At the same time I can look at it any time I choose. I'm not hounding them, asking them for special reports. I can generate those reports. If I look at it today and find everything is within the parameters I'm comfortable with, I go about my business. They are operating as if they were independent entities; I rarely need to bug them at the operational level, and yet I have more control.

USER EXECUTIVE:

It enables us to spot potential troubles much more quickly. We get an overall view of supply and demand. We can spot short-term fluctuations in demand or supply problems quickly. This saves money and lets us serve customers better.

USER EXECUTIVE:

The information center has enabled senior management to participate in key decisions when they should, but keep out of them when things are going well. It provides *management distance* from the day-to-day operations.

USER MANAGER:

A lot of our people have started installing the terminals at home. When they have a problem they sometimes sit up late at night working on it.

I like to check on things at 7 in the morning (at home). If I take any actions or send messages, these are available to people two seconds later. We can start the day in good shape.

INFORMATION CENTER EXECUTIVE:

Information center adapts the military command post and war room concepts to the needs of business executives. The information center is built around the dynamics of business decision making. To illustrate this point we can visualize a movie of a NASA mission control center. We may first be attracted to and impressed by the computers and technical support. However, when we watch "mission control," that is a complete mission—such as the recovery of the ill-fated Apollo 13, mobilization for a miltary alert, or an energy distribution crisis—rather than a still picture, attention shifts from technology to the total decision-making scene. Much frustration by executives and managers about management information systems can be traced to a misplaced and often distorted perception by systems people of information and processing needs in the real world of dynamic business decisions. Information can be systematically prepackaged so that it has the same strategic relevance and value that it must have in the "war room" context.

INFORMATION CENTER EXECUTIVE:

The president of the corporation likes graphs and charts. He believes that financial management and other management participate better in meetings when information is presented graphically. It enables the whole management team to participate. In 15 minutes you can get a picture of the entire situation.

Information presented graphically can enable you to spot problems quickly, and quickly understand the effects of "what-if?" questions. Graphics can highlight problem areas.

The success of the information center depends on the degree to which the business people accept it as a means of directly solving their problems. This is not too likely to happen if traditional DP technicians are in control. People with a business background need to be in control and greatly helped with the right technical support. They need to select user-seductive software and demonstrate the value of the tools throughout the organization.

Some information centers have been staffed by APL enthusiasts and have achieved only a very limited penetration. APL is an extremely powerful and valuable language, but most business people need Visicalc, graphics, relational data bases, powerful report generators, and simple-to-use decision-support tools.

Education of users is of paramount importance and was done on much too small a scale for real success on the early information centers. In addition to widespread courses for uses the information center should have rooms where users can select video and computer-based training courses like those from Deltak's Advanced Technology Library.

Above all, it is necessary for top management to understand the power and value of the information center concept in improving the procedures and decision making, and to ensure that it penetrates their entire organization.

Box 7.3 summarizes the reasons for success and the reasons for failure or disappointment with information centers.

INTERVIEWER:

Having created a successful information center operation yourself, what advice would you give to other organizations about how to succeed?

INFORMATION CENTER EXECUTIVE:

The concept needs to be extensively sold throughout the organization, and you cannot sell it on an intellectual basis. Users must try it, get their hands on the terminals, and roll it around.

We build pilots. We give demonstrations. We have given demonstrations to the president, to senior management, to DP personnel, and to all levels of end users. We have a demonstration center and have given so many that we are the longest-running show on Broadway!

INTERVIEWER:

I'm sure that's excellent advice. What else?

INFORMATION CENTER EXECUTIVE:

Pick the most important applications. Capture data for them, and show what can be done with them. Pick the best software packages, and particularly packages which give the best output—clear reports, really good graphics. Use these with the most important applications and demonstrate the results to those executives who will make things happen.

BOX 7.3   How to succeed with information centers*

Reasons for Success	Reasons for Failure or Disappointment
● Strong support by top management.	● Top management uninterested.
● Determination to change the use of computers throughout an organization.	● Insufficient commitment.
● Information center staffed with businesspeople (with appropriate technical support).	● Information center staffed with technicians only.
● Start-up staff having sufficient product expertise to ensure the first projects go flawlessly.	
● Information center employs new graduates who accept and spread new ideas.	● Information center is staffed with traditionalists only.
● Information center staff consists primarily of individuals with good interpersonal and communication skills, who can understand and react to users' problems.	

*Reprinted by permission of Technology Transfer Institute.   *(Continued)*

BOX 7.3 *(Continued)*

Reasons for Success	Reasons for Failure or Disappointment
• An appropriate mix of languages and generators is supported, with good support tools. (But unnecessary language proliferation is avoided.)	• A narrow view of languages, e.g., only APL or only IBM software.
• Good use of graphics.	
• Constant research of hardware. Information center staff should always be looking for better tools.	
• User-seductive software is sought out.	• Insufficient emphasis on ease of use.
• No advertising of capabilities until necessary expertise, experience, and facilities are acquired (although needs should be discussed with key end-user executives).	• Information center oversold at the beginning and does not deliver what it promises.
• Aggressive organizationwide selling of the capabilities once they are proven and powerful.	• Failure to sell capabilities aggressively throughout the organization once they are proven.
• Aggressive information center executive (once initial building of expertise is done) who is determined to change the entire culture of computer usage.	• Timid, nonaggressive, nonselling management.
• Management strongly oriented to business problems.	• Academic or technical management.
• Information center resource tied to the corporate strategic business plans, critical-success-factor analysis, and senior executive needs.	
• Knowledge of the machine performance criteria of the languages and generators.	• Applications which will not run economically on a given system.

BOX 7.3 (Continued)

Reasons for Success	Reasons for Failure or Disappointment
● Good monitoring of resource usage to ensure that adequate resources remain available.	
● Ability to tune applications which are frequently run, to improve machine performance.	● Excessive consumption of computer power. Insufficient computer power to support the 4GL approach.
● Thorough linkage to the information engineering design stages. Ability to provide users with subsets of the data models.	● Users create their own data bases without data administration controls, resulting in massive redundancy and inconsistency in data.
● Good understanding and use of data analysis.	● Failure to do thorough data analysis leading to integrity and inconsistency problems.
● Traditional DP organization is made to cooperate, providing data from production systems.	
● Ability to access internal and external data stores; good data extractors.	
● Guidelines for on-line documentation. Good on-line HELP facilities.	● Lack of adequate application documentation.
● Teamwork between users and information center staff to improve application creation.	● Uncontrolled technical mistakes by user developers.
● Users and skilled developers working hand-in-hand, when necessary, to create applications, or prototypes.	● Restrictive rules saying that information center staff may *never* develop applications.
● Thorough, widespread training of both information center staff and end users.	● Underestimating the education needs.
● Information center walk-in facilities and help for beginning users.	

(Continued)

BOX 7.3 *(Continued)*

Reasons for Success	Reasons for Failure or Disappointment
• Immediate access for users to video and computer-based training.	
• Good data cataloging and extraction facilities. Information center should act as a clearing house for data.	• Inability to locate and extract the data which users need.
• An excellent demonstration center with a projection screen.	• Failure to spread the gospel.
• Many demonstrations given to key executives and staff.	
• Demonstrations which are carefully constructed to address vital business needs.	
• Integration of end-user terminals, personal computers, office automation, and word processing functions.	
• User-group meetings to interchange experience and spread understanding.	
• Skilled psychological motivation of all potential users. Identification of early adaptors.	
• Eventual operation as a profit center. Clear simple formula for changing users. Information center should operate as a business within a business.	
• Design for an appropriate level of system availability.	
• Realistic assessment of the work needed.	• Excessive optimism.

8 AN IDEAL DP DEVELOPMENT FACILITY

INTRODUCTION There are now on the market many application generators and fourth-generation languages. They employ a surprising diversity of techniques, syntaxes, and semantic structures. None of them are perfect. Each one, although shrouded in the spectacular praise of its blurb-writers, has deficiencies. With some it is worth correcting the defects and improving the functionality because it is having a huge effect on DP productivity. Others are hardly worth the effort. Some will turn belly-up and float slowly to the top of the tank.

Given the experience with this software so far, we can describe what would now appear to be an ideal development facility for today's state of the art in *commercial data processing.* This chapter lists some of its desirable properties. Such properties are discussed in more detail in the author's *Fourth-Generation Languages* [1].

USES OF DATA The heart of the facility is a data-base management system, much more flexible than the data-base management systems of the 1970s, which are now regarded as traditional.

The user has an extremely user-friendly language with which he can create a data base. He can state what fields he wants in the records. The system will ask him to fill in details so that a logical data-base description is created.

The user can either create his own personal data-base structure, independently of other users, or employ a data-base structure derived from the corporate data model and dictionary which is maintained by the data administrator. He will be encouraged (or instructed) to employ the official data representations wherever possible.

The user can employ three categories of data base:

Category I   *A personal data base created independently of the corporate data bases.* The user may regard this as his own personal electronic filing system. Although this category is independent, the user will often employ data representations from the corporate dictionary. The system will make it easy for him to do this (on-line).

Category II   *A data base extracted from the corporate data bases.* This will contain data that have been updated by other systems. The user will employ them for his own information and possibly manipulate the data, doing calculations with them and developing answers to "what-if?" questions. The data may be extracted periodically. The user will not be able to modify the corporate data bases from which the extract is taken.

Category III   *Shared corporate data bases.* The user has access to corporate data bases which are updated by other systems. This form of access is carefully controlled for reasons of security, accuracy of data, and machine performance. Security controls may prevent the user from making any change to the data. In some cases the user will enter data with accuracy and integrity controls which have the approval of the data administrator.

BASIC FACILITIES

● Creation of a Data Base

The system will make it easy for the user to create or derive a data-base structure (schema) or to employ an existing data-base structure. For any such structures it will provide the following facilities as illustrated in Fig. 8.1.

● Creation of a Data-Entry Dialogue

The user can select the fields for which new values are to be entered. The system will request details of integrity checks that are to be applied to any data which are entered. These include range- and data-type checks, checks for permissible values, and checks involving cross-references to other data. The system will then create a well-human-factored data-entry dialogue that other uses may employ.

● Creation of a Data-Update Dialogue

The user can select fields in the data base which may be updated. The system will request details of integrity checks, as above, and will then create a well-human-factored data-update dialogue that other users may employ. This will use the same input panel design as the data-entry dialogue.

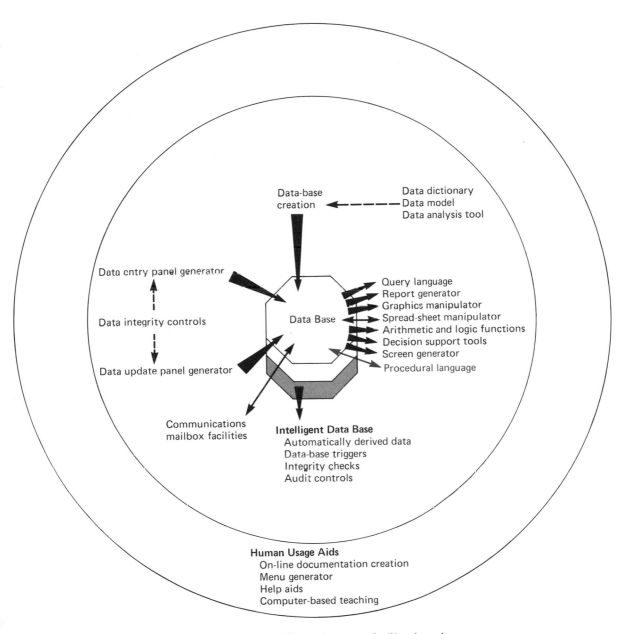

Figure 8.1 Components of a DP development facility (see also Figure 8.4.)

• Query Language

The system provides a very user-friendly means of querying the data base, either for simple queries that display a single record, or for complex queries that cause data to be projected, joined, or searched with various conditions applying. The query language incorporates data-update facilities. These make it possible to update many records with one command. Security and integrity controls regulate the use of such facilities. Complex queries and updates may be catalogued and referred to by name so that they do not have to be reentered every time they are used.

• Report Generator

A means is provided for generating and formatting reports. The report generator is a natural extension of the query language. The report formats specified may be catalogued, referred to by name, and easily modified.

• Graphics Generator

A means is provided of generating graphics charts of data, and of manipulating these charts. The user can adjust the formats, color, shading, and labeling of the charts to create well-designed presentations. The chart formats can be catalogued, referred to by name, and easily modified.

• Arithmetic Manipulation

The user can express arithmetic and mathematical operations to be performed on the data. Such operations often create new variables which the user can store in his data base and use in query, report, or graphics generation. This facility enables the user to ask "what-if?" questions about the data.

• Derived Data

The data base may contain fields which are derived from other fields, for example by employing an arithmetical expression. When a field in the input of the derivation expression is changed, the derived field will be automatically changed accordingly.

• Spreadsheet Manipulation

The system provides spread-sheet facilities (like Visicalc) which enable the user to create and manipulate tables of values. For more sophisticated users these can be multidimensional tables. These matrices are displayable with the graphics generator.

● **Communication**

The user can send messages to other users. Each user has a "mailbox." These messages may be reports or charts created with the generators. Specified messages can be designated "URGENT" and the system takes action to enforce these on the recipient's attention.

● **Data-Base Triggers**

Triggers can be expressed such that when a specified data value falls into a specified range, an action is taken. This action may be to notify a user, possibly with the "URGENT" message-sending facility. The action may be the execution of a named procedure.

The value to which a trigger applies will often be that of a derived field.

● **Procedural Language**

A procedural language is provided with which more complex procedures can be expressed. These may involve loops (or recursion), condition tests, nested routines, and calls to library routines. The procedural language is, as far as possible, compatible in syntax with the facilities noted above.

**USER
FRIENDLINESS**

All of the facilities described above use nonprocedural dialogues, with the exception of the last one for procedural coding. Nonprocedural dialogues can be designed to be highly user-friendly. The success of the development facility we describe depends to a large extent on the ease of use of its dialogues.

We can classify human computer dialogues as one-dimensional and two-dimensional. One-dimensional dialogues employ character strings which the user types and the machine prints or displays. Two-dimensional dialogues employ a two-dimensional space; the computer creates displays and the user reacts to them by moving a cursor around a screen, entering data or commands into it, and possibly pointing to it with a light pen, finger, or mouse. Two-dimensional dialogues give the capability to create many more user-friendly interfaces. The dialogues help with such dialogues though excellent monochrome dialogues can be created, employing reverse video and flashing characters. For some applications a large monochrome screen is better than a smaller, lower-resolution, color screen of the same price. The facilities for different aspects of the application backlog have a compatible syntax.

**DEFAULT
ASSUMPTIONS**

Report and graphics generation can be made easy by permitting the user to key in a brief simple statement of what he wants without giving full details of how it should be formatted. The software makes its own decisions about formatting.

In NOMAD2 (from National CSS), for example, the user may simply say "LIST" followed by the fields to be included on the report: for example, "list empno name address birth sex dependents." The system responds:

EMPLOYEE NUMBER	EMPLOYEE NAME	ADDRESS	BIRTH DATE	S E X	DEPEN- DENTS
42	FLYNN, HENRY	4 OAK TRAIL, HOBOKEN N.J.	01/23/33	M	3
48	STEIN, HARRY	3 MARSHALL CT., WESTPORT CT.	01/10/47	M	1
104	DISCALA, ANN	2 CENTER ST., NORWALK CT.	06/01/40	F	2
341	SHERWOOD, LESLIE	5 TRADER LANE, STAMFORD CT.	08/04/43	F	1
1328	RAND, PAUL	MULBERRY LANE, SCARSDALE NY	03/20/29	M	2
234	SMITH, KIM	119 DANBURY RD., WILTON PA.	02/21/45	F	0

In default of any more detailed instructions the system formats the report as above, putting page numbers on it if necessary, and putting an appropriate label at the head of each column. The label (e.g., "EMPLOYEE NUMBER") is obtained from the data dictionary.

Row totals, column totals, and subtotals for individual variables can be requested simply:

This requests a total for each row.

This requests a total for the entire report.

list by prodname skip 2 across months sum (sales)
rowtot total

PROD NAME	JAN SUM $SALES PER MONTH	FEB SUM $SALES PER MONTH	MAR SUM $SALES PER MONTH	APR SUM $SALES PER MONTH	MAY SUM $SALES PER MONTH	JUN SUM $SALES PER MONTH	TOTAL SUM $SALES PER MONTH
BLIVETS	$651.38	$556.91	$470.10	$497.56	$576.14	$316.16	$3,068.25
JARVERS	$400.68	$208.59	$442.18	$161.11	$282.21	$444.48	$1,939.25
LINKERS	$168.23	$204.12	$278.08	$253.55	$193.95	$243.36	$1,341.29
WIDGETS	$534.90	$473.40	$581.20	$1,327.45	$688.53	$885.77	$4,491.25
	$1,755.19	$1,443.02	$1,771.56	$2,239.67	$1,740.83	$1,889.77	$10,840.04

Some report generators give the user a screen from which he can select options for formatting the report. The report generator which is part of ADR's IDEAL package gives two option selection screens. The first relates to the overall report, and the user may fill in the report name, select the spacing between lines or columns, and so on. The second lists the fields to be included in the report and the user may indicate the sort sequence, and for each field whether totals and subtotals, maximum, minimum or average values are needed, column widths, column headings, and so on. Where options are not selected, the software chooses appropriate formats, column widths, and so on.

In NOMAD2 the user can say "PLOT" instead of "LIST." For example, instead of saying

LIST BY PRODNAME ACROSS MONTH SUM (SALES)

he can say

PLOT BY PRODNAME ACROSS MONTH SUM (SALES)

The user could have stated what type of plot is needed, for example LINE, SCATTER, BAR, or PIE chart. In the example above he did not state the type of plot, so the software determined what would be an appropriate chart type.

Figure 8.2 shows the plot that results from the command above. This plot may have too many products on it. The user could state "NEW PLOT" or "NEW COLOR" after "BY PRODUCT" to separate them.

The item following the word "ACROSS" is treated as the independent variable. When this is not numeric, NOMAD2 selects a bar chart if not otherwise instructed. For example, a bar chart would be produced from the command "PLOT SALES ACROSS BRANCH_OFFICE." On receiving such a result, the user could change the chart type, colors, textures, and so on, as required.

SUBSETTING

A comprehensive development language can become complex with a bewildering array of features and a thick manual. To make it easy for beginners it should be designed for subsetting. Raw beginners may be exposed to only a data-base query language, or report generator, or a facility for doing arithmetic on data, such as an extension of a pocket calculator. When they become *completely* familiar with such a subset, they are exposed to a planned follow-on subset. When they are completely familiar with this, the next level is revealed to them, and so on.

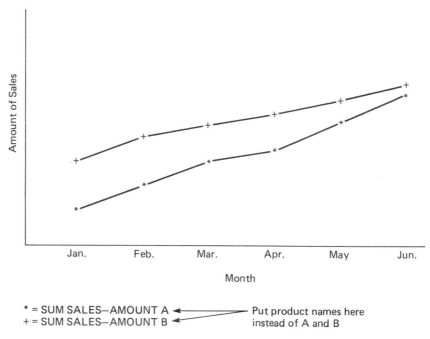

Figure 8.2   Use of the NOMAD PLOT command.

Subsetting of this type is very important for wide acceptance of a language. There have been innumerable cases of languages being rejected by people who could benefit greatly from them, because they appeared too complex at the start.

HUMAN USAGE AIDS   Even though the syntax of the system can be made very user-friendly, the users will often need help and training. The system should provide this to them on-line. They should be able to invoke a HELP function at any time. Using menus, the system asks them what type of help they require, and provides it.

Computer-based instruction in how to use the system should be built into it. This should be user-friendly and self-contained. (Computer-based instruction varies in quality substantially.) The user, after taking a short training course, should be able to expand his own knowledge of how to use the system.

When a user creates an application that is to be employed by other users, he should create on-line HELP and documentation for them. The system should have features that make this easy to do.

SPECIFICATION TOOLS The designer of applications needs ways of sketching his application before he builds it (except when it is simple enough that no sketch is needed). The generator incorporates a user-friendly sketching technique which is easy to learn and which allows the sketches to be edited on the screen and converted directly into code.

Simple queries or report generation need no sketch; procedures with loops or nested routines do. The form of sketching such procedures that is perhaps the easiest for end users is a *data-base action diagram* [2]: Figure 8.3 shows an example of this.

Each lozenge in the data-base action diagram (DAD) shows a data-base command. Each of these in Fig. 8.3 is a *read* or *update* of a single record. In

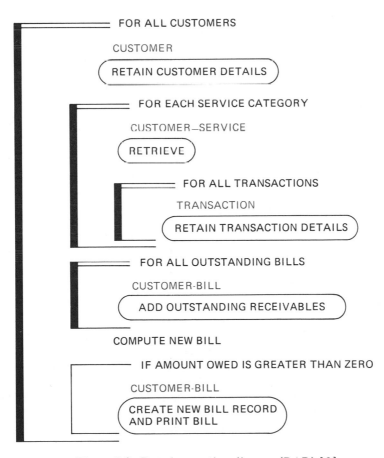

DATA-BASE ACTION DIAGRAM (DAD)

Figure 8.3 Data-base action diagram (DAD) [2].

some cases compound commands are used, such as the searching of a set of records. The vertical brackets of Fig. 8.3 show the control structure of the program. Brackets with a single line at the top indicate a group of operations that are done once, and controlled by some condition. Brackets with a double line at the top indicate a group of operations that are repeated. (A double line in a music score means repetition.)

Diagrams such as that of Fig. 8.3 were designed to translate directly into the code of fourth-generation languages, and to be as user-friendly as possible. The diagramming technique was developed by a psychologist to be as easy to learn and use as possible, while adopting the lessons of structured programming [3].

The development facility should provide a tool for sketching and editing the action diagrams on the screen and then converting them to code. This facility links directly to the data administrator's tools—the data dictionary and data model. The application developer can see the structure of the records he uses.

This linkage to the data administrator's facilities is designed to assist users or analysts in automatically using or creating the data bases they need, and helps to reduce the chances of creating incompatible data.

DATA BASE   The generator employs a *relational* data-base management system that is dynamically changeable, like the data base for IBM's SQL. The tool permits the definition of *logical user views* which are derived from the larger data structure. The user can refer to and employ these logical views. The user can view the data in either a relational or a hierarchical form.

A data-base management system requires many properties if it is to be fully useful [4], such as security controls, concurrency controls, access optimization, failure protection, checkpoint/restart, auditing features, and so on. The generator has all of these. It is much more than just a set of language interpreters and compilers. It has a complex infrastructure giving the system foundations that are needed.

The user can quickly create the data structure or schema that he wants to use, and with this data-entry panels can be generated for the input of any specific data. In existing products a good example of a system for data-base creation and generation of data-entry facilities is that in the language FOCUS from Information Builders Inc. An example of a data-base query and update language that is particularly well-human-factored is IBM's Query-by-Example. A good example of an easy-to-use report generator is that in ADR's IDEAL language. An example of powerful business graphics is TELL-A-GRAFF from ISSCO.

INTELLIGENT DATA-BASE FUNCTIONS

We may distinguish between dumb data bases and *intelligent* data bases. A dumb data base is *passive*. Operations against the data are specifically requested each time they occur by a user or by a program associated with a specific transaction. The dumb data base does not initiate any actions of its own. All logic is associated with the transactions and applications, and none with the data base itself.

An intelligent data base has logic associated with specific data as well as that associated with specific transactions or applications. This logic may be invoked automatically when certain changes are made to the data. It is invoked independently of what application or transaction causes the change. This logic associated with the data may be used for integrity controls, for the automatic updating of derived data, for audit controls or for trigger operations. A trigger operation occurs automatically when the value of a field falls into a specified range. It may send an urgent message to a user; it may invoke a program operation. An intelligent data base can thus be an *active* facility as opposed to merely a *passive* data base. The bottom of Fig. 8.1 indicates intelligent data-base functions.

DATA ADMINISTRATION AIDS

The system should provide on-line data-administration aids. It should have a data dictionary and means of representing the data model used, showing the associations among data items.
In all commercial application design, data analysis should be done before procedures are designed [4]. The facility should have a tool for this built into it.

SEMANTIC DISINTEGRITY

The ability to perform relational joins and projects is an essential aspect of relational data bases. When users employ relational languages they often use join or project operations. Unfortunately, these can give invalid results under certain circumstances. The use of the language appears correct and the results appear plausible, but the results are, in fact, wrong. The term *semantic disintegrity* is used to describe this [5].

It is possible to devise mechanisms that warn the user when he enters statements to which this problem might apply [5]. Unfortunately, many of today's nonprocedural languages do not do so, and this makes them dangerous.

Protection from the danger of semantic disintegrity depends on the data relations being correctly modeled. All functional dependencies must be correctly represented (a subject beyond the scope of this report). Semantic disintegrity warnings can then be generated. For this reason the development facility *should include a tool for data analysis.*

The user may encounter two situations: first, the data are fully modeled, in which case semantic disintegrity warnings can be issued for potentially incorrect use of the data; second, the data are *not* fully modeled, in which case a general caution may be given to users who do joins and projects, like the Surgeon General's warning on U.S. cigarette packets.

SYSTEM CONTROLS A variety of other system controls is needed, many of which are more obvious than the semantic disintegrity trap. Mechanisms are needed to permit multiple users to employ the system at the same time. This required concurrency controls to prevent invalid updating of the data.

Security controls are needed. There must be means of recovering from failures and system crashes, which ensure that data are not damaged or lost. When failures occur, operations must be backed out to a point at which they may be safely restarted. Appropriate restart points or checkpoints are needed.

Tools are needed for the auditors to ensure that they can investigate system usage appropriately. Audit trails may be created automatically.

CODE GENERATION AND CHECKING The development facility has an interpreter to convert into executable code the syntax, which is designed for human beings. The interpreter produces code while the user is at the terminal so that it can then be executed and tested. As with a human interpreter of foreign languages, this interpretation allows immediate interaction between the user and the system.

As well as an interpreter, the development facility should have a compiler that produces optimized code. A compiler operates in batch fashion and may go through multiple stages to produce optimized code and allocate machine resources in an efficient fashion.

If the code will be run many times or will produce large throughputs, a compiler is needed to achieve machine efficiency. If the code is used for personal decision making, an interpreter is needed to achieve direct interaction between the decision maker and the computer, and optimized code is generally not needed. The same development facility should be usable for both decision-support computing and for production runs, so both an interpreter and compiler are needed.

Some interpreters and compilers generate a third-generation language such as COBOL, FORTRAN, or Pascal. This then has to go through another interpreter or compiler to produce machine code. This is generally undesirable except to achieve portability. It is more efficient to produce machine code *directly*.

The intermediate code is sometimes thought to help developers who are familiar with COBOL, FORTRAN, and so on. In practice, it does not help them. The COBOL is strange and hard to read, and should never be modified by the developers because this introduces bugs and severe maintenance difficulties.

PORTABLE CODE   The only good argument for generating code in a third-generation language is to achieve portability (i.e., programs that can be run on different vendors' machines). Unfortunately, most third-generation languages are not completely portable to different types of machines. DEC's FORTRAN does not run on IBM without modification, and so on.

One exception to this is Ada. The intent is that Ada source code specifications should be exactly the same for all machines. Compiling to Ada should give truly portable code. This is highly desirable for some applications. It is desirable for a software company that wishes to sell its programs to customers with all types of computers.

CODE CHECKING   There are many ways in which the input of the developer may be checked. All possible syntax and semantic checks should be made before the executable code is generated. When these checks detect inconsistencies, errors, or incompleteness, the system should give the developer a full and complete explanation which is easy to understand.

PROVABLY   The next chapter discusses a technique for creating
CORRECT CODE   code which is mathematically provably correct. It is desirable to apply such a technique wherever possible.

The creation of provably correct specifications and code represents a change from ad hoc methods to true engineering in software. It is particularly important for specifications with complex logic and systems where modules created by different developers must work together. In the latter case the interface between modules must be provably correct.

LIBRARY   A library is needed of functions, data types, screen panels, subroutines, and previously developed applications. A "software factory" environment is needed for some development organizations, which enables applications to be created quickly from previously built modules.

As time goes by, higher-level library modules come into existence. It is desirable that, if possible, the linkage to these should employ rigorous verification to avoid interface errors.

THEORETICAL PRINCIPLES

Most fourth-generation languages today are being created and improved by craftsmen-programmers with no interest in the theory of languages. Most computer scientists who specialize in languages have taken no interest in fourth-generation languages and do not even know their names. This is similar to previous technological history. Newcomen produced the first steam engine with a piston in 1712. For decades Newcomen's successors in this field were craftsmen-mechanics. The scientists of the era took no interest in the principles or theory of steam engines. Forty years after Newcomen's death an engineer, John Smeaton, did meticulous research in the area and this resulted in much better steam engines. Later, the theoretical principles of thermodynamics and the Carnot cycle enabled engineers to design steam engines of maximum efficiency. Eventually, computer scientists will direct their attention to high-productivity languages and we will probably see major improvements.

INFRASTRUCTURE

Fourth-generation languages or application generators require a substantial infrastructure to support them. The cost of creating the infrastructure is often greater than the cost of the language interpreters and compilers. A good development facility needs this infrastructure to be excellent as well as the languages being as user-friendly as possible.

The infrastructure requires a good data-base management system that is as flexible as possible. It should provide multiple *logical user views* of the same data, differing at the field level. The data base needs to handle multiple users at the same time without integrity or deadlock problems. The accessing of data needs to be optimized to give good machine performance. The system needs security, recovery features, checkpointing, and protection from crashes. The auditors need facilities for investigating how the system was used. Figure 8.4 shows the infrastructure needed to make the development facility fully usable.

MULTISYSTEM INFRASTRUCTURE

Often the system in question will need to access other systems. It will often be necessary to use data that reside in other systems, for example. The interconnection of systems will become more common as data networks be-

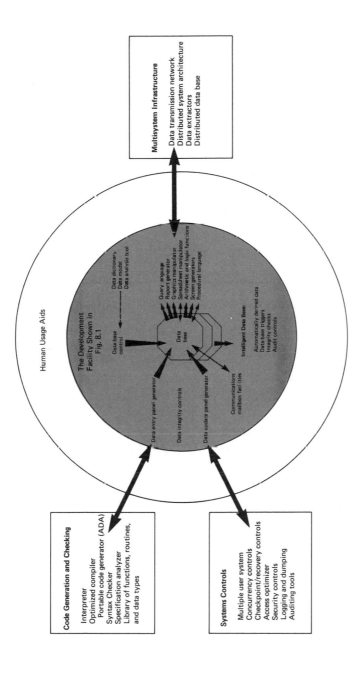

Figure 8.4 Infrastructure needed to make a development facility fully usable.

come more widespread and distributed systems and small computers continue to proliferate.

The right-hand side of Fig. 8.4 shows the infrastructure needed for multisystem linkage. The development facility may stand alone or may be linked to other systems.

Particularly important in some systems is a *data extractor* with which data can be extracted from other (often older) data-base systems for use in the new system. The data will be transmitted and restructured in the data base of the development facility. The extraction may be periodic, real-time, or ad hoc. Periodic extraction is appropriate for many information systems.

9 MATHEMATICALLY PROVABLE SYSTEM DESIGN

Program designers generally use ad hoc, undisciplined methods far removed from the precise disciplines of most branches of engineering. This results in code that is impossible to debug completely. We have learned to live with the idea that programs sometimes do strange things because it is not possible to detect all of their hidden anomalies.

This chapter describes a software breakthrough with profound implications for the future of computing. It gives the capability for ordinary (nonmathematical) people to generate programs which are mathematically guaranteed to be bug-free.

MATHEMATICAL PROOFS OF CORRECTNESS

Many authorities have expressed the view that mathematical approaches to program design must eventually be the solution to building better-quality software.

Ever since Dijkstra's early writing about a programming calculus [15,20], a small number of researchers have attempted to apply mathematics to programming to produce provably correct code. A variety of different approaches have been used to derive correctness proofs [8–21].

Mathematical techniques have been applied to proving programs correct and to creating specification techniques for verifiable programs. The techniques have worked with certain fairly small programs. A variety of approaches have been used. These are summarized in Fig. 9.1, which is designed to act as a guide to the literature. A concise summary is given in Berg et al. [1].

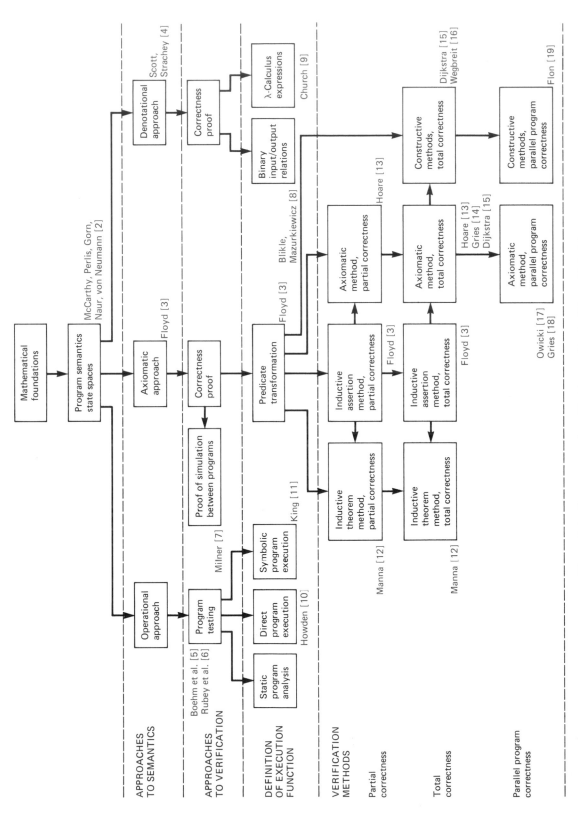

Figure 9.1 Taxonomy of verification methods. (From Ref. 1.)

Almost no programmer uses such techniques in practice for two reasons. First, they require a high level of mathematical sophistication. Even for simple programs a level of mathematical maturity is needed far beyond that of ordinary DP analysts and programmers. The mathematical proofs involved are often several times longer than the program derived. So the whole subject has tended to be relegated to the world of exotic research, with almost no attention being paid to it by DP executives and staff. Second, they do not work with most real-life programs because these programs are too complex and unruly. The programs do not fit the mathematics.

Today's programming languages permit all manner of constructs which defy mathematical verification. They were not designed with mathematical verification in mind.

The approach described in this chapter is different. Instead of applying ad hoc programming constructs, it employs only constructs that are built with mathematical axioms and proofs of correctness. A library of provably correct *operations* is built. The operations manipulate precisely defined *data types* by means of provably correct *control structures*. As the library of defined operations and data builds up, complex systems can be linked together. Most important, the mathematics is hidden from the typical user so that the method is easy to use. Non-computer professionals quickly learn to think about the systems they need using the basic approach.

The approach begins, then, by ignoring existing programming languages. However, the software used automatically generates code which *is* in conventional languages such as FORTRAN, Pascal, COBOL, and Ada.

Although it was generally thought that mathematically provable software was a long way in the future, this new technique, which emerged from the work of Margaret Hamilton and Saydean Zeldin, is both highly powerful and practical [21–27]. The technique has been automated so that bug-free systems can be designed by persons with no knowledge of either mathematics or programming. The software automatically generates logically guaranteed program code. Whereas mathematics like those of Dijkstra have been applied only to small programs, Hamilton and Zeldin's technique has been used successfully with highly complex systems. Furthermore, the technique is used not only for program design but for high-level specification of systems. The design is extended all the way from the highest-level statement of system functions down to automatic generation of code.

This methodology is so powerful that it needs to be regarded as a major new technology for creating systems which in a sense obsoletes earlier structured techniques.

IMPOSSIBILITY OF CONVENTIONAL DEBUGGING

The following illustrates the difficulty of conventional debugging:

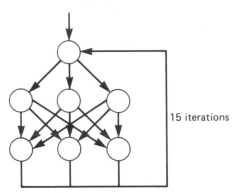

15 iterations

There are over 206 trillion unique paths through this module. If it were possible to test each of them in a millisecond, the total time taken for the complete test would be over 6000 years.

It is clearly impossible to perform a complete test. We would therefore saturation-test the module, checking as many different unique paths as we could, hoping that if the ones we have tested are correct, the ones that we have not tested are also correct.

Conventional structured design seeks to lessen the number of unique paths that have to be tested. It does this by making the modules small (modular design), keeping the interfaces between modules simple, and limiting the control structures to ones that are easier to test. With nontrivial programs, however, there are still too many paths for complete testing. Furthermore, changes to the program, which often have to be made, cause unpredictable effects. Complex programs remain a mine field in which we can never be sure that all the mines have been removed.

Mathematically provable design takes a different approach. It limits the designer to the use of constructs that are rigorously verifiable. The use of hierarchies of such constructs permits the building of highly complex systems which are logically correct. Because mere human beings cannot be trusted to follow the rules, each step in the design is meticulously checked with software.

HIGHER-ORDER SOFTWARE

The technique created by Hamilton and Zeldin is called *higher-order software* (HOS) and software that implements it is available from a corporation of that name [28]. The software automatically generates program code, thus eliminating the need for conventional programmers. A systems analyst or specially trained end user can generate the program he requires.

The technique is really a basic way to think about systems and system specifications. It can be applied to any systems—not only software, but hardware or organization systems.

HOS BINARY TREES   The HOS methodology represents systems by means of binary trees. Each node of a binary tree has zero or two subordinate nodes. The node at the top of the tree is called the *root*. The nodes with no subordinates are called *leaves*. The following are binary trees:

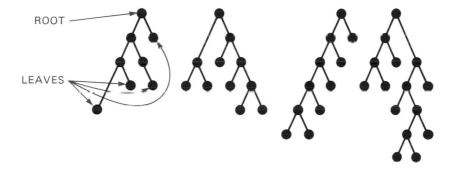

This is a six-level tree:

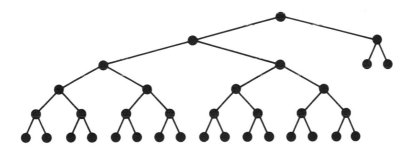

The following are *not* trees:

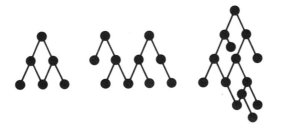

Each subordinate node is drawn below its superior in our diagrams. A branch is described as *entering* a node if it comes from above. It is described as *leaving* a node if it goes to a subordinate node.

If a branch leaves node A and enters node B, node B is referred to as the *offspring* of A. Node A is the *parent* of B.

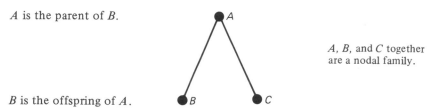

A is the parent of *B*.

A, *B*, and *C* together are a nodal family.

B is the offspring of *A*.

A node of a tree may be regarded as the root of another tree—a tree within a tree. The tree of which an intermediate node is a root is called a *subtree*.

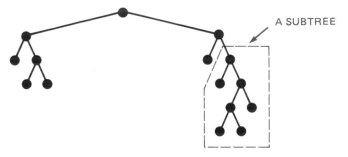

A SUBTREE

FUNCTIONS   Each node of an HOS binary tree represents a *function*. A function has one or more *objects* as its input and one or more *objects* as its output.

An object might be a data item, a list, a table, a report, a file, a data base, or it might be a physical entity such as a circuit, a missile, an item undergoing manufacturing scheduling, a train, tracks, switching points, and so on.

In keeping with mathematical notation, the *input* object or objects are written on the right-hand side of the function; the *output* object or objects are written on the left of the function.

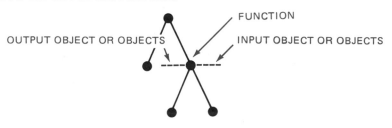

FUNCTION

OUTPUT OBJECT OR OBJECTS   INPUT OBJECT OR OBJECTS

The function may be a mathematical function, for example:

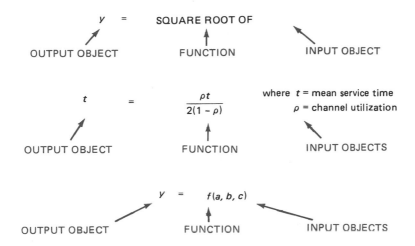

The function may be a programmed algorithm. For example:

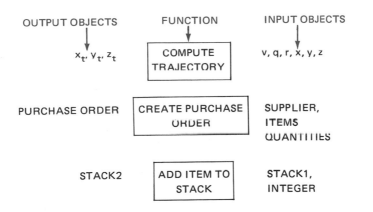

It may be a statement in a nonprocedural language:

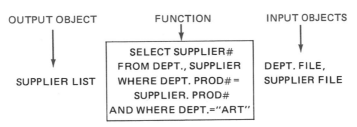

The function may be a program or subroutine specification. For example:

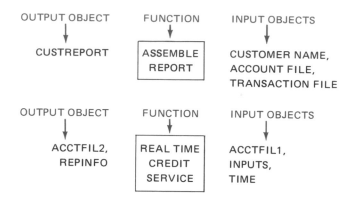

It may be a very broad statement of requirements.

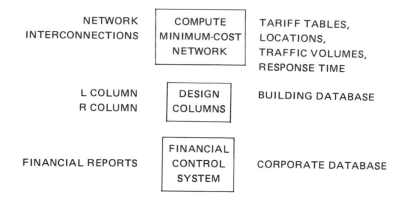

In fact, the notation can express (and decompose) operations which are not necessarily related to computing.

In some cases the object that is the output from a function can be the same item type as the object that is the input. The value of the object is transformed by the function. Thus

| TIME2 | INCREASE BY ONE HOUR | TIME1 |

TIME2 is the same data type as TIME1, but its value has changed.

| CAR2 | WRECK | CAR1 |

CAR2 is the same type of object as CAR1, but it is a different version.

| STACK2 | POP | STACK1 |

When a computer stack is "popped," this means that the top item in the stack is removed so that the next item down becomes the top item. STACK2 is similar to STACK1, but modified.

To add an item to a stack, we use the function PUSH. The following inserts an integer into the stack.

| STACK2 | PUSH | STACK1, INTEGER |

The top function of the stack is represented with the function TOP:

| INTEGER | TOP | STACK1 |

In mathematical notation we would write

$$STACK2 = PUSH (STACK1, INTEGER)$$

and
$$INTEGER = TOP (STACK1)$$

If the stack is empty when we do the latter command, the output would be a REJECT value.

In mathematical notation the output of one function is sometimes used as the input to another. Thus if we do PUSH (STACK, $INTEGER_1$) we obtain a stack with $INTEGER_1$ at the top. Applying the TOP function to this gives us $INTEGER_1$.

We could write these two operations in one statement thus:

$$INTEGER_1 = TOP\ (PUSH\ (STACK,\ INTEGER_1))$$

Note that we read such mathematic statements from right to left. In $y = f(x)$ we start with x, then we apply function f to it, then we obtain output y. With the previous example we start with the inputs STACK and $INTEGER_1$, then apply function PUSH to these variables, then apply function TOP to the result, then receive $INTEGER_1$ back as output. This notation is used to state some behavior of the relation between the functions TOP, PUSH, and STACK.

FROM REQUIREMENTS STATEMENTS TO DETAILED PROGRAM DESIGN

The HOS tree charts (which are called "control maps") show how broad functions like those above are decomposed into subfunctions. The *root* of the tree is the broadest overview statement. In the tree that results from the final design, the leaves are functions which do not need to be decomposed further. The leaves may be primitive functions, functions already existing and stored in a library, or functions obtainable from an external source.

Design may proceed in a top-down or bottom-up fashion. With top-down design the broad overview is successively decomposed into functions that contain more detail. With bottom-up design, detailed modules are aggregated to form higher-level modules until the overall goal of the system is reached.

In many methodologies the requirements statements, the specifications, the high-level design, and the detailed program design are done with different (and usually incompatible) languages. With HOS one language is used for all of these. An appealing feature of the methodology is that the binary tree, formally expressed, goes all the way from broad requirements statements to detailed program design. Automatic checks for errors, omission, and inconsistencies are applied at each stage. The resulting tree is processed to create the application code automatically.

THREE PRIMITIVE CONTROL STRUCTURES

Unlike most structured methodologies the HOS decomposition of a function into subfunctions (in other words, the relationship between a node in the tree and its two offsprings) is mathematically precise. It is this formality that leads to provably correct code.

When a function is decomposed into its two offspring, this is done with a *control structure. Three primitive control structures* are used. They are called JOIN, INCLUDE, and OR. Other control structures can be defined as combinations of these three.

JOIN

Suppose that a high-level function is BUILD-A-STOOL. The stool is to be made from two types of wood: TOPWOOD and LEGWOOD.

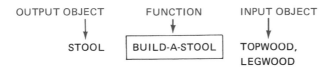

We write $y = f(x)$ in mathematics, where y is the result of applying function f to data x. Similarly, to describe our requirement for building a stool, we write

STOOL = BUILD-A-STOOL (TOPWOOD, LEGWOOD)

In order to build a stool, two operations are needed. We have to make the legs and the top, and then assemble these parts. The BUILD-A-STOOL function can be subdivided into a MAKE-PARTS function and an ASSEMBLE-PARTS function. Two objects are *output* from the MAKE-PARTS function: TOP and LEGS. These objects are *input* to the ASSEMBLE-PARTS function.

STOOL = BUILD-A-STOOL (TOPWOOD, LEGWOOD)

is then composed of the following two functions joined together:

TOP, LEGS = MAKE-PARTS (TOPWOOD, LEGWOOD)
STOOL = ASSEMBLE-PARTS (TOP, LEGS)

In the tree notation we represent this as follows:

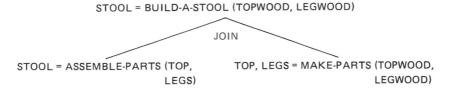

This is an illustration of the use of a JOIN control structure. Here one offspring depends on the other. The output of the right-hand function (i.e., TOPS, LEGS) must be the input to the left-hand function.

This input to the right-hand function is the same as the input to the parent. The output from the left-hand function is the same as the output from the parent. The effect of the parent function is thus reproduced.

The diagram must be read from right to left. (TOPWOOD, LEGWOOD) is the input to MAKE-PARTS, which results in TOP, LEGS. This is the input to ASSEMBLE-PARTS, which results in STOOL. Data enter each function from the right and leave it on the left.

(Mathematicians sometimes do things differently from ordinary people. The tree is read right to left, not left to right, and it has its root at the top and leaves at the bottom.)

INCLUDE

The MAKE-PARTS function can be decomposed into two functions, MAKE-TOP and MAKE-LEGS. The top must be made with TOPWOOD and the legs must be made with LEGWOOD. The two functions composing make parts are thus

TOP = MAKE-TOP (TOPWOOD)
and
LEGS = MAKE-LEGS (LEGWOOD)

These are combined by means of an INCLUDE control structure, thus

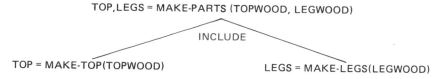

In this control structure the two offspring are independent of one another. They can operate separately and could even be executed on separate machines. Together both offspring use the input data of the parent function, and together they produce the output data of that function.

OR

Let us suppose that the legs can be made in one of two ways, either with a TURN function or with a CARVE function. We have *either* LEGS = TURN (LEGWOOD) *or* LEGS = CARVE (LEGWOOD). In order to decide which to do, a Boolean expression is used which can be either true or false. An OR control structure is used as follows:

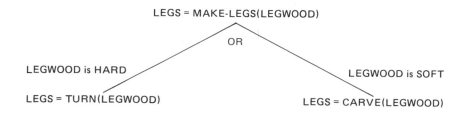

In this control structure, one or the other of the offspring, achieves the effect of the parent, but not both. The resulting output of each offspring is the same as that of the parent (i.e., LEGS).

Figure 9.2 summarizes the three primitive control structures.

CONTROL MAPS   We can combine the three control structures above into one tree as shown in Fig. 9.3. Diagrams like Fig. 9.3 are called *control maps.*

GENERATION   By breaking functions down with binary decompo-
OF CODE   sition with the JOIN, INCLUDE, and OR con-
structs, control structures can be achieved which are mathematically provably correct ⌊24⌋.

The functional decomposition continues until leaf nodes of the binary tree are reached which are *primitives* which are known to be correct or *subroutines* which have themselves been created with this method. When all parts of the tree reach such leaf nodes the design is complete. *Program code can then be automatically generated from the resulting structures.*

At each step in the design its correctness can be checked automatically.

FOUR TYPES OF   The tree structures have *functions* as their nodes.
LEAF NODES   The *function* is also called an *operation.* Every function is decomposed into lower-level functions showing more detail, except for those which are leaf nodes of the tree.

There are four types of leaf nodes:

P: Primitive Operation

This is an operation that cannot be decomposed into other operations. It is defined rigorously with mathematical axioms.

OP: Operation Defined Elsewhere

This function will be further decomposed in another control map, which may be part of the current design or may be in a library.

R: Recursive Operation

This is a special node that allows us to build loops.

XO: External Operation

This function is an external program which is not written with HOS methodology. It may be manufacturers' software or previously existing

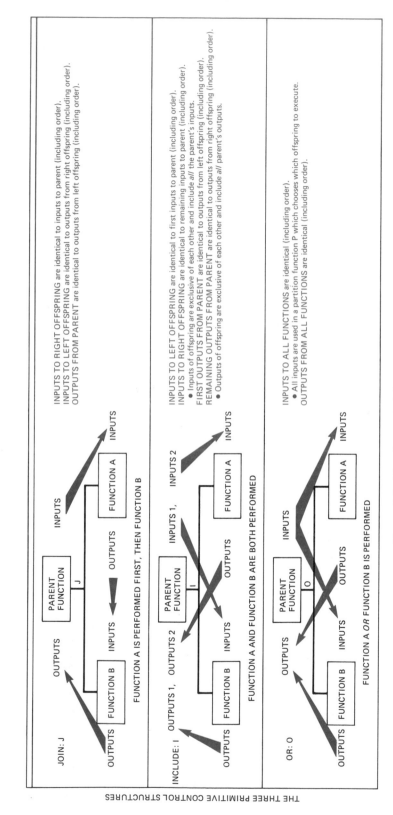

Figure 9.2 The three primitive control structures.

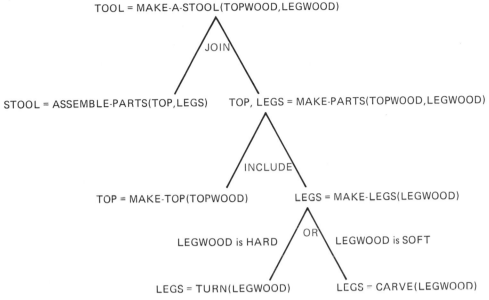

TOOL = MAKE-A-STOOL(TOPWOOD,LEGWOOD)

JOIN

STOOL = ASSEMBLE-PARTS(TOP,LEGS) TOP, LEGS = MAKE-PARTS(TOPWOOD,LEGWOOD)

INCLUDE

TOP = MAKE-TOP(TOPWOOD) LEGS = MAKE-LEGS(LEGWOOD)

LEGWOOD is HARD OR LEGWOOD is SOFT

LEGS = TURN(LEGWOOD) LEGS = CARVE(LEGWOOD)

Figure 9.3 An HOS binary tree using the three *primitive* control structures: JOIN, INCLUDE, and OR. Other control structures can be defined as combinations of these three. Diagrams like this are called *control maps.*

user programs. Needless to say, the HOS software cannot guarantee its correctness.

If there is no non-HOS software (external operations), every operation is ultimately broken down into *primitive operations* which are described mathematically.

The repetitive use of predefined functions is essential. Without this the binary structures would have too many nodes to be practical for human design. Complex programs require the building of libraries of functions and defined operations (e.g., subroutines). These include completely general functions such as user-specifiable *loop* control structures, mathematical operations, elaborate application-independent functions such as data-base operations and report generators, and operations which are specific to given applications, such as a backorder subroutine.

STATIC AND DYNAMIC TESTING OF PROGRAMS

We may distinguish between static and dynamic program testing.

Dynamic program testing is necessary with all programs not built with a rigorous mathematical technique (which includes the vast majority of programs in existence today).

Each branch and usable combination of branches must be tested. As discussed earlier, there are usually so many combinations of branches that it is impossible to be sure that all have been tested. Consequently, saturation testing is done, but in practice, not all combinations of paths are exercised and not all possible errors in the code are revealed. Complex software is notorious for containing subtle bugs which can be extremely difficult to track down. Most large programs never become completely bug-free.

Static testing refers to verification that the functions, data types, and control structures have been used in accordance with rules that guarantee correctness. This verification can be performed by a computer with absolute precision. When this static verification is done there is no need to test dynamically *all* of the control paths in the control map through the hierarchical structure. A few instances of control paths will be checked to ensure that correct results are being produced.

It is still necessary to check that the specifications are correct and are what the users really need, and that nothing has been omitted. Does the example above represent completely the building of a stool, for example, or is there something else needed other than legs and a top? The HOS method eliminates most of the effort in saturation testing and tracking down obscure logic errors.

The dynamic testing which we normally perform does not *guarantee* that code is error-free. You may search for flying saucers, but just because you cannot find any does not mean that they do not exist, especially as you do not know what you are really looking for.

EMBELLISHMENTS

We have now described the basic structures of the HOS methodology. Logic created with these structures is provably correct. However, much embellishment is needed to make the technique easy to use and powerful.

It has been proven that a computer could execute all arithmetic and logic with only three instructions. However, if you programmed such a computer you would need tools to make the programming easier—compilers, macroinstructions, libraries of subroutines, report generators, and so on. The same is true with the HOS language. Now that we have the sound foundation we can build higher-level control structures out of the three primitives. We can have libraries of defined operations. We can convert data-base models into HOS notation. We can use the HOS language to build report generators, create data flow diagrams, or translate other problem definition languages into computable HOS terms. We can specify a computer designed to implement the HOS constructs which can take advantage of future VLSI circuit costs and use multiple parallel processors.

It is possible to build other control structures out of the primitives. In fact, a long-term question for HOS product developers is: What types of control structures would benefit the users most?

Other control structures can be created in two ways. First, they can be new primitives created with new axioms and mathematics which proves them correct. This would require considerable mathematical skill and is not likely to be attempted by HOS users in general.

Second, they can be built out of existing control structures and invoked when needed. Employing this approach a user can build his own control structures. They are called *defined structures.*

There are two ways of extending the power and usability of the HOS tool. The most common is to build a library of operations, for example, a library of subroutines and callable programs. Almost every HOS control map contains blocks labeled OP (operation defined elsewhere) or XO (external operation). The user creates OP blocks all the time for operations that he has not yet specified in detail, or which he has already specified elsewhere. As time goes by a large library of defined operations grows up.

The second way of extending the usefulness is to create defined structures. This is rather like *creating one's own language,* or at least *dialect,* in HOS. Some classes of users already have languages or language constructs which they want to use. They may want to use DO-WHILE or REPEAT-UNTIL loops, for example. They may want to use menu selection. They may draw data-base action diagrams [29] and want to convert them into HOS. There are a variety of such constructs with which different users are familiar, and they would like to employ them to make HOS system development easier.

An important aspect of the future of HOS is the building of higher-level constructs or languages for special purposes, which employ HOS. Unlike other computer languages, they would have two important properties, first rigorous verification of the resulting control structures, and second the ability to drop from the higher-level constructs down to control maps for building detailed and often complex logic.

By building other constructs with HOS, we can create techniques that are user-friendly, or employ variants of methodologies which are already familiar, and hide all of the mathematics under the covers but know that it is there to protect us.

HOS SOFTWARE

This technique for generating rigorous control structures would be tedious to do by hand. Its general usability depends on automation with user-friendly software.

Software for applying such techniques requires the following components:

1. A language for expressing functions and their decomposition into other functions.

2. An interactive screen facility for constructing and manipulating the control maps and helping the user to correct errors.

3. A library of data types, primitive functions, and previously defined modules.

4. An analyzer routine for automatically checking that all the rules that give provably correct logic have been followed.

5. A generator that automatically generates program code.

HOS software provides all of these. It may be regarded as a system specification tool which, unlike other such tools, precisely checks the logic of the specification. It is much more than this because it automatically generates the required code.

It may be regarded as an application generator. Most generators can generate reports, or data-entry software or data-base operations, but cannot create *any* type of software. They can usually generate only a specified class of applications. The HOS system can generate *any* application and is particularly useful with highly complex logic.

The key to making the HOS method easy to use is an interactive graphics editor. The HOS tree structures can be displayed on a screen and manipulated in a quick-and-easy manner.

The designer can work in a top-down fashion decomposing high-level functions, or in a bottom-up fashion combining low-level functions. At each stage the design is checked for correctness. The designer can add comments to any node. Rather like a film editor he can cut out subtrees and save them, hanging them on a "hook" for future use.

A designer working at a low-level node may discover the need for a data type that is not included in the nodes at the top of the tree. He can add this data type and quickly include it in the higher-level nodes.

The graphics editor is easy and enjoyable to use. Its syntax is simple but powerful. Most commands are entered by only one keystroke. A systems analyst can build a complete function tree quickly if he understands the application well enough, and can check it for consistency and completeness. He has available to him a library of data types, primitives, previously defined operations, and previously defined control structures.

The HOS software employs multiple different code generators so that it can create code in various languages which can be executed on various types of computers.

A WAY TO THINK ABOUT SYSTEMS   The systems design methodology of HOS has been applied to a startling diversity of situations. The technique provides a powerful way to think about axioms and logic generally, not only in computer systems.

The technique has been used to design hardware as well as software. It has proven valuable in the design of integrated circuits and electronic hardware [30]. A technique for provably correct design is essential with future chips and wafers of great complexity, containing millions of components.

A complex radar system was specified with it. It was used to specify a portion of the NAVPAK satellite communications system. Its Boolean logic can describe basic electronic functions such as NAND and NOR circuits. These primitive structures can then be combined into complex circuits which are guaranteed bug-free. The behavior of such circuits can be simulated before the hardware is built.

Front-end system specification methodologies have been adjusted so that they can be converted into HOS control maps. This provides a rigorous semantic foundation for an already established user community, and helps automate the generation of programs from these methodologies by formalizing an already existing syntax into a syntax with computable semantics.

The control maps can be used to specify a logically consistent design for noncomputer systems, or systems that involve people as well as machines. They have been used for project management, assigning tasks, resources, and relationships. They clearly identify sequential and parallel activities. The methodology was used for designing a system with multiple robots in operation in a hospital in France.

Its use was proposed in Harvard Law School for the study of laws and their relation to the U.S. Constitution. Complex branches of law, for example tax law, could be clarified and made consistent. Computerized aid to both lawmakers and lawyers could lessen the ever-growing burden of legal costs.

The technique was used to analyze the programming language Ada [31,32] and found subtle faults in its specification. Such analysis assists in compiler, interpreter, or implementation design, but it goes beyond that. It gives a context-free grammar (syntax) showing the structure of strings of a computer language which guides the assigning of semantic values to the strings. This could produce a language specification that is completely formal. The language specification using HOS is completely machine-independent and is logically verifiable. A compiler or optimization of a compiler could be simulated with HOS tools. This provides a powerful way to study and specify new languages.

The HOS technique has been used to design a microprocessor. Particularly intriguing is the possibility of designing a computer intended to run programs created with this method. It is desirable that future computers should use multiprocessing with many cheap microprocessors combined to form a larger machine. Such multiprocessor architectures have been built, but it has proven difficult to break down programs so that they can employ multiple processors operating in parallel. Programs designed with HOS may be broken down for parallel operation. The INCLUDE construct, for example, requires that two activities be performed which are independent. A large system has many INCLUDEs, which permit parallel processing.

New machines need new operating systems. The operating systems of the past have been plagued with subtle bugs which are sometimes extremely difficult to find. Seemingly trivial modifications to operating systems have triggered chain reactions of unanticipated problems. Flaw fixing introduces new flaws and more and more time is spent on fixing these secondary problems rather than correcting the structure that caused the original problem. After his experience in building OS 360 Fred Brooks lamented: "Program maintenance is an entropy-increasing process, and even its most skilful execution only delays the subsidence of the system into unfixable obsolescence" [33]. When complex systems are designed with a technique such as HOS, this is not true. Changes can be made without triggering chain reactions of bugs. Logically guaranteed code removes most timing, deadlock, and other problems. A library of provably correct system modules steadily grows. Complex software can at last be based on a sound engineering discipline.

To build complex software without such a technique is like building a bridge without stressing calculations. The early bridge builders used massive superstructures just to be sure. Even then, their bridges sometimes collapsed. The massive quantities of code in today's operating systems could be replaced with much smaller, tighter, provably correct constructs.

The author recently examined a set of highly complex system specifications created with conventional techniques, which were later redone with HOS. The rigorous tool revealed thousands of errors, omissions, and inconsistencies in the original specifications (over a hundred person-years of work). Most complex specifications are similarly inadequate. The time has come to insist that more automated and more rigorous tools are used for creating complex specifications.

10 THE IMPACT OF COMPUTER-AIDED SOFTWARE DESIGN

THE REVOLUTION Techniques such as that described in Chapter 9 portend a fundamental revolution in computing. They are analogous to the design revolution in engineering, microchip design, etc., that has been brought about by CAD (Computer-Aided Design). We *must* apply CAD to software. There are two aspects to the revolution: first, the effect on coding and debugging, and second, and perhaps more important, the effect on the specification of systems.

EFFECT ON The ad hoc coding process, which is so vulnerable
PROGRAMMING to the frailties of the human coder, disappears. This is how the computer world *must* progress. Program coding as we know it today *must* disappear. It is too error-prone, too expensive, and creates results that are too difficult to modify. In the typical programming department Murphy's Law has become a Constitutional Amendment. Programming is an inhuman use of human beings because it asks them to do something beyond their capabilities—produce perfect, intricate, complex logic which can be easily understood and modified. That is a task for computers, not human beings.

Our brain cannot handle complex logic and intricate detail without making mistakes. We need an intimate partnership between our brain, which is creative, and an electronic machine, which is precise at handling immense detail.

Complex software created with ad hoc methods has an amazingly large number of combinatorial paths that must be tested. In practice there is no way they could possibly all be tested thoroughly. An attempt is made at saturation testing, in which the system is flooded with large numbers of test cases. In saturation testing it may be difficult to notice or track down an error if it occurs, and many errors may lurk in paths that the saturation testing does not happen to reach.

Because of this most large systems are never fully debugged. They occasionally do mysterious things. A high-level check is placed on them so that they do not lose bank transactions or have dramatic errors. Most of their minor disasters can be caught when they happen and recovered from. On some software there is a lengthy list of bugs observed but not yet caught. There are probably many others not yet observed.

When this report was being written, *MIS Week* reported in a headline that only 30 bugs remained in a certain system [1]. We could ask: "How do you know?" If there are 30 bugs that you cannot find, there are probably many more hiding in the woodwork. In a later issue the publication said that 600 out of 900 bugs had been fixed on the same system.

One of the more extraordinary phenomena of the present computer age is the Big Eight accounting firms charging large sums for "certifying" certain programs when there can be no possible assurance that these programs work correctly. If they were created with HOS-like tools, they could, honestly, be certified.

When a complex system is developed with HOS, including one with many loops, all possible paths are built from primitives which are mathematically verified. *There are no unknown paths.*

Dynamic program testing is necessary with all programs not built with a rigorous mathematical technique (which includes the vast majority of programs in existence today). Each branch and usable combination of branches ought to be tested if this were possible. With code generators most errors are caught with *static* verification, and some with tests of specific instances to ensure that correct results are being generated.

EFFECT ON SPECIFICATIONS   An improvement in programming techniques, even a dramatic improvement, is not enough by itself.
The biggest problem with most programming is that the specifications are inadequate. The technique of Chapter 9 is a form of specification language. Specifications are created with the aid of a graphics tool which reveals their inconsistencies and errors. Where the statement of specifications is inadequate (as they all are in the beginning), it is adjusted and broken into more detail until provably correct code can be generated from it.

Programmers have an irresistible desire to start coding something, and managers have a comfortable feeling that work is under way if code is being produced. To produce code without rigorous specifications, however, is ultimately very expensive. The code has to be modified and the cost of modifying it is usually much higher than the cost of creating it in the first place.

A basic principle of structured analysis is that more work is needed at the front-end specifications in order to save time later in expensive code modification and maintenance. The problem with most structured analysis techniques, however, is that they are not rigorous. When using them it is still true that most of the errors in delivered code are caused by imprecise specifications. The method of Chapter 9 forces the specifications to be rigorous and bug-free.

The human being needs user-friendly nonprocedural techniques with which he can express his desires to a computer. Because most of his requirements statements are not computable, the computer must help the user to successively refine his requests until they *are* computable.

As automation of programming matures, the specification languages which predominate may be different from the one described in Chapter 9, but they need to have the property that they *translate broad human thinking about requirements into a computable form and successively refine it until it is possible to automatically allocate the resources needed and generate correct machine code.*

WHAT DOES "PROVABLY CORRECT" MEAN?

Just what do we mean when we say that programs or specifications are "provably correct"?

"Provably correct code" does not mean that the program is necessarily without fault. We can still tell the computer to do things that are stupid. If we create a forecasting program based on the phases of the moon and the behavior of groundhogs, no mathematics will help. Provably correct code will not improve my stockbroker's predictions.

However, the majority of bugs in programs today are caused by the mechanics of programming, inconsistent data, sequence errors, and so on. These can be eliminated. We can create a machine in which the gears and levers mesh correctly.

Mathematics do not eliminate errors in the *concept* of what a program should do. The methodology can create correct code for a stupid operation. In old fairy stories a magic device such as the *Monkey's Paw* executes its users' wishes but does not check that the effects will really be good for the users. The fairy stories warn us, philosophically, about wishing for the wrong thing.

We can give wrong instructions to specification tools, not because of any philosophical problems but because we are careless. This is a new version of garbage-in-garbage-out. Ill-conceived requirements or misstated requirements lead to correct code for executing those wrong requirements. It is perfectly possible to create a correct control map in HOS for solving the wrong problem. The software checks that the control map is correct according to its mathematical rules, but the result is wrong because the wrong problem was solved.

SYNTAX AND SEMANTICS

We can distinguish between syntax and semantics in languages. *Syntax* refers to *how* something is being said. *Semantics* refers to *what* is being said.

The *Oxford English Dictionary* defines *syntax* as "sentence-construction; the grammatical arrangement of words (in language); set of rules governing this." It defines *semantic* as "relating to meaning in language."

Most compilers and interpreters check for *syntax* errors—misspelled words, commands without the required variables, missing END statements, and so on. They cannot check the *meaning* of the language. Languages of higher level than programming languages can make some checks on *what* is being said, not just *how*. The HOS software carries out as much verification as it can of *what* is being said. Do the operations and data references obey the basic axioms? There may be garbage-in-garbage-out, but the internal logic can be checked for what it is doing. This type of internal semantic check is a major step forward in automated design verification.

It is desirable to represent specifications in a technology-independent fashion because machines and software change. A fixed semantics is necessary for this. This semantics may be expressed with different forms of syntax, such as COBOL, FORTRAN, Ada, and so on. In historical methods the opposite is true. The languages have a fixed syntax but uncontrolled semantics. Specification languages have controlled semantics that can be translated into multiple syntaxes.

INTERNAL AND EXTERNAL SEMANTICS

We might distinguish between internal semantics and external semantics. *Internal semantics* relates to whether what is being said obeys the rules that are established in the basic axioms. *External semantics* relates to whether the system is solving the right problem. Techniques for proving program correctness can deal with internal semantics, not usually with external semantics.

We might say to a science-fiction robot, "Get me a dry blartini with a twist." It will tell us there is a *syntax* error, and ask whether the word "blartini" should be "martini." If we tell it to get a dry martini made with Seven-Up it will tell us we have a *semantics* error. Our instruction violates a basic axiom of martini-making.

If we want a vodka martini and only say, "Get me a dry martini with a twist," it might bring a gin martini. Now we have an *external semantics* error which the software has not caught.

You might say that the robot should have detected that our specifications were incomplete. It should have known that there are two types of martini and asked "vodka or gin?" There are other options. It should say "With ice or straight up?" But where does it stop? It might say "Gordon's, Juniper, Beefeater, Boodles, Tanqueray, Bombay, Schenley, Skol, London, Mr. Boston, Burnett's, Crystal Palace, Seagram's, Calvert, Booth's, Fleischmann's, S. S. Pierce, Five O'clock, Gilbey's, . . . ," and we lose patience and say, "Fetch the damned thing."

Specifications, to be computable, have to have much detail, or else *default options*. Default options are common in the simpler forms of non-procedural languages, such as report generators. They are useful elsewhere. We would like the software to use its own intelligence as far as possible in comprehending our requirements and filling in the details so as to save us work and avoid specification debugging.

A WAY TO THINK   Specification languages and graphics tools provide
ABOUT SYSTEMS   *a way to think about systems* which leads to higher-precision specification and design. At its different levels they should be understandable by both skilled end users and computer professionals. They should provide a way to bridge the gap between these different communities.

The concepts of accountants and double-entry bookkeeping can be mapped into HOS or other specification charts. The ideas of planning business resources, or scheduling production, or controlling projects can be drawn as such charts. Complex engineering operations, robot functions, or the operation of trains on a railroad can be mapped into these charts. Other types of charts that help human communication are also desirable, but if they are to become the basis of system specifications, enough rigor ought to be imposed on them for them to be convertible into a form from which correct code can be generated.

STANDARDS   The author was recently in communication with a standards committee concerned with the rapidly evolving standards for data networks. The committee produced a document of several hundred pages specifying the draft standard in fine detail. Its object was "to ensure compatibility between equipment made by different manufacturers." To accomplish this it provided specifications "that establish common interfaces and protocols." Like all such standards, it was not provably correct or even provably computable. Among other notations it contained state diagrams which could easily be transformed into the rigorous notation of HOS. Once in that notation these could be manipulated by the graphics editor, and code automatically generated, and tested. Computer standards committees everywhere should be upgrading their notation to provably correct forms.

Now that we know that it is possible, future standards, future network interfaces, future operating systems, future data-base management systems, and so on, all ought to be built with rigorous provably correct design that helps eliminate redundancies and enforces rigorously correct interfaces between modules.

Software of all types ought to have a certification stamped on it saying whether it was built with a rigorous mathematical foundation.

VERIFICATION AND TESTING

We can distinguish between *verification* and *testing*. By verification we mean checking a system's specification for logical completeness and consistency and that it obeys rigorous rules. By testing we mean checking the correctness by demonstrating that the system really works as it was intended to work. *Verification* is performed automatically and statically by code generation software. *Testing* requires instantiations of the target system's behavior to be checked. Test cases are fed to the system to ensure that its algorithms give the results the designers intended.

In conventional systems development almost all testing has to be done after programming. This is expensive to do and it is even more expensive to correct the errors found at that late stage. Figure 5.2 illustrated that if errors are caught early they are less costly by one or two orders of magnitude. With the best new languages most of the errors can be caught early. The software analyzes the high-level specifications and they can be successively reanalyzed as they are broken down into detail. The designer will also do case tests on modules as he proceeds.

Verification ought to take place at every stage in a design process. Hamilton and Zeldin express this as follows: *Design* means to think. *Verify* means to think back. For each step of design there should be a counterstep of verification. At times, the process of design is the same as the process of verification. This occurs when certain design characteristics are included for the purpose of preventing unnecessary verification. In such a case, some types of verification requirements are designed out of the system [2].

In order to verify automatically, one has to translate a design into a computable form. Rigorous verification should be applied at each step of the design process.

BUILDING HIGHER LEVELS OF TRUST

Modules that are verified and tested are stored in the system library. These are then regarded as proven modules that do not need to be verified again. They are verified *one time only*. Their application may be tested when they are used in newly defined systems.

The library of verified modules grows and these modules may become linked to form larger modules. All new design should use as many of the library modules as possible. This lessens the amount of verification and testing required.

Systems can thus be defined using techniques that eliminate the need for certain types of verification. If techniques are enforced that eliminate data and sequence errors, there is no need to look for these errors. When you use a computer as part of a system, you do not check its internal wiring. You assume that is correct. We should similarly be able to trust as many software modules as possible, and link them together into larger trustworthy modules.

The growth and maximal use of the library of verified modules is thus a very important part of the overall reduction of testing time and costs.

**IMPROVEMENTS IN
PRODUCTIVITY**

The early experiences with the HOS tools show major increases in application development productivity. There are several reasons for this:

1. There is no program coding; the code is generated automatically.

2. Most dynamic testing and error correction, which consumes so much time, is avoided.

3. When an error is corrected or a change is made, the effects of this on other parts of the system are *rigorously* detected and quickly modified with the graphics editor.

4. The control maps, although they become large and complex, are highly modular and are created and manipulated quickly and easily with the graphics editor.

5. *Defined operations and defined structures* are created to form a powerful macrolanguage for specific application areas or system viewpoints.

6. Early feedback helps to make the system specifications consistent and complete.

7. The library facility largely eliminates interface problems among separately created system modules.

8. The library facility encourages the maximum repetitive use of code modules and the minimum redundant code creation.

There are now many nonprocedural languages and code generators in use. It is typical to observe an order-of-magnitude improvement in productivity with the good ones [3]. Most generators generate relatively simple applications. Some can generate exceedingly complex logic, and can interlink many separately developed library modules in a correct fashion.

COST SAVINGS

Figure 10.1 shows the typical breakdown of costs of a large software project using the classical life cycle. Using code generators, the programming costs disappear and the costs of testing largely disappear. There is less maintenance because the original system was thoroughly specified. Maintenance is much easier and faster to perform.

Much more care has to go into the specification stage. It might be thought that specification will take longer because it has to be thorough. In early examples of HOS usage, like other forms of computer-aided design, however, specification and design costs have been halved because of the top-to-bottom communication with the tool, the speed of using the graphics editor, and the automatic detection of errors, inconsistencies, and incom-

PERCENTAGE OF COSTS

	DEVELOPMENT EFFORT	FINDING AND FIXING ERRORS	TOTAL
INITIAL DEVELOPMENT			
Specification and Design	5	5	10
Programming	5		5
Verification and Testing		10	10
TOTAL	10	15	25
MAINTENANCE			
Residual Errors		7.5	7.5
Specification and Design	13.5	13.5	27
Programming	13.5		13.5
Verification and Testing		27	27
TOTAL	27	48	75
OVERALL TOTAL	37	63	100

Figure 10.1   Classical life-cycle costs. (Derived from Ref. 4.)

pleteness. A committee using imprecise methods takes *much* longer than a small group using precise and powerful methods.

EFFECT OF PROGRAM SIZE   Lower programmer productivity is achieved with large programs than with small programs. Figure 10.2 shows a typical distribution. The productivity achieved with very large programs is almost one-tenth of that achieved with small programs [5].

There are several reasons why productivity with large programs is worse than with small ones. First, the programming team is larger. This requires more formal interaction between people and gives more scope for miscommunication. There is substantial overhead required to fit together all the pieces of a large program.

Small programs are often created by one person who has all the pieces in his head. With large systems, planning and paperwork is needed to control the development cycle. The various forms of paperwork with large systems sometimes contain an aggregate of over 50 English words for each line of source code in the system [6,7].

In large systems where the programmer works on one project for more than a year, his interest and productivity often decline substantially. On a small program the programmer can keep working fast to complete the work quickly.

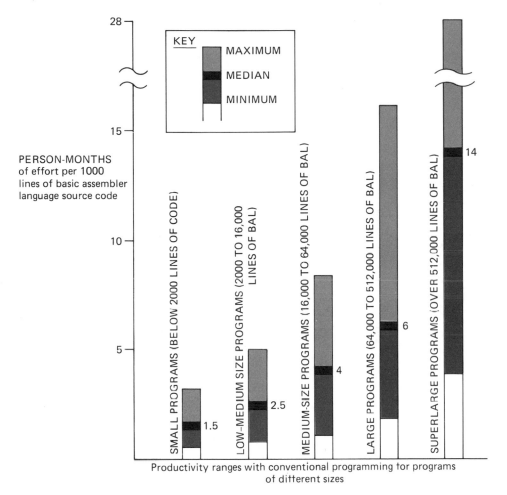

Figure 10.2 Lower programmer productivity is achieved with large programs than with small programs. (From Ref. 5.)

The testing is disproportionately time-consuming with very large programs. The number of combinations that need to be tested tends to increase roughly as the square of the program size. The problems with interfaces between modules become numerous and severe on large programs. Saturation testing becomes lengthy and unsatisfactory in that many bugs are not found. When a bug is corrected, it can have unforeseen consequences in other parts of the program, which in turn are difficult to find.

Code generators with rigorous verification have a direct effect on all of these problems. They rigorously control the interfaces among modules. The modules fit together in a correct fashion. The generation of code is so much faster than hand coding that a large team of people is not needed. One person can replace 10 programmers. Three people can replace a team of 30. This shrinkage greatly reduces the problems of communication among people. The different members of the team all interact with the same computerized representation and library. When any change is made, the consequences of that are automatically shown on the screen and can be quickly adjusted. The finding of most errors is brought to the front of the development cycle. Saturation testing is largely replaced by static verification. Individual modules, or portions of the system with missing modules, can be tested on-line in a simulated fashion.

In a typical large development project a programmer sits at his desk and is greeted each morning with a set of memos or documents about changes. He often regards them cynically feeling that he has neither the time to read them nor the ability to remember to react to them. Somebody, he hopes, is filing them. With the new tools, change control is largely automatic. The areas affected by each change are revealed automatically and the system ensures that all consequential adjustments are made. These adjustments then reside in the on-line representation of the system which every developer uses.

With nonprocedural languages and code generators, many team programming efforts shrink to one-person projects. This can be enhanced by firm high-quality data administration techniques [8].

ERROR STATISTICS   On some large projects detailed analysis has been done of the errors made. It is interesting to look back and estimate how many errors could have been avoided with the technique described in Chapter 9.

Figure 10.3 shows statistics of the preflight software errors in NASA's moonshot, Project Apollo. These were errors discovered *after* implementation and delivery of code. Far more errors were presumably caught by programmers during implementation. A total of 73% of the problems were software-software interface errors. This is common on large projects. If all software for a project were developed with a methodology such as HOS, there should be no interface problems discovered *after* implementation. The interfaces are defined with mathematical precision and details of all modules and their interface definitions are in the library. Forty-four percent of the errors were found manually and many by *dynamic* testing runs. With the new tools most could be found in *static* verification.

It was estimated that 30% of the errors would have been avoided with better programming style—a good structured programming method. Eighty-seven percent of the errors in the bottom chart of Fig. 10.3 would have been caught by HOS-like verification methods, before code delivery. Thirteen percent of the errors were conceptual problems or problems of changing requirements which would not have been caught by mathematical verification.

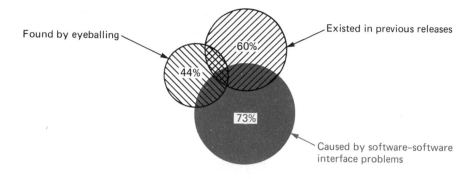

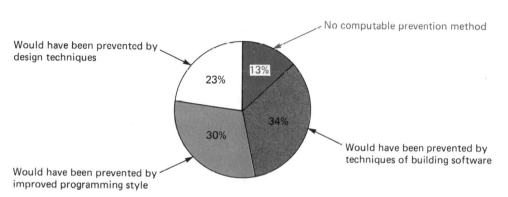

Figure 10.3 Breakdown of the official preflight software anomolies of Project Apollo. (From Ref. 4.)

Typically, the specification was incomplete or inconsistent with the original intent of the designer.

Hamilton and Zeldin refer to this residual 13% of errors as the "13% problem." If code generation and verification are automated, and precision is enforced in specification, developers can spend more time at the front of projects checking the high-level system description with the end users and management, trying to flush out any specification faults and omissions.

Seeing results as quickly as possible and being able to perform simulations at the terminal help developers to catch external semantics errors. Better front-end methodologies for helping to achieve accurate system conceptualization may reduce the 13%. These include thorough data modeling and event diagramming.

HUMAN SYSTEM COMPONENTS A particularly interesting error occurred on Project Apollo Mission 11. Just prior to landing on the moon, a warning signal informed the astronauts that the capsule should not land. This hair-raising signal was incorrect.

The error was caused by an incorrect entry in the astronaut's checklist of procedures. This caused the astronaut to take an incorrect action with the hardware, which in turn caused the software to think something was true which was not true. Here we have a system error where the system includes interacting hardware, software, and human beings.

Techniques like HOS can be applied to broad systems, in which the interaction of the hardware, software, and human beings is diagrammed, so that human checklists can be provably correct as well as other system components. This would have prevented some of the problems with nuclear power station operating procedures, for example.

SOFTWARE FACTORIES   As computers become increasingly numerous and cheap, it is necessary to create software factories, where software can be created in a professional, engineering-like, low-cost fashion. A methodology is needed with which standard bug-free building blocks can be created, cataloged, and linked together in a manner that avoids interface errors. The building blocks will become larger and more comprehensive as higher levels of trust are developed.

The methodology needs to make certain building blocks modifiable so that they can be adjusted to customers' needs. Some of the building blocks should be highly flexible report generators, document generators, screen handlers, and data-base facilities.

Software factories will often need to produce portable code which runs on all machines. This may best be achieved with an Ada generator, assuming that all manufacturers conform to a single standard specification of the Ada language.

Box 10.1 lists the ways in which rigorous specification languages and code generators provide solutions to the problems of traditional software development.

BOX 10.1

Problems with Traditional Development	Effects of Rigorous Specification Languages with Code Generators
Development takes too long. ⟶	Development is much faster.
Development costs are too high. ⟶	Major reduction in development costs.

BOX 10.1 *(Continued)*

Programming is manual.	→ Programming is automatic.
Most errors are found *after* coding.	→ Most errors are found *before* implementation.
Most errors are found manually or by *dynamic* runs.	→ Most errors are found by *automatic* and *static* analysis.
Some errors are *never* found.	→ Almost all errors are found.
Mismatch between requirements and specifications. Mismatch between specfications and design. Mismatch between design and coding.	→ Each level is a precise expansion of the previous level.
Incomplete and inconsistent specifications.	→ Internally complete, consistent specifications are enforced.
Many interface errors and mismatches between subsystems (73% of the errors on Project Apollo).	→ Rigorous, provably correct, interfaces between subsystems.
No guarantee of function integrity after implementation.	→ Guarantee of function integrity after implementation.
Large developer teams: severe communication problems.	→ Small or one-person teams: few communication problems.
Massive paperwork for management control.	→ Elimination of most paperwork.
Much redundant code development.	→ Identification of common modules. Use of common modules made easy.
Separate developers reinventing the wheel.	→ Library mechanism with rigorous interfaces encourages the building of reusable constructs.

(Continued)

BOX 10.1 *(Continued)*

Difficult to maintain.	⟶ Easy to maintain.
Modifications trigger chain reactions of new bugs.	⟶ The effects of all modifications are made explicit and clear.
Successive maintenance degrades the code quality.	⟶ High-quality code is regenerated after each change.
Portability problems.	⟶ A design can be regenerated to different environments.

11 THE CHANGE IN THE DEVELOPMENT LIFE CYCLE

INTRODUCTION   Most of the methodologies referred to in this book completely change the traditional development life cycle. The life cycle is illustrated in Fig. 11.1. Various organizations have their own version of it. Figures 11.2 and 11.3 show two of them.

Formal management of system development requires that certain documents are created and reviews conducted at each stage. The phases of the life cycle are decomposed into subcycles and checklists as illustrated in Fig. 11.4. These components of the cycle are important for telling development staff what to do, giving them guidelines and ensuring that nothing important is forgotten.

Management standards associated with the life cycle have acquired the force of law in many organizations. And yet there are obviously great problems associated with the traditional life cycle. The historical life cycle grew up before the following tools and techniques existed:

- Nonprocedural languages
- Techniques that generate program code automatically
- Computable specification languages
- Rigorous verification techniques
- On-line graphics tools for design
- Formal data modeling tools
- Strategic data planning techniques
- Information engineering
- Languages for rapid prototyping
- Languages for end users
- Distributed processing and microcomputers
- The information center concept

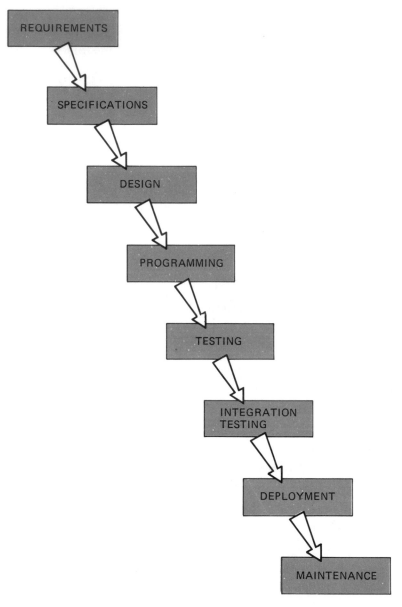

Figure 11.1 Traditional development life cycle.

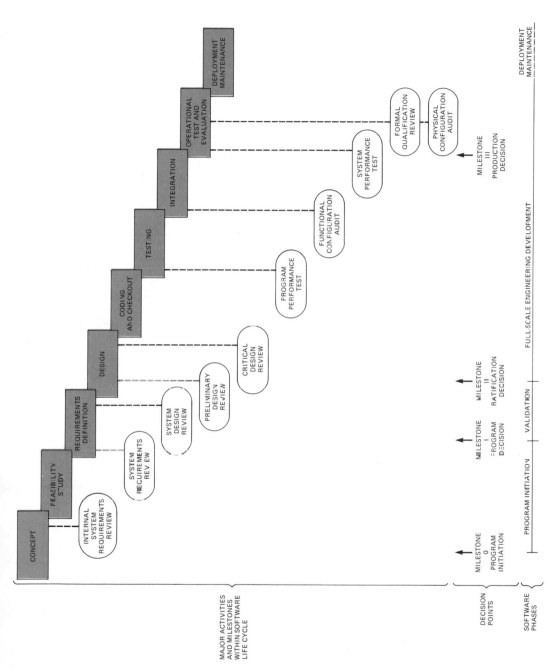

Figure 11.2 Traditional system development life cycle. The reviews and milestones shown here are those required in the U.S. Department of Defense.

SYSTEM DEVELOPMENT LIFE CYCLE

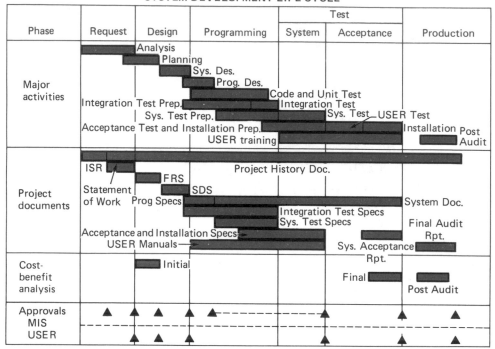

Figure 11.3 System development life cycle in a commercial organization.

All of these tools and techniques have a major impact on the effectiveness of computer usage. Any one of them would change the historical life cycle. In combination they render it obsolete. It needs complete redesign, retaining those checklist items that ensure thorough planning. At each stage the life cycle needs to be reexamined to *maximize the degree of automation* of systems engineering, *build in thorough data modeling* which is often independent of specific projects, ensure flexibility so that systems can be *easily changed when necessary,* and provide end users with facilities for *extracting and themselves manipulating* the information they need.

With application generators the program coding phase disappears, testing and integration testing are radically changed and shortened, and the requirements, specification, and design of the logic are completely changed and integrated. The time taken to create applications falls from years to months with complex applications, and from months to hours with simple applications.

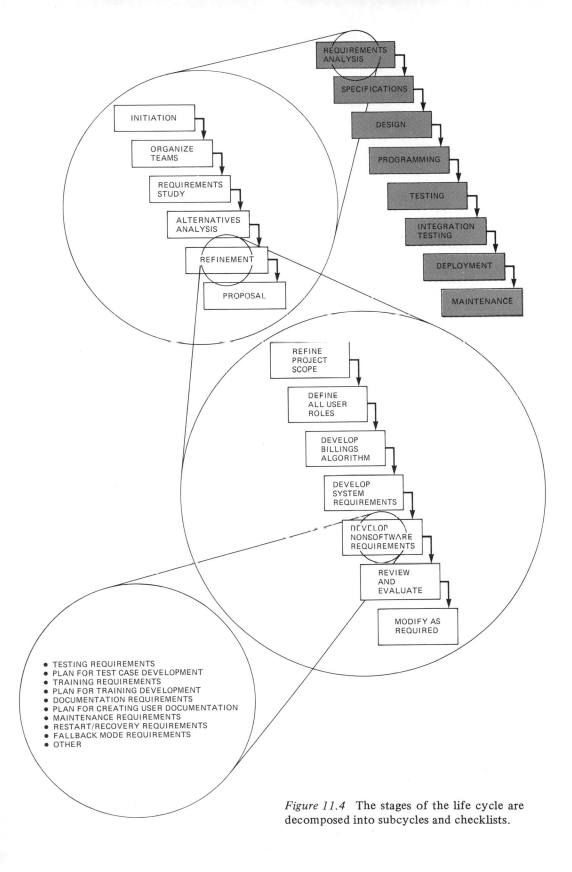

Figure 11.4 The stages of the life cycle are decomposed into subcycles and checklists.

THE METHODOLOGY ZOO

Realizing the seriousness of the problems in DP, many organizations have undertaken to create and sell "methodologies" for system planning and development. Methodologies are sold by manufacturers, software houses, consultants, accounting firms, university professors, and new companies formed for this purpose. Managers reading *Computerworld* are confronted with such a zoo of methodologies that they often ignore them all and continue to do what they are familiar with.

Many of the methodologies are utterly obsolete, including some of those with high prices, voluminous documentation, and impressive salespeople. To use them guarantees low productivity, high maintenance costs, and inability to change. They formalize the ways of the past, fail to automate system development, and encourage excessive, unnecessary bureaucracy.

The DP executive should be aware that computing is going through the greatest changes in its history and should meticulously avoid methodologies that fossilize the manually oriented techniques of the past.

What should a manager look for in new methodologies? Above all, *automation.* We must automate the job of the analyst and programmer as fully as possible. This automation needs to harness the knowledge of end users, communicate well with the end users, and be adaptable to their changing needs in a flexible fashion.

Box 11.1 lists properties that are needed in DP methodologies. It is sometimes commented that systems analysts are prone to automate every job except their own.

BOX 11.1   What do we need in DP methodologies?

- *Automation.* As much as possible of the analysts' and programmers' jobs should be automated.

- *Avoidance of hand programming.* Hand programming is too slow, clumsy, and error-prone. The maximum use should be made of code generators.

- *Speed.* Techniques are needed that obtain results very quickly.

- *Changeability.* Techniques are needed that enable programs to be changed quickly without the cost and slowness of traditional maintenance.

- *Verification of correctness.* All syntax and internal semantics errors should be caught automatically. Maximum assistance should be provided in catching external semantics errors easily.

- *Avoidance of most dynamic testing.* Dynamic testing is slow, expensive, and does not catch all errors.

BOX 11.1 *(Continued)*

- *Techniques that facilitate communication with end users.* The knowledge of the users must be harnessed and their needs responded to flexibly. Users should be able to check every stage of system evolution.

- *User-driven computing.* Users should be able to employ their own query and update languages, report generators, decision-support languages, and specification languages.

- *Stable data-base design.* Automation of data modeling is necessary, linked to techniques to make the data bases a stable foundation stone.

- *Fast data-base languages.* Languages should be adopted which enable new information to be extracted from the data bases for management as soon as they need it.

- *Enterprise-wide data planning.* Data should be planned to avoid the Tower of Babel effect of different analysts creating the same data incompatibly.

- *Overview planning.* Complex organizations need overview planning for converting to and streamlining on-line procedures.

- *Aids to eliminate redundancy.* A methodology is needed that avoids redundant development and reinventing the wheel.

- *Modularity.* Systems should be divided into easily comprehensible modules. Changes should be able to be made locally *within* a module. Any effect of changes outside a module should be *rigorously* traceable.

- *Control of interoperability.* A formal, rigorous technique is needed to ensure that separately developed systems and modules operate together correctly.

- *Truly usable library control.* There should be an ever-growing library of program modules with a methodology for making these known to and usable by all developers.

- *Automated change control.* When changes are made the consequences of these should be revealed automatically and the complete set of consequential corrections should be represented in the library.

- *Evolving power.* The methodology should encourage an evolving set of more powerful mechanisms, built with lower-level mechanisms.

- *Alternative dialects.* Alternative means for conceptualizing, drawing, and designing systems may be permitted where helpful and linked automatically to the basic representation.

- *An integrated set of tools.* Tools that achieve the objectives listed above should work together and avoid manual bridges which introduce errors. They should use common syntax and graphics where possible.

In the traditional life cycle the numbers of persons employed grows toward the end of the cycle, as shown in Fig. 11.5. There are more programmers than specifiers, and much effort is needed in testing. Sometimes concern builds up about a project slipping its schedule and additional programmers are added late in the cycle (often with disastrous results).

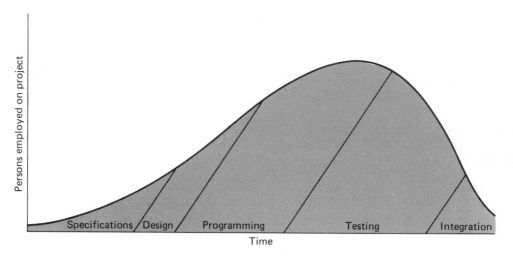

Figure 11.5   People requirements with the traditional life cycle.

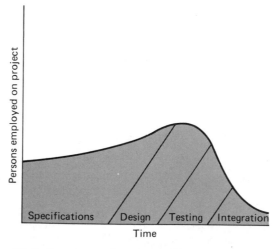

Figure 11.6   People requirements with more automated tools.

Structured analysis grew up in the 1970s because of concern that the front end of the cycle was inadequate. It was clear that poor quality and incomplete specifications were giving rise to inappropriate coding. Poorly defined specifications cause the wrong thing to be coded, make testing difficult, destroy management control, and often cause project failures.

The analysis phase was often glossed over because it did not lend itself to the use of precise tools. As more precise tools and techniques have evolved, more attention has been paid to front-end analysis. The shape of Fig. 11.5 changed somewhat. More effort at the front resulted in less effort later. Structured analysis, however, was still far from being a precise discipline. It is only with computable specification languages that we begin to see high precision at the front end. This has a high payoff at the back end and substantially shortens the entire cycle.

Figure 11.6 shows the timing and people consumption with more automated tools. Program coding has disappeared. Program testing has been reduced to a low level. Verification is moved to the front of the cycle, where it is much lower in cost. The overall development time is much shorter, and the costs drastically reduced.

ELIMINATION OF UNNECESSARY TOOLS AND PROCEDURES

As traditional life-cycle management has evolved, many procedures and tools have been created to solve its problems. The procedures have become rigidified in order to achieve management control of the life cycle. Many of the original problems disappear with computer-aided design tools and code generators and hence the procedures associated with them are no longer needed. The life-cycle procedures need to be examined critically and eliminated where appropriate. This eliminates much time-consuming work.

Among the problems that gave rise to time-consuming procedures and tools were:

- Problems of managing large teams.
- Nonautomated change control.
- Management of manual documentation.
- Problems of dynamic testing.
- Tools for saturation testing.
- Difficulty of tracking the effects of changes or bug correction (the ripple effect); correcting one bug often gave rise to other bugs.

- Difficulty of controlling source-code changes.
- Communication problems among programmers.
- Interface errors.
- Mismatch of requirement language (normally English), specification diagrams, and program design.
- Errors in converting the design to coding.

These problems are taken care of to a large extent by computer-aided design tools with code generators. Elimination of time-consuming, tedious, or expensive procedures is an important part of the life-cycle change.

Not only can procedures be deleted but also much software. Much software is performing tasks that are unnecessary. High-level programming languages, compilers, testing aids, maintenance aids, and many operating system functions become unnecessary. Compilers for languages such as FORTRAN have complex functions to deal with the problems that FORTRAN causes. These problems can be made to disappear. Operating systems have functions to deal with uncontrolled interrupts, deadly embraces, and other problems that can be removed in the original design. Networking software has highly complex functions to help recovery from subtle deadlocks and interference problems. Many such problems should not occur with HOS-like design. Testing tools spend much time testing over and over again for errors that should be provably absent.

A challenge, then, of computer-aided design techniques and nonprocedural languages is to throw overboard as much unnecessary baggage as possible. We should eliminate as much of the procedures, documentation, maintenance, training, computer time, compilers, testing aids, unnecessary software mechanisms, recovery aids, and people time as is practical. Some of these can be eliminated by new development methods; some go to the heart of complex software and require new generations of such software to evolve.

USE OF OTHER FRONT-END METHODOLOGIES

The HOS software can be made more acceptable and easy to use by linking it to familiar, powerful, or user-friendly front-end methodologies. The extent to which the computer-aided design encompasses such methodologies is likely to determine its level of success.

Various different methodologies are powerful for the overall planning and design of computer systems. It is often desirable to retain these and enhance them, but to link them into rigorous verification techniques, graphics editors, and automated code generation.

Although powerful front-end methodologies exist which can enhance the conceptual clarity of systems design or create overview designs for corporate data processing, many of these methodologies are not rigorous. The specifications they create (contrary to the sales claims) are inconsistent, incomplete, redundant, and ambiguous. HOS-like tools reveal these deficiencies. The step of translating their designs into HOS is very valuable. It allows problems to be found at the front end, where they are easily correctable, rather than at the back end, where they are disastrous.

In one case a module that was part of a battlefield intelligence system [1] was documented with a mixture of English, equations, and the SREM specification language [2]. Translation of this into HOS revealed and removed multiple design inconsistencies [1].

The U.S. Department of Defense has extensively funded a set of methodologies for improving and integrating the manufacturing processes of its suppliers. This is called ICAM (integrated computer-aided manufacturing) [3]. A specification technique was created for ICAM, called IDEF [4]. It uses a type of diagram which represents complex flows and relationships and is easy to use and understand. It is not completely rigorous from a computability point of view. HOS was used to create a computable version of IDEF so that this valuable technique becomes rigorous [5]. A graphics tool was specified which might be described as an IDEF-O typewriter [6]. A single keystroke can produce a box, an arrow path, an arrow end, a shift to the next location, and so on. The arrows fall along uniform and predictable paths. This chart becomes part of a computable specification, linked directly to HOS control maps which can be analyzed and from which correct code can be generated.

Adjusting front-end methodologies to make them computable has two very important effects. First, it enforces the creation of specifications which are rigorous; it flushes out the inconsistencies, vagueness, and incompleteness. Second, it permits the automatic generation of correct code, and so speeds up the life cycle as shown in Fig. 11.6 and greatly reduces development costs.

This linking of methodologies can allow user-friendly specification facilities such as report and graphics generators to be incorporated. It allows the benefits of familiar methodologies to be retained and permits users to "speak their own language."

DATA MODELING AND THE LIFE CYCLE

The DP development life cycle of the 1970s usually encompassed the design of the data. It became realized that data need to be planned on a corporate-wide basis, and that this is practical because the data entities do not change much, even though the ways data are used change greatly. Efficient data administration, then, began to separate the planning and modeling of data from the life cycle of individual projects [7]. As we saw in Chapter 6, data modeling expresses the inherent associations in data which are largely independent of any one application of those data.

Once canonical data models exist the design of applications becomes easier and quicker, and another class of errors is removed. Well-executed data administration shortens the front end of projects' life cycles. Code generators shorten the back end. Where the code generators are very easy to use, the life cycle, in the normal sense of the term, disappears for some projects. We find applications being generated from a previously existing data base in days, and reports being generated in hours.

A CONTINUUM OF INFORMATION RESOURCE BUILDING

Rather than thinking of a succession of projects each with a discrete life cycle, an enterprise should think of an ongoing continuum of information resource building. There will be some big projects with a lengthy life cycle, but many of the new needs of users will be met with nonprocedural languages employing previously existing data bases. Often data are extracted from existing files or data bases, restructured with relational data management systems, and manipulated with powerful nonprocedural languages. Some of the languages are sufficiently easy to use that end users can employ them, with help from information center staff. Some applications are too complex for the users in question to build but can be quickly prototyped by DP staff.

Figure 11.7 illustrates the continuum of planning and design that is needed, extending from higher management strategic planning down to application building. The left of Fig. 11.7 relates to functions and the right relates to data. The top relates to top-level planning. On the left an overview of the entire enterprise is created with strategic planning of what information systems are needed. On the right strategic data planning is done and a chart is produced of the data entities in the enterprise [7].

The entity chart at the top right of Fig. 11.7 is expanded into detail in the middle right-hand block. This is the task of the data administrator—to build stable canonical data models, obtain agreements about the definitions of data, and represent these in a data dictionary.

The middle left-hand block relates to the requirements planning of applications and the creation of specifications. The specifications are decomposed into detail until an application can be generated. The lower left block shows the application design.

Applications are designed using the data model. A submodel of the data for that particular application is extracted from the overall model, and a data access map is drawn showing the access paths through the data. The data model and the control maps for the applications reside in the library.

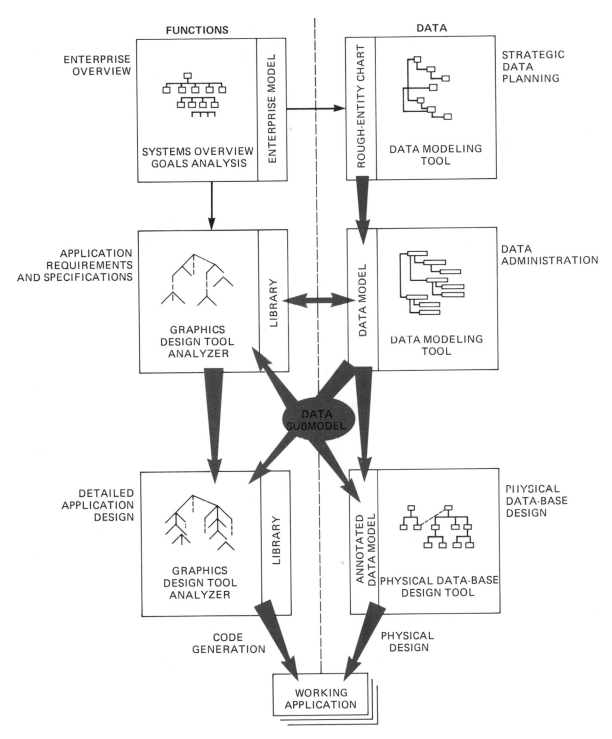

Figure 11.7 Design extending from the highest-level strategic planning down to working applications. The arrows show automatable links.

The collection of data access maps for one hardware system forms the basis for *physical* design and layout of the data base, indicated in the bottom right block of Fig. 11.7. Annotations on the data model, such as cardinality (on a one-to-many association, *how many* of one record are associated with another), assist in the physical design.

In some uses of data the middle left block of Fig. 11.7 is bypassed. Reports are generated, information is extracted and manipulated, or decision-support aids are created, directly from the data bases with easy-to-use languages without the need for detailed specification or design.

The red arrows in Fig. 11.7 represent automatable links. A compatible family of tools is needed for strategic data planning, data modeling, data dictionary representation, extraction of submodels and data access maps, representation of requirements, specifications, and application design, design verification, generation of code, and physical design. This family of tools, all using interactive graphics, will constitute the systems engineer's workbench of the future and will provide a quantum leap in the efficiency of system building.

MINIMIZING INTERACTIONS AMONG DEVELOPERS

When there are complex interactions between the work of different programmers, progress slows down. A complex programming project which is behind schedule usually cannot be helped by adding more manpower. Fred Brooks, in his book *The Mythical Man-Month* [8], stresses that men and months are interchangeable commodities only when a task can be partitioned among many workers *with no communication among them* (Fig. 11.8). This is true of picking oranges or painting a battleship; it is far from true of large conventional programming projects.

When a task cannot be partitioned because of sequential constraints, adding more manpower would have no effect on the completion time (Fig. 11.9). Having a baby takes nine months no matter how many women are assigned.

In a programming project the training is like having a baby; it cannot be speeded up. The more people added to the project, the more must be trained in the goals and details of the project. Intercommunication is worse. If three people have dinner and clink wine glasses, that is three clinks; with four people it is six clinks; with five people it is ten. With 46 people it is over 1000 clinks; they will spend all of their time clinking instead of drinking. Brooks draws Fig. 11.10 to show how the project completion time can become longer, not shorter, if there are too many workers with complex intercommunications.

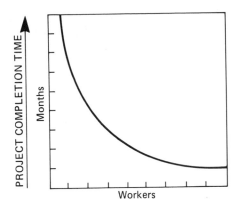

Figure 11.8 Time versus number of workers —perfectly partionable task. (From Ref. 8.)

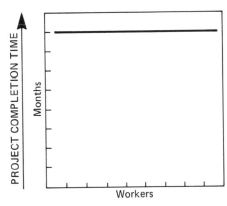

Figure 11.9 Time versus number of workers —unpartionable task. (From Ref. 8.)

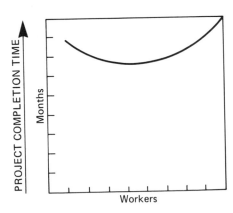

Figure 11.10 Time versus number of workers —task with complex interrelationships. (From Ref. 8.)

To increase productivity on complex system development, it is necessary to minimize the interactions among developers. This can be done in several ways:

- Use the most powerful development software. Fourth-generation languages enable one developer to achieve what would have needed 10 with third-generation languages. A 10-person project can become a one-person project.

- Use the most capable and productive people (with the highest salaries). A small team of fast-moving developers is much better than a large team of slow-moving developers.

- Employ the principles of information engineering. This permits commercial data processing to be subdivided into one-person projects. The separate projects are interlinked via the common data model which is created in advance of the process development.

- Employ a development tool which enforces rigorous interfaces between the modules created by separate developers.

ONE-PERSON PROJECTS

The ideal is to achieve one-person projects. Information engineering combined with fourth-generation languages, computable specification languages, code generators, and so on, makes this possible. As well as lessening the manpower needed for intercommunication and meetings, one-person projects are appealing in other ways. The one person can be carefully selected. He is responsible for his own work. He has no excuses about other team members lessening his effectiveness. He cannot pass the buck. He is more likely to be proud of his work. He can be measured, motivated, and rewarded appropriately.

Particularly important, a skilled developer can become excited about what he is doing. He has more freedom for creativity, more freedom for excellence. When people are excited about their work and proud of it, they tend to work much harder.

There is much to be said in all complex human endeavor for having one-person projects where that one person has the tools to achieve elegant or powerful results. Tools that give a person the power to build systems by himself greatly encourage his creativity. He can have ideas and make them work. He is cut free from bureaucratic inhibitions.

PROTOTYPE CYCLES

We have commented that there are very strong reasons for building prototypes of systems. These prototypes often supplement a preliminary specification. Sometimes they replace the specification entirely. It is easier, faster, and much more satisfactory for an analyst to build a prototype, given the right tools, than to work out detailed written specifications.

If data models exist, prototyping is generally faster. If not, data analysis is an essential stage in good prototype design. The prototype often needs to be modified after the end users employ it. To a large extent that is the point of prototyping. A second prototype is then created. In some cases many versions of the prototype are built.

One highly complex financial management system went through six levels of prototyping. The first prototype took about three months to build. The users tried it out for a week. Many changes had to be made and it took about two weeks to create the second version. Each subsequent version took somewhat less time. Eventually the system settled down with its sixth prototype. The comment was made that the final system was of such complexity that it almost certainly could not have been created with COBOL.

In this type of development the traditional life cycle is replaced with a cycle of prototypes which are successively refined. The refinement can be an ongoing process, like maintenance. This is sometimes referred to as a "prototype cycle" or "protocycle." If heavy-duty computing is involved in this type of development, it is necessary to have a language which makes changes easy and which can be compiled to give highly efficient code.

MULTIPLE TYPES OF LIFE CYCLE

It is clear that there is no longer one formal type of system development life cycle. There are different types of life cycles suitable for different types of development methodologies and tools. At the start of a major project it is desirable to sketch out the life cycle appropriate in the methodologies and tools selected.

12 STRATEGIC PLANNING

A CAUTIONARY TALE   The U.S. Department of Defense (DoD) built many systems in the 1970s, which are referred to as battlefield automation systems (BAS). Each system considered by itself was impressive, and most worked well. Unfortunately, the systems would not work *together* as they should. If anyone actually had a war, it would be necessary for the systems to exchange certain information, and for higher-level command-and-control functions to extract information from multiple systems. Major changes were needed to make the systems interoperable and enhance their value to commanders. These changes, however, were very expensive and difficult to make. (When the military says "expensive," it means outrageously expensive!)

Sometimes the experience with complex systems in the military is years ahead of corporate computer application, and lessons learned with military systems filter down to civilian practice. SAGE and AUTOVON, for example, taught the world much about real-time and transmission systems. The enormous expenses incurred because of the incompatibility of multiple systems is also happening in corporate and government MIS, especially with the spread of minicomputers and separate network systems.

The DoD systems were independently developed, as indeed they must be, and the problems of information exchange requirements were addressed in various studies and directives under the general guidance of the Army Tactical Command and Control Master Plan (ATACCOMAP) and the ARTADS Interface Management Plan (AIMP). However, after separate systems had been implemented it became clear that these studies were not detailed enough.

There had been a large-scale proliferation of independent systems, but insufficient detail in planning how the systems would work together. The Department of the Army described the result as "an inefficient and uneconomical situation" where necessary information exchange between automated systems is often not possible [1].

A solution was devised: the Army Battlefield Interface Concept (ABIC) [2]. The ABIC was devised to identify interface and interoperability requirements among U.S. army battlefield systems. It provided architectural guidance for system developers. It addressed the retrofitting of existing systems so that they could cooperate. It organized the funds needed to develop software *and hardware* facilities that would enable separate systems to interface and work together. The 1978 ABIC addressed 48 battlefield automation systems. The 1979 ABIC addressed 100 systems.

FUTURE PLANNING   The expense of retrofitting was great, and the danger of having systems that would not work together was alarming. To prevent this situation recurring in the future the ABIC plans in detail the interfaces and interoperation of systems for seven years in the future. Each year the top-down plan is rolled forward. The 1980 ABIC addressed all systems required to interwork in 1987; the 1981 ABIC addressed 1988; and so on.

Future planning of information resources is vital in a corporation. Failure to do strategic planning in DP has resulted in *extremely* expensive modifications and rebuilding, and has kept senior management from obtaining information they need.

An objective of strategic planning is to make the pieces of information systems fit together where they need to. Most systems will evolve and as they evolve they still must be able to interchange data. This requires both logical and physical compatibility. The need for interfaces and interchange among separate systems has often been grossly underestimated. Because of incompatibility, changes have to be made, and these changes can be very expensive.

THE NEED FOR   It would be unthinkable to build an opera house
TOP-LEVEL   without an overall plan. Once the overall plan
PLANNING   exists, separate teams can go to work on the components. Corporate information engineering is not much less complex than building an opera house, yet in most corporations it is done without an overall plan of sufficient detail to make the components fit together.

The overall architect of the opera house cannot conceivably specify the detailed design of the organ, stage machinery, sound equipment, or other subsystems. These have to be developed by different teams working autonomously. But imagine what would happen if these teams enthusiastically created their own subsystems without any coordination from the top.

The DP world is full of inspired subsystem designers who want to be left alone. Their numbers are rapidly increasing as small computers proliferate and end users learn to acquire their own facilities. In many cases they are doing an excellent job. However, the types of data they use overlap substantially and this is often not recognized. The subsystems need to be connected together, but often this cannot be done without conversion. Conversion, when the need for it becomes apparent, is often too expensive to accomplish and so incompatible systems live on, making it difficult or impossible to integrate the data that management need.

Good system design avoids excessive complexity. Corporate information systems ought to be composed of discrete modules, each of which is simple enough to be efficiently designed, completely understood by its design team, low in maintenance costs, and susceptible to high-productivity development methods (such as the use of high-level data-base languages). But the modules must fit together and they will not do so unless designed with planning from the top, with appropriate design tools.

THE DANGER OF INTEGRATED SYSTEMS PLANNING

With ABIC, the Army moved from individual systems development to a functionally integrated approach to development. Integrated network planning and management is done, standards are developed and enforced, and data formats, definitions, and exchange requirements are planned. Common software and commonality of systems configurations are used where necessary to aid the horizontal and vertical interoperability of systems. A philosophy of optimization of the whole is advocated even where it may be at the expense of one or more individual systems.

The danger with highly integrated systems planning lies in our inability to understand in detail the future system requirements. Although it is desirable to design systems so that they can work together, it is *entirely impractical* to plan or understand all the systems that an enterprise will need. Totally integrated systems are far beyond our capability, and almost all attempts to build them have failed catastrophically.

What is needed instead is freedom for user areas to employ their own initiative in creating the systems they need, but they still must obey certain laws. They make *their systems conform to a set of rules that permit them to interchange data, now and in the future.*

TOO MUCH GOVERNMENT

In some corporations users and senior user management rebel vehemently against any suggestion of central planning of DP. They have learned the advantages of building their own systems. The faraway DP department, they would say, does not and cannot understand their real needs. They want their own information resources. They want to be able to create and modify their own procedures, and to do it quickly.

My own view of life is that I do not want to live in a world with too much government. I want to be free to do my thing and solve my own problems. But I do not want to live in a society with no government. I want the sewers and telephone to work. Society needs an infrastructure which provides law and order and certain services, and leaves its members as free as possible to build their own lives.

In DP, users are rapidly acquiring much more capability. This trend will continue with user-friendly software. But, as with the DoD battlefield systems, it is necessary that separately developed systems can interchange data.

To permit interoperability, two design characteristics are needed:

1. The separate systems need to have an interface to a common network so that they can interchange data.

2. The separate systems should employ compatible data in their files or data bases, structured according to a common data model.

If appropriate standards for networking and data can be created so that they are reasonably stable, then individual systems can be created by relatively small teams covering areas of operation each narrow enough to be well understood and sharply focused.

The object of future planning then should not be a grand all-embracing design, but rather a stable infrastructure into which small modular designs can be connected. The grand all-embracing design is too complex, with vast numbers of interactions doomed to vast numbers of changes all entangled and expensive. The infrastructure should be the *minimum* set of standards needed to enable the separate modular systems to interoperate. A good corporate network and stable corporate data models increase, not decrease, the freedom of user groups to create the information resources they need. Productive individualism is made possible by an organized society.

THREE TYPES OF STRATEGIC PLANNING

Strategic planning for information technology needs to take place at three levels, as shown in Fig. 12.1.

1. Strategic Business Planning

Most businesses have a strategic business plan, and all businesses *ought* to have one. It describes the basic goals, strategies, and targets of the enterprise. It is largely independent of technology except that now, technology is changing all aspects of corporations and in some cases is changing the types

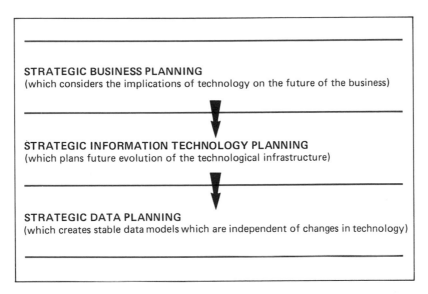

Figure 12.1 An enterprise needs to do three types of strategic planning. These are illustrated in Figure 12.2.

of business that a corporation is involved in. Technology is changing the products, the fabrication techniques (and hence the product opportunities), the services, the flow of information and decision making, and hence the management structure. New opportunities and new competition are arising fast in many businesses.

2. Strategic Information Technology Planning

The growth of computer networks in an enterprise needs to be planned. So does the spread of distributed systems, data bases, and office automation. If there is no planning, a ragged mess of incompatible systems will grow like weeds taking over a garden. Unlike weeds, the incompatible systems are extremely difficult to get rid of once they take root.

3. Strategic Data Planning

As discussed in Chapter 6, the data entities and their attributes which are shared in an enterprise should be defined independently of the applications and systems. We know that the technology is going to change beyond recognition, but the data, if thorough data analysis and data administration are done, remains stable. The data models will be viable with relatively minor adjustments and additions for many years and will be used in many different types of systems and data bases.

Figure 12.2 breaks this planning into more detail.

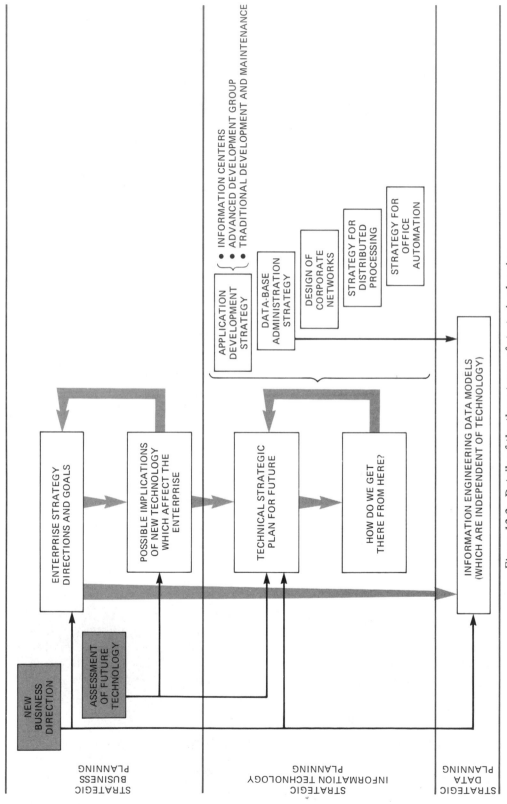

Figure 12.2 Details of the three types of strategic planning.

STRATEGIC INFORMATION TECHNOLOGY PLANNING

Strategic planning of the technology infrastructure needs to look some years into the future, create a view of what facilities will be needed at that time, and then ask the question: "How do we get from here to there?"

Getting from here to there needs to be done in a succession of projects each of which has a high chance of success. The facilities created by each project should link together where necessary, but the interactions between the projects should be minimal, as described above. Each project should be as small and modular as possible, able to be completed by a small team in a reasonably short time. Strategic planning should seek to subdivide the enterprise requirements into small projects, each autonomous except for the conformity to the overall plan.

The view of the future cannot identify all user needs with clairvoyance. What we need instead is to design an infrastructure that permits the autonomous growth of independent projects. If we were designing a new form of city for the future, we could not possibly know how people would live or what type of houses they would want. We *could* design the street layout, the transportation system, the public utilities, the library facilities, the shopping areas, the theaters, and services. People and entrepreneurs would be free to build their own houses and design their own life-styles within this planned infrastructure.

ASPECTS OF THE TECHNICAL STRATEGIC PLAN

There are several aspects of technical strategic plan shown in Fig. 12.2:

- Application development strategy
- Data-base administration strategy
- Planning and design of corporate networks
- Strategy for distributed processing
- Strategy for office automation

For each of these areas the planning needs to be done in sufficient detail that it gives implementable standards or guidelines for the individual project developers. The knowledge required is different in these five areas, so a different person may be responsible for each. The skills required for the information engineering planning described in Chapter 6 are, for example, quite different from the skills required for network planning or office automation planning. In some large corporations separate efforts have been conducted relating to these planning areas.

The *application development strategy* relates to what Part I of this book is all about—changing the methodologies of application building so that there is much higher productivity, low maintenance costs, user-driven development, fewer bugs, and fast creation of decision-support tools. It should relate to the selection of fourth-generation languages, relational data bases and development tools, and the establishment of information centers and advanced development groups.

Closely related to the application development strategy is the strategy *for information engineering* described in Chapter 6. This set of techniques (Fig. 6.4) is designed to help get the right information to decision makers and application builders. If done well, it has a great effect on lowering maintenance expenses.

Network planning should be concerned with all telecommunications—voice, data, electronic mail, teleconferencing, wide-area networks, and local area networks. It needs to plan the protocol conversion mechanisms which permit devices with different link control procedures to intercommunicate [3]. Eventually, a ubiquitous, highly flexible, data networking facility needs to be built in an enterprise. There are multiple options for how this might be done and they need long-term planning. In the past many enterprises have planned their networks inadequately. This has resulted in multiple incompatible teleprocessing systems and the need for later conversion, which is sometimes extremely expensive.

The conversion (maintenance) due to an absence of planning is often much more than mere access method conversion. The terminals have to be changed to achieve common networking protocols and this causes the terminal dialogue to have to be changed in application programs. Changing the terminal dialogue often results in changes to record structures. These records are used by multiple applications.

Distributed processing standards [4] are broader in scope than network standards. The architectures for distributed processing encompass complex functions over and above the transmission subsystem. The planning for distributed processing includes selection of the software architectures to be used. Proliferation of software needs to be avoided because different architectures tend to be incompatible at the higher levels and are often evolving in different ways. If more than one type of architecture is used, the planning needs to design which zones of the enterprise use which architecture and how they interlink.

Office automation planning attempts to determine what office-of-the-future facilities will be required. Word processors, electronic mail systems, electronic filing and archiving systems, intelligent copying machines, terminals for document display, and so on, need to interconnect and hence need top-down planning. Random uncoordinated purchase of office systems leads to high future expenses for conversion or replacement. The office terminal of the future needs to access data-processing facilities as well as office automation facilities. Combined software is often needed for office automation and DP. Both classes of facilities need to share local area networks, exchanges, and often wide-area networks. Failure in top-down planning of office automation has resulted in DP facilities having to be changed as well as office automation facilities, with consequent costs in program maintenance.

DESIGN OF DISTRIBUTED SYSTEMS

The designers responsible for distributed systems in an enterprise should have two contrasting images in their minds. One is of a plate of spaghetti on which if you pull one piece of spaghetti every piece on the plate is moved. The other is an image of separate autonomous nodes, each appearing to be simple to its users—the complexities hidden under the covers. The network interconnecting them is standard, flexible, and also appears to be simple, like the telephone network, its complexities hidden under the covers. The complexities under the covers are much greater than most systems analysts imagine, so they should not be modified or tampered with in any way.

NETWORKS

Desirable properties of a computer network are that it should be autonomous, trouble-free, and easy to use, like the telephone network. Machines should be able to plug into it simply at any location and transmit to any other location it serves. Unfortunately, much software for networking does not have these properties. Some software is complex, needs careful network planning, and is rapidly evolving. Many machines cannot connect to it. Worse, it is incompatible with network software from other vendors.

Because of this, careful planning is needed to avoid maintenance problems [3]. It is often tempting to solve the problems of incompatibility by writing teleprocessing monitors, modifying the network software, or writing software to interlink machines. This activity is almost always doomed to expensive maintenance later because the vendors' software is rapidly evolving. From all the experience we can observe we believe that customers should never modify vendors' networking software or write their own if they can possibly avoid it. Find off-the-shelf software solutions even if they restrict, for the time being, the configurations that can be used. The attempt to create unique network solutions has almost always turned out to be far more expensive than expected and often in the long run does more to restrict the configurations that can be used than following the vendors' evolution.

How, then, can two vendors with incompatible network software be employed? Their networks should be kept separate, and where records must be passed between them this should occur in a simple, *loosely coupled* fashion. There are various ways in which networks can be loosely coupled. Tapes or discs may be passed off-line between the machines. A machine of one network may emulate a standard input/output peripheral of a computer on another network. Simple start–stop or binary synchronous links may connect the different machines (with software support). Both types of machines may connect to a local area network. There may be a computerized branch exchange which does protocol conversion.

MIGRATION PATH   Both software and hardware are likely to continue to evolve rapidly. Although improving what is possible with computers, this evolution can worsen maintenance problems if not handled appropriately. To lessen the problems, most manufacturers have a migration path planned for their customers' systems evolution. The total elapsed time to create a new-architecture computer is typically about six years, so manufacturers have their product lines planned some years ahead without necessarily revealing them.

If a customer follows the migration path of a major vendor, this will usually lessen the system maintenance costs. It pays a customer to try to understand the migration paths of his vendors. The more he understands the future evolution, the more he can design to minimize maintenance.

Some vendors, including IBM, do not reveal their future product plans except in generalizations. The customer then needs to decide whether a partially blind commitment to the vendor's migration path is worthwhile. With IBM it often *is* in reducing system maintenance but has other effects on application creation which need to be evaluated.

Often, a customer locks himself out of his vendor's migration path without understanding the maintenance implications. A vendor may be designing complex software to link distributed systems, for example, and the customer installs foreign front-end processors that will not operate with the new software when it arrives. The vendor may be planning an active data dictionary designed to drive a future data-base management system, teleprocessing facilities, and very-high-level languages, but the customer installs a foreign data dictionary which cannot be used in this way.

Migration path planning should be discussed with the vendors, with the objective of avoiding expensive maintenance later.

SYSTEM KLUGES   It is desirable to avoid lashing together hardware and software combinations that are each evolving separately. One bank installation, for example, has a mainframe without its own data-base management system. A DBMS from a software house is used with no data dictionary. A different teleprocessing monitor is used with terminals from still other vendors. This combination is clumsy and fraught with software problems. It is a nightmare to make any changes. The middle-level managers of the bank became very dissatisfied at not obtaining the applications they needed, and adopted a policy of implementing microcomputers.

These, however, needed to extract data from and pass data to the mainframe, so further linking of systems became needed.

System kluges—hardware/software combinations that incur high future maintenance costs—tend to arise because of absence of strategic planning. Box 12.1 lists examples of system problems that lead to expensive maintenance but which can be avoided with top-level planning.

BOX 12.1 Examples of system problems that lead to expensive maintenance but which can be avoided with top-down planning

- Machines are difficult to interconnect by telecommunications because they use different line control procedures.

- Computer network architectures of different manufacturers are fundamentally incompatible.

- Even if compatibility can be achieved in the transport network, fundamental incompatibility exists between manufacturers' software external to the transport network.

- Different types of data-base software are incompatible (even without considering distributed data bases).

- File structures are expensive (sometimes prohibitively so) to *convert* to other file structures or to data-base structures.

- Technology is evolving rapidly, and migration to better technology may be difficult in a distributed environment unless planned for.

- Even if all the software is compatible, severe problems may arise from incompatible data fields and data structures due to inadequate data administration in an organization.

- Office automation terminals cannot be connected to data-processing facilities.

TOP MANAGEMENT INVOLVEMENT Strategic planning needs top management involvement for two main types of reasons.

First, the plans which are put together are often counterpolitical—they cut across separately managed areas and middle managers are often jealous of their empires. Without top management directives, all manner of arguments will be devised for deviating from the plans.

Second, the enterprise, its information needs, strategic direction, and geographic locations are likely to change. Top-level managers know best what changes are likely or desirable. They know what new business areas are possible. They understand the factors critical for success of the enterprise, which relate to the planning of information resources.

Just as in the Department of Defense ABIC approach, the top-down plans need to be reviewed every year and rolled forward. ABIC looks forward seven years. This may be too long a planning horizon for some corporations, especially as the rapid rate of technology evolution makes the future more blurred. Five years seems an appropriate horizon for most corporations. The strategic infrastructure takes a long time to build, so a horizon shorter than five years may be insufficient for network and distributed system planning.

SUMMARY   In general when systems are built, the better the view of the future, the lower future maintenance costs will be. End users, especially with fourth-generation languages, need a high level of spontaneity in creating new procedures and generating information. This can happen much better when network, terminal, and data system planning has been thorough and well implemented. Strategic planning for information resources is an activity that should involve the highest levels of management.

13 MANAGING A REVOLUTION

RESISTANCE TO
CHANGE
Fundamental changes in methodology meet great emotional resistance. Napoleon refused to believe in steamships 20 years after the first one was working, even though he could have left Nelson's fleet standing on a windless day.

Some of the methodologies in this report are a quantum leap from conventional programming but will encounter resistance. Many programmers will reject them because they seem alien to the God-given order. Many systems analysts will be unaware of them because they are too busy putting out fires caused by the use of inadequate methodologies. In many installations at least some of the DP professionals want to introduce new techniques but are prevented from doing so by DP management.

ARGUMENT
AGAINST CHANGE
Many computer executives hear the reasons for change but do not know what to do about it. They have too much invested in present systems to be able to change, or so they think. The argument becomes stronger with time as more becomes invested, and the old systems become more difficult to change.

This argument is a lethal trap. The old systems become steadily worse and DP becomes even more unable to respond to needs for changes and new systems. Newcomers have a major competitive edge by moving directly into high-productivity techniques.

Many DP executives are in the trap illustrated in Fig. 13.1. There is a growing demand for new applications because the end users are becoming more knowledgeable about computing. They learned about computing at

DP EXECUTIVE

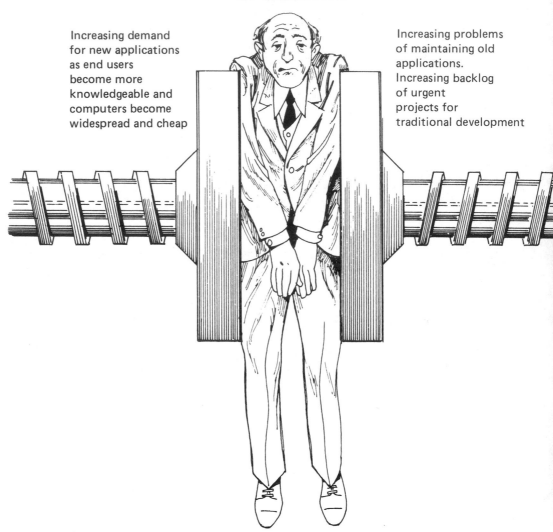

Increasing demand for new applications as end users become more knowledgeable and computers become widespread and cheap

Increasing problems of maintaining old applications. Increasing backlog of urgent projects for traditional development

Figure 13.1

college. Their kids have a hobby computer. They know that computers are dropping in cost so their imagination goes to work on how better information or use of terminals could help them. Meanwhile, the overworked DP department has to spend ever more time on maintaining the old systems and handling urgent projects. The urgent projects have a tight deadline, so the DP executive dare not experiment with untried methods. On the critical projects he will use the methods that he is familiar with, and which he knows work.

NEW DEVELOPMENT CHANNELS

The trap in Fig. 13.1 will squeeze steadily tighter unless we find some way of relieving the pressure. The solution for most old-established organizations is to set up alternative channels of development which will use new high-productivity techniques. The new techniques will be applied to certain selected new systems which are not on the critical path.

Where radically new techniques are used, it is desirable to establish a separate development group. We will refer to this as an Advanced Development Group. It should be managed by a person with DP experience who has made himself an expert with the new technique. Many of his staff may be new graduates, because new graduates learn new techniques fast.

System development in a large organization cannot be switched from traditional methods to a radically new technique overnight. The new technique needs to be introduced a stage at a time, and must find its place among other powerful new facilities, such as query languages, report generators, application generators, and languages designed for end users.

The use of the new method should not be regarded as *research*. It should be regarded as application building of higher productivity. If the group has "THINK" signs on the wall, replace them with signs that say "FINISH IT!" The objective is to finish building certain applications and *measure* the resulting productivity. If the new technique proves to work better than the old, more applications will be switched to that form of development.

The intention is that this new-technology group will grow, finding the best methods and using them on increasing numbers of systems. The old-methodology group should be steadily migrated across to new techniques. As old systems become too expensive to maintain, or need major changes, they are rebuilt with high-productivity methods.

INFORMATION CENTERS

It is desirable in most organizations today to establish information centers, as described in Chapter 7, to encourage, support, and control user-driven computing. This is another form of channel of system development, deliberately bypassing the DP backlog of conventional development.

The software and methodologies that are appropriate for information centers, user-driven computing, and personal decision support, are different from those which are suitable for routine heavy-duty computing. Information center management needs to be quite different from that of an advanced development group building production systems, routine computing, or systems with complex logic. The information center channel of development should be separate from the advanced development group. The former supports ad hoc development by, or in cooperation with, end users; the latter supports development by DP professionals.

THREE CHANNELS   An MIS executive may divide his organization into three areas as shown in Fig. 13.2. He may have a manager who oversees all information centers, and another who oversees all advanced development groups.

The objective should be progressively to minimize and ultimately to eliminate traditional programming, because of the problems we have discussed. This will not be done quickly in old-established DP organizations because of the mass of existing programs that have to be maintained or converted, and because of the difficulty of making traditional DP staff adopt new methods.

The three areas in Fig. 13.2 should, in effect, be in competition with one another. The ones that produce the most satisfactory results should be made to grow the fastest. The ones that produce slow, expensive, inflexible, or unsatisfactory results should be progressively replaced.

A DP executive who is not putting a certain proportion of his budget into methodologies which give faster development and a higher level of automation is not giving himself a chance of escaping from the slowly closing trap of Fig. 13.1.

DIFFICULTIES OF   There is one factor about the powerful new lan-
UNLEARNING THE   guages and techniques which is slightly alarming
OLD METHODS   for the DP professional. New graduates often learn
and become skilled with the new techniques faster than many established programmers.

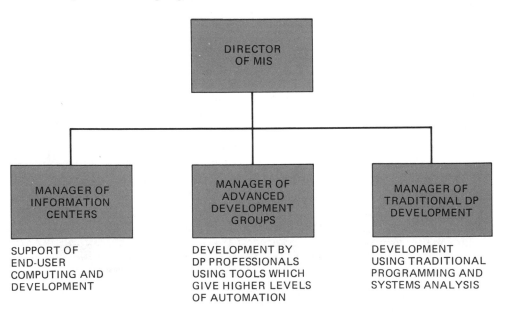

Figure 13.2   Three separate channels of development.

This phenomenon has been observed and measured with many application generators and fourth-generation languages. IBM uses ADF extensively for its own internal DP development. It has measured the performance of many ADF users and discovered that new graduates do much better, on average, than experienced programmers. National CSS staff members sometimes refer to the NOMAD programs written by old COBOL programmers as "NOBOL" programs. The COBOL programmers, thinking in COBOL-like terms, fail to use the powerful but different constructs in the NOMAD language. HOS have had certain non-DP persons achieve startlingly fast results in generating provably correct programs, while experienced programmers often describe the technique as user-unfriendly because their hard-learned experience of loops, branches, debugging techniques, and so on, does not apply to the new tool.

The new development software requires a new way of thinking about systems. The established programmer or analyst has to do much *unlearning* of his current thought patterns. However, the established programmer or analyst does have much experience that is valuable, so he is challenged to put his knowledge to work with a methodology that will make him far more powerful. He needs to set aside his hard-learned preconceptions about systems design and think about the future. The new techniques are easier than conventional programming once familiarity with them is built.

Appendix II-E is a manifesto for programmers. They should think about their career and determine to make themselves as powerful as possible with the new techniques. This needs a commitment to a substantial amount of learning. Some of the best programmers of new languages, such as RAMIS and FOCUS, that the author has met *have* been ex-COBOL coders who have thoroughly learned the new techniques. Their previous experience gives them a broader understanding than that of newcomers, which enables them to avoid mistakes.

When organizations first try out application generators or new types of application development software, they should be aware of the culture-shock phenomenon, and the difficulty that experienced programmers and analysts have in *unlearning* old techniques. For the new types of development an organization should select employees who have the ingenuity to adapt to new techniques quickly, and employ new graduates, perhaps from a business school, to work with them.

NEW GRADUATES   The change in DP culture, then, can be most quickly brought about by setting up separate channels of development employing many new graduates who are strongly motivated to learn the new techniques and obtain results with them as fast as possible. These new channels should be managed by highly innovative DP professionals who can understand the new methods, make them work, and be aware of their dangers.

There have been catastrophes with new software for DP development. Sometimes after man-years of effort a project fails because the software does not fit the application or cannot give the machine performance required. Sometimes, fast development neglects the controls that are needed, such as security protection, checkpoints, integrity controls, or auditability. Experience and professionalism are needed to watch out for these dangers and avoid them. A combination of innovative experienced leadership with creative, young, new talent is needed.

The creative talent to employ the new software often comes from the end users. The managers of the new channels should be on the lookout for users with this potential.

REVOLUTIONS COME FROM THE OUTSIDE

In many of the most spectacular case histories the author can find, the introduction of dramatically different DP methods have been from outside DP. The end users have found ways to solve urgent problems with the new methods.

Looking at the history of revolutions in general, drastic changes are not usually initiated by the establishment. Revolutions normally come from the outside. Monks do not dissolve monasteries.

Nobody in the entire steam-engine industry was involved in the design and introduction of electric motors. The United States had a large and successful industry manufacturing electronic vacuum tubes. *None* of these great corporations is a major player in the semiconductor industry, which swept away vacuum tubes. Not a single person in any telephone company was involved in the design and introduction of the first packet-switching networks (Arpanet and Telenet). The initial fourth-generation languages did not come from the computer manufacturers, who had vast staffs doing research on languages.

The establishment can quickly accommodate itself to the revolution once it is a *fait accompli*. The steam-engine-based machine-tool companies bought electric motors. The giant telephone company GTE bought the packet-switching company Telenet. DP departments sometimes link to or encompass the user-developed systems.

An MIS executive wanting to bring about fundamental changes might set out to recruit people from the outside who have acquired the talent to get results fast and competently with the new languages and tools. He should note that in certain cases top management has replaced or bypassed their MIS executive by doing the same.

CASE STUDY OF A DP REVOLUTION

A particularly spectacular example of a revolution in systems building occurred at the Santa Fe Railroad.

The Santa Fe is a U.S. railroad with 12,000 route miles of track, almost 2,000 locomotives, 66,500 cars, and 34,000 employees. Its revenues exceed $2 billion per year.

In the 1970s its "piggyback" operations were growing rapidly. This involves the loading of highway truck trailers on to railroad flat cars so that the trailers are sent by train. It saves fuel over highway cartage. To keep this lucrative business the railroad has to provide consistently excellent service; otherwise, the traffic will revert to highway transport.

Piggyback service generates blizzards of paperwork. The Corwith yard at Chicago is the world's largest piggyback facility, and the paperwork was becoming catastrophically out of control. Corwith is not much smaller than the world's giant container shipping terminals such as Rotterdam or San Francisco. Trains leave every 50 minutes at the peak period, and there is often as little as an hour between the trailer arriving at the checkpoint and the train leaving. It was almost physically impossible to type 100 bills in that hour. Waybills had to be sent by teletype to a central computer at Topeka, Kansas. Waybills from Chicago often arrived at the computer center barely hours before the train arrived at Los Angeles or San Francisco.

The bills of lading had to be matched to the movement waybills after the train left. A clerk might be processing the bill of lading while a clerk at the next desk had the movement waybill, but the two clerks would not make the proper paperwork connection. The indexing and locating process had become overwhelming. As Corwith became buried in paperwork the railroad was receiving large fines from the Interstate Commerce Commission for incorrectly assessing charges for storage of trailers.

The traffic was rapidly growing. It was clear that other yards would soon have problems as bad as those at Corwith. Adding more clerks worsened the difficulty of matching up the huge stacks of paper.

While Corwith was drowning in paperwork, DP was drowning in programming problems. A new ultramodern gravity-operated railroad yard was being built at Barstow in California to operate under full computer control. The huge cost of this dictated that the Santa Fe's Information System Department dedicated almost everybody to having its programs working on time. Traditional analysis and programming techniques were being used. The Information System Department, like many others, had its hands more than full.

Corwith formed a crisis committee, the OX ("Operations Xpeditor") committee to deal with its problems. There were four staff on the committee:

- An accountant
- A person in the freight train operations section with an operations research background but no DP experience
- A management trainee
- The head clerical supervisor at Corwith

The first two of this group had been looking at some new software from Univac called MAPPER, which at the time was in a very early stage of development. MAPPER is an on-line system that allows its users to create files, reports, and processing procedures at display terminals. MAPPER employs a relational data base which can be thought of by the end users as being a set of electronic filing cabinets. The users can design the files and data entry screens, merge, sort and search the data, do calculations, and generate reports and printouts.

The Santa Fe used only IBM computers in those days and the Information System Department could see no reason to take on a then unproven software system based on a revolutionary concept on a strange vendor's equipment. So the end-user group received opposition and no support. They obtained the cheapest possible computer that would run MAPPER, a used 1106. They were on their own!

The first application built by this user group was a billing system. It slowed the billing down too much during the critical peak period, so after five days it was abandoned and the clerks reverted to the old manual system.

Univac made some software modifications. Disasters such as deadly embraces in core had to be avoided. The system designers worked on a better way to handle file updates. The clerks were given better training. A second attempt at cutover was made five weeks after the first. This time it worked and the manual billing typewriters were stored away in the basement for good!

That was the beginning of what was to become one of the world's spectacular DP success stories. Almost every clerical function in Corwith was computerized in 17 months by an end-user team of never more than four full-time people. None of these users had had any previous DP experience. Meanwhile, at the new yard at Barstow 20 full-time professional programmers worked for two years to complete only one system of the many developed at Corwith—the yard system.

The Corwith applications were spread to many other railroad yards across the country. Other end users, observing the success, developed ways of solving their problems with MAPPER. A variety of management reports were generated. The marketing staff had to produce a source book each year for salespeople in the field, showing Santa Fe's largest customers, what they ship, where the volume is growing or shrinking, and so on. This used to be a three-month project with word processors to create several hundred pages. The users learned how to do it on MAPPER and now the operation takes about a week.

A few years after the start of this story the system used about 2000 visual display terminals and 800 printers. It processes about 60 million input/outputs and 600 million report lines per day. Users initiate 420,000 runs per day. At the peak it handles about 100 transactions per second.

The error rate on waybill keying at Corwith dropped from 3% to 0.2% (one-fifteenth of the previous rate). The system had terminal microcomputers added so that vital functions kept in operation when there was a mainframe or telecommunications failure.

The applications developed by end users, at the time of writing, consumed six of Univac's largest mainframes, the 1100/82, and many terminal microcomputers, whereas the applications created by the Information Systems Department consumed one IBM 3033 and one Andahl V8.

The freight handled at Corwith doubled in the years after the applications there came on-line, and there were no increases in administrative staff. The railroad's standard measure of productivity is revenue ton-miles per employee-hour. For the five years before the system was implemented this index rose 13%; for the five years after the implementation it rose 28%. A large part of this improvement was due to the user-developed applications. A Wall Street analyst stated in his research report that the system had in effect added $1½ to the value of the shares.

CREATIVITY

There are many other examples of users solving their own problems with computing. They differ greatly in their nature. Many are complex, interesting, and different from conventional DP. Almost all employ languages other than the traditional DP languages: COBOL, PL/1, FORTRAN, and Assembler. This is one of today's most valuable trends in computer usage.

Many of the major examples of user computing have been stories of rebellion. As in the Santa Fe case they would not have happened by following the DP guidelines, just as the electric motor would never have come from the steam engine industry. More new interesting uses of technology grow in environments where entrepreneurship is encouraged and the rebels are not suppressed. Rebels, entrepreneurs, and inventors often seem naive to the establishment. Large-company development staff people laughed at Jobs and Wasniac when they built the first Apple computer in their garage. Anderson and Sheppard, the originators of the Santa Fe project, say that it happened because they were too naive about DP to know that it was supposed to be impossible.

Creativity tends to happen, then, when we set free the rebels. However, the creative urge needs much help. Invention is 1% inspiration, 99% perspiration. End users who want to use computers to solve their own problems need training, help, budgets, and tools. When they create something large, as at Santa Fe, they need professional design of the hardware configuration, networks, data bases, and so on. End users can make all manner of mistakes when they create systems—sometimes expensive mistakes.

CREATIVE PARTNERSHIP

To deal with these concerns a creative partnership is needed. Users should be encouraged to devise solutions to their problems, and DP professionals should help to engineer the solutions to be efficient and really work.

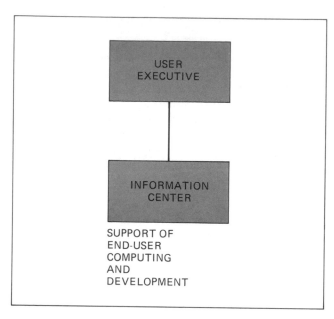

Figure 13.3 It is sometimes felt that the information center should be outside DP, reporting to a user executive, rather than reporting as shown in Figure 13.2.

The information center is a mechanism for this creative partnership. Sometimes, however, the users feel strongly that the information center should report to a user executive, as in Fig. 13.3, rather than to a DP executive as in Fig. 13.2. DP is sometimes perceived as having problems and the center servicing user computing should be outside DP, away from these problems. It should be free to select hardware, often minicomputers or micros, separate from the mainframe and its army of systems programmers.

This viewpoint is much advocated by the vendors of computers other than those installed by DP. Other vendors often perceive that the only way to sell hardware to a company with IBM-dominated DP is to sell it directly to end users and advocate the organization in Fig. 13.3.

The argument for the organization in Fig. 13.2 is that the information center needs to be wired in to the data administration, networks, and information resources which DP designs and controls. For this to work well, the director of MIS in Fig. 13.2 needs to run the information center so that a high level of creativity is possible and events could take place as revolutionary as the Santa Fe story was in its time.

EARLY ADAPTERS   We are creating changes in culture. The new DP development methods are a change in culture for the analysts and programmers. The office-of-the-future is a change in culture for management and administrative staff. User-created computing is a change in culture for everyone involved.

Most people do not want to have their culture changed. They prefer to relax in the comfort of familiar procedures. A few people in almost any environment, however, are more adventurous. They want to explore the frontiers, try out new ideas, and test innovative approaches. To introduce a change in culture it is necessary to identify these people. It is usually clear who they are.

These early adapters will try out the new systems, attempt to adapt them, and enjoy doing something different. They can be motivated to make the new ideas work and often become excited about them. They are proud to think of themselves as pioneers. They contrast strongly with the ordinary mass of people, who do not want to pioneer.

Management should try out pilot schemes on these early adapters. If the schemes do not succeed at first, management can work with the early adapters to modify them. Once they are working well, they are taken to the next level of culture changers, the early-adapters-minus-one; then the early-adapters-minus-two. Eventually, the most conservative people will feel—reluctantly—that they have to adapt because their colleagues have done. Only peer-group pressure moves the late adapters.

MOTIVATION

In revolutions there are extremely strong motivations; otherwise, the risks would not be incurred. Sometimes the motivation comes from a passionate or very unusual individual. Often it arises because the current state of affairs is intolerable. In the Santa Fe the worsening paperwork chaos at Corwith led to desperate measures. Sometimes revolution occurs because those in authority are aloof, arrogant, oppressive, and cannot be communicated with. In desperation, end users say "To hell with DP" and go their own route.

If management wants to bring about a revolution, it must create the motivation. Well-calculated psychological motivations can be used to direct the changes needed. In many of the most aggressive case examples of moves to revolutionary methodologies, one finds engineered motivations of the individuals. The individuals are told they are making history. A user-of-the-month may be selected each month and visibly rewarded for innovation. The leaders are paid according to their success. The best participants are selected to join a prestigious club which has a symposium in a glamorous resort once a year. An atmosphere of excitement is created in which the participants work extremely hard to change their world.

DIRECTIVES TO CHANGE NEED TO BE SPECIFIC

DP staff will not necessarily change to new methods of their own initiative. The old methods are too deeply engrained.

In one organization a first-class DP executive

with a budget of $18 million had attended one of the author's seminars. His organization was using third-generation languages exclusively, mainly COBOL. He resolved to achieve some of the step-function changes in productivity which the author described.

He used management by objectives throughout his organization and quickly changed the objectives of *all* DP staff so that their highest objective was to find a project where application generators or fourth-generation languages could be introduced with a consequent large increase in development productivity. This was made the highest objective of everyone in DP. Even if it resulted in their own project being shelved, they would achieve the highest MBO rating by initiating such a project. This high MBO rating directly affected their salary increases and chances of promotion.

The result was zero! There were no such projects introduced by DP staff in the entire vast organization.

Meanwhile, end users who had problems of not obtaining the applications they needed had discovered RAMIS II, a moderately user-friendly fourth-generation language. A culture was spreading like a fever throughout substantial end-user areas of building applications with RAMIS II. The productivity of obtaining results with RAMIS II was 1000% greater than that of the traditional large projects in DP.

In many of the most spectacular case histories the introduction of dramatically different DP methods has been from outside DP. The end users have found ways to solve urgent problems with the new methods.

A DP executive wanting to change the methods of DP has to take much more direct action than changing the MBO objectives. He must find specific projects that can be developed with new software, select the software, and charge appropriate individuals with learning and using the software to build the applications in question. Rather than saying "We must change our ways," he must say: "Project X will be developed with software Y, and person Z will manage it, with the following deadline for completion." He will often need a staff assistant to select the software and the projects.

WINDING DOWN LOW-PRODUCTIVITY DEVELOPMENT

The objective of the organization in Fig. 13.2 is that the two left-hand channels should grow until they take over all application development. The right-hand channel—traditional COBOL or PL/1 development—should be wound down until it does not more than maintenance of systems which have not yet been converted. This maintenance is expensive, so systems requiring substantial maintenance should be redeveloped with the new methods.

A problem with the organization in Fig. 13.2 is the morale of the executive on the right, who sees his organization dwindling. In most areas of human endeavor it is sometimes necessary to have an executive in charge of a withdrawal. This can be an important and responsible task. The military sometimes needs a general in charge of a retreat. The executive on the right of Fig. 13.2 needs to understand that this is his task. He needs to be motivated to conduct the withdrawal well and to be paid accordingly. Some DP executives prefer to have this position because they can manage something they understand. An executive five years away from retirement might find this a relatively comfortable end to his career.

The problem in many installations is that the executive in charge of traditional DP is not told that he is to conduct a withdrawal and be motivated for it. He is hanging on to his empire, perpetuating the traditional methods and their problems.

The alternative to shrinking the right-hand area is to move it to much higher productivity methods. Measures of results achieved by all three areas in Fig. 13.2, and the individuals in them, should be published for all to see. This causes the individuals on the right to clamor to obtain the power tools themselves. They need to be motivated is this way to raise their own productivity. Without such visible competition the group on the right are likely to remain content and comfortable with the old slow methods.

PART **II** THE FUTURE

14 ENTREPRENEURS WHO WILL GET RICH

THE OPPORTUNITY The computer, microelectronics, and software industry has made many people rich beyond the dreams of avarice. When those who have made it get together in some late-night bar they sometimes refer to their associates with a number that is an exponent of 10 to represent their guessed-at wealth. There are many thousand 6's, several hundred 7's, a healthy number of 8's, and at least three 9's. Not too many of these people work for IBM and the vintage mainframers. Most are entrepreneurs or work for smaller corporations, where they had a piece of the action. Apple Computers alone bred several hundred 6's.

In the next 10 years there are going to be more entrepreneurial opportunities in information technology than there were in the last 10. The typical reader should ask himself if he is content to remain a mere 5?

NEW DIRECTIONS There are clearly gigantic changes ahead in computer technology:

The automation of automation
Powerful nonprocedural languages and generators
New hardware designed to execute these languages
Powerful relational data-base languages
New hardware designed to execute relational data-base operations
Data-base machines
Microcomputers with enough memory to handle powerful languages
User-seductive software
Personal computers of great power linked to networks
Highly distributed systems using local area networks
Major changes in person–machine communication
Software and hardware (combined) for decision support

Personal tools and games using the digital audio disk
Provably correct design techniques for software creation
New hardware to execute these techniques at high speed
Software factories using automation of software building
Provably correct design techniques for microchips
Microelectronic wafers of great complexity
Applications of artificial intelligence techniques
Expert systems
Knowledge-based systems
Inference and learning systems
Hardware designed to execute the above
Personal knowledge-based computers
Highly parallel machines taking advantage of VLSI
Non-von Neumann computers
Intelligent robots
Knowledge-based microelectronics for robots
Automated factories
Advanced CAD/CAM
New hardware designed for the above
Portable and pocket terminals and computers
Data broadcasting and packet radio
New types of information utilities
Advanced computerized education (including videodiscs)
The marriage of computers and television

The new directions of which this is a brief sampling give massive opportunities for entrepreneurs.

ENTREPRENEURIAL SUCCESS   The entrepreneur has several advantages over large corporations. He can move nimbly in new directions, and information technology today is streaking in new directions like a herd of gazelles meeting a lion. He is not locked in to existing products, procedures, and standards. He has minimal overheads. He can improvise freely. He can exercise the maximum originality. Creative and brilliant people can be given their head with no bureaucratic constraints. There must however be the constraint that the marketplace will really buy what is being created for a price that will make the enterprise profitable. This criterion needs to be constantly and ruthlessly tested. Every employee in a new company needs to be measured against this criterion as far as possible.

The entrepreneur also has severe disadvantages over large corporations. He is usually short of finances. He has to make do with less than perfect equipment. He does not have the resources of a large enterprise. He does not initially have a sales force. If a large project fails, it might sink the new company, whereas it causes only a minor wrinkle in the growth curve of a large company.

Many technical entrepreneurs create excellent products but fail because of shortage of capital, inadequate sales capability, lack of management skills, key employee groups leaving and setting up in competition, or general over-all lack of perspective. Because of these management problems, good venture capitalists select which small companies they will invest in by judging the management more than by judging the ideas or products. It is better to invest in people than ideas, although the ideas are very important.

Entrepreneurs who win work very hard and so does their entire team. Together they are going into battle. All of the excitement of war is present. The risks and the rewards are high. There is no place for the chicken-hearted, the bureaucrats, the slow-movers, or those who do academic work divorced from marketplace reality. To good entrepreneurs, life is an adventure. They have fun.

DEVELOPMENT DIVORCED FROM REALITY

In Australia there is a somewhat vulgar word for doing intellectual work which produces no practical usable results. The word is "wank" [1]. Curiously, I could find no equivalent word in my American dictionary or in my colleagues' vocabularies of slang. The word describes a very real problem. There are increasing numbers of intellectuals who do research, write papers, or assemble ideas which are unlikely to be translated into reality. These people often believe that they are in the real world when they are far from it. Their ideas are never customer tested. One single phrase in these groups can represent complex sets of ideas, but when they hear such phrases from other departments explained in detail, they nod politely without understanding. Herman Kahn commented that educated incapacity may well be "the single most important problem facing the developed world" [2]. He states that since World War II there has been an amazingly high correlation between having a better education and a lack of reality testing.

If we cannot verbalize a phenomenon we usually do not think about or discuss it. A popular publishable word is needed for "wankers." Once this word becomes known among executives, they tend to quote endless examples. When the problem is verbalized, entrepreneurs resolve to fight it. One corporate president sent a cable to the author stating that he was "CONSOLIDATING DEVELOPMENT AROUND THE WORLD TO PURGE THE RANKERS" (Western Union spelled it wrong). Perhaps it is because there is no popular word for the problem that the problem is so extensive.

BUREAUCRACY

All creative organizations have to fight against two forms of cancer—wanking and bureaucracy. Given the slightest chance, the wankers and bureaucrats spread their activities.

Unfortunately, computers and office automation both act as powerful amplifiers of these activities. Computing appeals to graduates who want to live in an intellectually rich environment such as that of their universities, removed from grubby considerations of making a profit. White-collar automation appeals to bureaucrats, who create rigid procedures and forms to fill in.

The entrepreneur struggling to make a profit and keep his cash flow positive needs to have the sharpest nose for the onset of activities that do not directly feed the bottom line—and stamp them out. He should instantly detect unnecessary form-filling, research for the sake of research, pretentiousness, papers being written for entertainment, useless newsletters, employees in search of immortality, and activities done because they are intellectually interesting, glamorous, ego-satisfying, computable, or high fashion. The test for all such activities is their demonstrable effect on market revenue and cash flow.

SOLUTIONS TO BIG-MONEY PROBLEMS

A time-tested formula for success is to find solutions to serious problems which exist, especially problems that have a high revenue figure associated with them. Box 1.1 listed DP's problems. A general problem with computers is that for the vast mass of people they are too difficult to use. They are not being put to work as they should be.

NEW SOFTWARE

The first 13 chapters have discussed solutions to DP's problems which are being used in practice today. There is much money to be made in implementing these solutions and improving the software which they need.

The computer industry is at the edge of a cliff. After 20 years of use of third-generation languages we now understand that there are dramatically better ways to build systems. The new ways we have discussed are a potential gold mine for entrepreneurs. Most of the new languages, like the electric motor in its day, are not coming from the computing establishment.

The language LINC, much advertised by Burroughs, was created by two men in New Zealand, one acting as the technician and one as the executive. They started this originally as a spare-time activity to solve the backlog problems in their installations. Burroughs, which had developed no such languages or generators themselves, bought LINC (after consulting with the author of this book) and made its two creators millionaires.

Some of the new languages and generators permit the building of software factories which can produce software of much higher quality but also produce it much more quickly and cheaply. The further a software factory evolves in building up its library, the more power it has in creating software for its customers.

HARDWARE CHANGES

It has always been the popular wisdom in the computer industry that the hardware is way ahead of the software. Now, in one sense, the software is ahead of the hardware. The fourth-generation languages, application generators, the ability to create provably correct logic, relational data-base languages, knowledge-based software, natural English query languages, and CAD/CAM languages all present a challenge to change the hardware so that they operate far more cost-effectively.

At the same time the hardware design process is evolving dramatically. Microprocessors are plunging in cost. We know that we can produce much more powerful 32-bit microprocessors. Their speed will increase greatly, and mass production can make them very cheap.

When traditional computer architectures evolved it was true that the larger we built the processor, the cheaper the cost of executing one instruction. The cost per instruction used to be inversely proportional to the square of the size of the machine. Now the cost per instruction on a small microcomputer is far cheaper than that of a large computer. At the time of writing a large computer costs about $300 per kips (thousand instructions per second); a microcomputer costs less than $1 per kips. That is an unfair comparison because the large computer has a much richer instruction set than the microcomputer. We are comparing oranges and apples (if you will forgive the pun). However, chips have been constructed which do have the rich instruction set of a large computer. IBM has demonstrated a 370 on one chip. Such chips will drop in cost rapidly when mass-produced. Furthermore, for most purposes the microprocessors which operate in parallel in the computers of the future will not need the rich instruction set of today's mainframes. Different processors will execute different functions. Nonprocedural functions will be decomposed for execution with relatively simple but fast processors. A major challenge of the future, then, is to find hardware architectures that can employ large numbers of cheap, fast microprocessors operating in parallel.

A variety of highly parallel machines has been built, and others have been simulated. They have been useful for highly specialized applications like seismic array processing, but have not generally been used for bread-and-butter data processing. A major reason for this is that data processing applications have been written in von-Neumann-like languages.

NON-VON-NEUMANN LANGUAGES Von Neumann, the greatest of the computer pioneers, created the machine architecture that we all know and love. It executes instructions one at a time in sequence, carries out tests, and branches to other locations in the sequence. Using the tests and branches we can employ loops of instructions. Von Neumann did not invent COBOL, Ada, PL/1, or Pascal, but these are von-Neumann-like languages in that they use a stream of sequential instructions similar to those of von Neumann with tests, branches, and loops. They were invented to be efficient with von Neumann machines. Most programmers have these constructs so engrained in their way of thinking that they do not realize that there are other useful ways to instruct machines.

The 1980s brought the first *widespread* use of the nonprocedural languages which enable us to achieve results fast and so are important for productivity in computing. These non-von-Neumann languages challenge us to design non-von-Neumann hardware to assist in executing them more efficiently.

There are a variety of types of non-von-Neumann-like languages which yield to parallel computing—languages that process sets, such as SETL, or relations, such as SQL and the numerous other relational data-base languages; languages for simulation, such as SIMULA; languages for string processing, such as SNOBOL, or text processing, where different parts of the string or text can be processed in separate machines simultaneously; languages for graphics; languages used in artificial intelligence such as LISP, or PROLOG, where multiple separate inferences can be processed simultaneously. Some languages use a fundamentally different type of instruction from von-Neumann-like languages, for example, the HOS language for generating provably correct code, discussed in Chapter 9. The first examples of non-von-Neumann machines for executing such languages are now being built.

MICROCODE

Most application generators provide standard types of building blocks which the user can link together to create applications rapidly. Such building blocks include menu-selection screens, report generation functions, standard data management access methods, data-entry screen generation, security routines, validity checks, data searching, data sorting, prompting screens, and so on.

Hardware designers can capitalize on this commonality of routines and subroutines. One approach is to microcode the generator routines. This is done, for example, on Microdata's SEQUEL system for implementing the generator ALL (Application Language Liberator). Applications generated in this way run faster than they would if written with conventional programming.

TANDEM-LIKE ARCHITECTURES

The first major use of parallelism in commercial DP was in the systems from Tandem Inc. The Tandem system was designed for processing a transaction stream in such a way that transactions could be directed to any of up to 16 processors. If one or more of the processors fails, the system as a whole is still operational, so Tandem's main claim to fame is that its systems are *nonstop*—they do not cease to function periodically like conventional systems. Efficient parallelism required an operating system quite different from that in traditional computers. Each Tandem processor *had its own memory*, whereas in traditional multiprocessor configurations they shared memory. The Tandem operating system was *message-driven*. The processors exchanged messages continuously on a high-speed bus, duplexed in case of failure.

Tandem demonstrated to the world that on-line data-processing systems could be built that did not fail. This is extremely important for many of today's uses of computers. The Tandem concept could be extended to more than 16 parallel processors, each designed for mass production and hence relatively inexpensive as VLSI grows in chip density and drops in cost. An extension of the concept could have separate front-end processors handling data transmission and back-end processors handling data-base operations.

Although a parallel configuration, the Tandem processors were nevertheless von Neumann machines designed to execute von-Neumann-like languages. Tandem compiles and interprets its nonprocedural code into von Neumann-like instructions.

RELATIONAL MACHINES

With the growth of relational data bases, relational languages evolved. Some of these are well humanfactored and enable users to explore a mass of data in valuable ways. They form an essential component of future decision-support systems.

Some relational languages are character-string languages such as IBM's SQL. Some employ English user dialogues such as the Artificial Intelligence Corporation's INTELLECT (now sold by IBM). Some are screen languages where a user interacts with two-dimensional displays of data, as in IBM's Query-by-Example. Some enable users to build their own electronic filing cabinets and design business procedures for themselves, as with Univac's MAPPER.

The relational languages are crying out for new hardware. The user statements often trigger a *search* or *sort* of data, or relational *join* or *project* operations. With conventional hardware each record is accessed one at a time and the search, join, and so on, are performed with a conventional instruction set. This is very time consuming and relatively expensive. It often gives unacceptably long response times.

Instead, the data should be organized so that many read heads can read parts of it simultaneously. These separate streams of data should be taken into separate microcomputers all of which perform the required operation. If the user's request is

```
SELECT RETAILER, DATE, QUANTITY
FROM DELIVERY, LINE-ITEM
WHERE DELIVERY . ORDER# = LINE-ITEM . ORDER#
AND PRODUCT = EXTRA-STRENGTH-TYLENOL
```

all of the microprocessors would simultaneously search their portion of the data stream for retailers who had had deliveries of Extra-Strength Tylenol.

The first commercially available relational engine to use parallel processors in this way was ICL's CAFS. This machine gave surprisingly fast responses to requests that required much data searching. It had several interesting effects on the early installations that used it. There were far fewer batch runs and sorts. Lengthy paper listings tended to disappear in favor of data available from terminals. The capability to browse through data and extract information existed without MIS programs having to be written. One personnel department with three programmers had them transferred as they were no longer needed. Unpredictability of information requirements, which had been a great problem on early MIS systems, now was no problem. The enquiries could be easily refined and changed. The data had much greater visibility, which led to more effective auditing. There was better consistency checking. A parallel relational back-end machine seems an essential component to many future information and decision-support systems.

AN HOS MACHINE   A parallel relational processor is a relatively well understood hardware improvement for a certain class of nonprocedural language. Some other types of nonprocedural languages also need a drastic change in hardware.

The HOS technique (Chapter 9), which is in use for creating provably correct code for complex systems, implies three primitive control structures which are quite different from those of conventional computers: JOIN, INCLUDE, and OR. More elaborate control structures are all decomposed into these three primitives. A machine could be built to execute these three primitives, together with primitive *operations* such as mathematical functions.

Such a machine could be much faster than today's computers. Speed could be gained in three ways. First, the code generated would relate directly to the machine. The substantial waste of matching today's machine instructions to the entirely different language operations would be avoided. Second, because the microprocessor chips would have a narrow instruction set, they could be made much faster. Third, the HOS control maps reveal where operations can be executed in parallel.

The INCLUDE primitive allows two operations to proceed in parallel, independently. The JOIN primitive shows that two operations could execute sequentially, possibly on separate processors if the output of the right-hand operation is passed from one processor to the other, where it becomes the input to the left-hand operation.

The HOS decomposition thus clearly states what can take place in parallel, and what can take place sequentially on separate processors. The possibility thus arises of a highly parallel machine built of many fast mass-produced processors each designed to execute the HOS primitives.

If such a machine comes into existence (whether with HOS techniques or any equivalently rigorous technique) the operating system and data-base management system should not be separate facilities independent of the hardware architecture. The hardware and controlling software should be one integrated design, built together with control maps which represent both hardware and software design and allow trade-offs between them to be explored. The intriguing possibility thus arises of a computer that is relatively inexpensive, fast, and enforces bug-free logic.

GRAPHICS PROCESSORS

A picture is worth a thousand words. The problem with pictures is that they take a lot of processing.

If handled by conventional computers, the more elaborate forms of graphics have required expensive mainframes.

Picture processing yields naturally to parallelism. Different parts of a picture can be examined or composed at the same time. Different processors may carry out different functions at the same time. Many people have watched a graphics screen for a minute or more while a computer creates an elaborate drawing or image a tiny step at a time. A group of relatively cheap processors working simultaneously can create it much faster. Parallel processors have been used, in research, for pattern recognition, for processing images from robot eyes, and so on.

KNOWLEDGE-BASED PROCESSING

As highly parallel processors drop in cost, different types of uses of computers will become economic.

Various applications from artificial intelligence research need parallel computing. A particularly important one is the building of *expert systems*. As discussed in the following chapter, knowledge-based technology is used for creating expert systems. A knowledge-based system stores logical inferences and needs to process many such inferences to arrive at the conclusions needed in an expert system. Separate inferences can be processed on separate processors simultaneously. An inference-processing engine needs to be linked to a relational data-base engine which will perform relational algebra operations in hardware at high speed.

A personal computer with multiple parallel processors can be architected for inference processing. Small personal knowledge-based computers will become available. They will have a major effect on the way computers are used for certain types of decision making. A major challenge of today is to determine what types of expert systems are likely to be valuable, and how they should be linked to other information systems. Some entrepreneurs are preparing now for a new wave of computing technology: expert systems and knowledge-based systems.

HUMAN LANGUAGE

Making computers as easy to use as possible by non-DP-trained people is a vital goal. Human language processing will aid this greatly. Our own language is surprisingly ambiguous and complex. Much knowledge is needed by a computer if it is to unravel our illogical sentences.

In some subway systems there is a notice saying "DOGS MUST BE CARRIED ON THE ESCALATOR." If this is interpreted in a literal computer-like fashion, all persons wishing to use the escalator must find a dog they can carry. Our language is full of such problematical shorthand and ambiguities.

Nevertheless, progress is being made in making machines interpret human language and render it computable. Knowledge-based technology will become an important means of accomplishing this so that the hardware and software we need for building expert systems will also be used for interpreting human input.

If typed English were to be a major part of the input to terminals, mass-produced circuitry could be created for recognition of words and simple grammar rules. This cheap dictionary circuitry is in the inexpensive pocket-calculator devices which are sold in department stores for foreign-language phrase translation. Again, the use of mass-produced micros is cheaper than employing a mainframe, so we could have work stations designed for English input.

OPERATING SYSTEMS AND SOFTWARE

Drastic changes in mainframe architecture are clearly needed and along with them there must be drastic changes in operating systems and related software such as data-base management systems and network software.

When comparing the speed of machines we often quote the mips rate (millions of instructions per second) and do not look hard enough at the associated operating software. On some mainframes the processing of one on-line data-base update of a transaction received on a network requires more than 100,000 instructions to be executed in the operating system, data-base management system, and network control software. Possibly the same transaction will require less than 1000 *application* instructions executing. The overhead has become two orders of magnitude greater than the substance. On other smaller computers a similar transaction needs only 5000 instructions of overhead.

Not only is the operating software costly in machine resources, it is costly in people. System programmers are needed with highly elaborate skills. They are expensive, hard to find, and often difficult to manage. It is perfectly possible to have complex computers without the need for systems programmers. A few machine architectures have demonstrated this. They contain aids that enable ordinary people to change the system configuration and optimize its performance.

The complexity of major operating systems has grown out of hand. However, they are very expensive and difficult to change. Changes tend to be made incrementally a step at a time. Many such changes add yet another component to the overall complexity.

SOFTWARE-HARDWARE COMBINATIONS

In the past some entrepreneurial companies have been innovators in hardware; some have been innovators in software. Few have been innovators in both. In the future fortunes will be made by packaging software and hardware innovations together, with integrated design.

The new computers may come from new companies. It seems likely that such companies will grow even faster than Tandem or the early minicomputer vendors if they are targeted directly at solving the problems we have discussed in Part I of this book. We need user-seductive nonprocedural techniques which are highly machine-efficient because they use many mass-produced microprocessors in combination. The urgent business need for computers that can be put to work more directly is one of the greatest challenges to today's entrepreneur.

The new hardware and software architectures need to be developed in conjunction with one another. The combined logic ought to be designed in a provably correct manner. Computer-aided design tools have been used for designing hardware as well as software, and can be used for combinations of these.

Software for highly parallel machines will necessarily be intricate and tricky. When the software development has problems they will not be solved by the emergency addition of hordes of coders. The design needs to have a rigorous basis from the start. The hardware and software are really parts of the same design and an integrated approach needs to apply to both.

The challenge of the computer industry today is to architect fundamentally better machines, in which highly complex mass-produced microelectronic wafers and software are designed with an integrated technique that is rigorously based. There are clearly many ways to achieve parallelism in support of powerful end-user languages. Eventually, the conventional computer that executes one sequential instruction at a time will give way to or be supplemented by machines using many cooperating microprocessors acting together. Today's computer is like a lone violinist who will be replaced by a full orchestra.

15 WILL THE NEXT GENERATION BE JAPANESE?

A DISCONTINUITY IN IDEAS
The second, third, and fourth generations of computers were each an extension of the previous generation, implemented with dramatically better technology. These generations of computers originated largely in the West. The original design of the fifth generation appears to have come from Japan. For this next generation, in the words of the Japanese Fifth Generation project director Kazuhiro Fuchi: "*A discontinuity in ideas seems inevitable*" [1]. The discontinuity referred to is dramatic, exciting, and expensive to develop. It will fundamentally change the computer industry and society's uses of computers.

The Japanese have long had a reputation for copying and improving Western technology. There is, perhaps, something of an inferiority complex about this in Japan, and various technology leaders in Japan express the urge that Japan should lead in technology innovation rather than follow. For the keynote speech of a conference on the Fifth Generation, T. Moto-Oka and his associates wrote "It is important to stop playing 'catch-up' and to set goals of leadership and creativity in research and development. . . . This [fifth generation of computers] will greatly influence the way in which research and development will be made in other industrial fields" [2].

The Japanese Fifth Generation took the Western computer development laboratories by surprise when it was first announced. As far as the author can find, there was then nothing quite like it under development or planned. A range of machines so different from conventional computers is perhaps more likely to be built and marketed first by the Japanese than by large traditional computer companies because these established companies have such a massive financial commitment to their existing market base.

Some presentations on the fifth generation by the Japanese have started with the statement that Western computer technology is locked into certain traps:

Von Neumann architecture

Vast operating systems

Dedication to third-generation languages

Nonrelational data-base management systems

Huge customer investment in existing programs

Financial vested interests in avoiding revolutionary (as opposed to evolutionary) change

The Japanese perceive these traps as preventing the West from fundamentally rethinking the next generation of computers. They view Western computer industry as a giant in a quagmire struggling to escape while the Japanese computer industry runs nimbly past.

Technology is dropping in cost to a level where all people in society ought to employ computers. There are many social problems and opportunities that would benefit from this. However, present-day computers are too difficult to use for many of the socially valuable functions. The fifth generation must find solutions to this problem. Pictures, speech, and human language should be employed to provide natural interaction between the machine and its users. Means of representing and processing knowledge in computers is necessary so that the computer can appear intelligent and provide expertise far beyond the capability of the human brain for certain highly specialized areas.

**KNOWLEDGE-BASED
TECHNOLOGY**
In the 1970s the artificial intelligence community created some financially attractive applications. These employed "knowledge-based" technology. A data base contains data; a knowledge base contains both data and assertions about those data. The assertions are represented symbolically in computer-processible form. The computer organizes and stores the assertions and can process them to make inferences.

Examples of assertions are:

COW is an ANIMAL

COW produces MILK

3083 is a COMPUTER

3083 is manufactured by IBM

PATHOGENS associated with GASTROINTESTINAL TRACT are ENTEROCOC-CUS, CLOSTRIDIUM-GANGRENE, BACTEROIDES, KLEBISELLA, PSEUDO-MONAS, E. COLI, ENTEROBACTER, PROTEUS.

A knowledge-based system stores such assertions and can combine them to deduce other assertions. For example:

FOR ORGANISM 1: (The MORPHOLOGY of the ORGANISM is COCCUS) is FALSE.

The deductions are the result of syllogistic inferences carried out on the assertions. A syllogistic inference is one that is supported by two assertions. One assertion contains a term that is the *subject* of the conclusion; the other assertion contains a term that is the *predicate* of the conclusion. Both assertions contain a term that is excluded from the conclusion. A typical form might contain the two assertions "All A is B" and "All B is C," and produce the conclusion "All A is C."

Just as a data-base system can contain a vast amount of data, so a knowledge-based system can contain far more assertions than a human expert, such as a doctor, could possible store in his head. It can process inferences that employ these assertions extremely rapidly.

The human expert can ask the computer questions about its deductions:

DOCTOR: DID YOU USE RULE 163 TO FIND OUT ANYTHING ABOUT ORGANISM 1?

COMPUTER: RULE 163 WAS TRIED IN THE CONTEXT OF ORGANISM 1, BUT IT FAILED BE-CAUSE IT IS NOT TRUE THAT THE PATIENT HAS HAD A GENITOURINARY TRACT MANIPULATIVE PROCEDURE (CLAUSE 3).

A target of the Japanese Fifth Generation project is to produce a knowledge-based machine by 1990 that can access up to 100 million data items (each of which might require a thousand bytes of storage) and 20,000 assertions (called "rules"). Initially, the knowledge-based machine will employ a separate inference machine for processing the assertions. Later the inference machine will be fused with the knowledge-based machine. The inference machine will be able to process 100 million to 1 billion logical inferences per second. To a large extent the inferences can be processed in parallel. A highly parallel architecture capitalizing on the costs of future microcomputers will therefore be used. The control mechanisms and software for this are highly innovative and complex.

In addition to large fifth-generation mainframes, *personal,* knowledge-based, inference-processing computers will be produced. These will be produced earlier and much valuable feedback is expected from their many potential users.

As knowledge-based systems become economical a large service industry is expected to develop codifying human knowledge into computer-processible form. Just as fortunes were made with TV games and personal computer software, so fortunes will probably be made in creating knowledge bases.

EXPERT SYSTEMS   Some types of knowledge-based systems are referred to as *expert systems.* They codify the knowledge of a specific domain of expertise. This computerized expert may then be used by another expert in the field to supplement his own knowledge, or it may be used by persons not expert in that area to provide them with expertise. An example of the former would be a doctor. He is himself an expert, but medicine is so complex that he needs the help of a "specialist" to supplement his knowledge in given areas.

One of the most famous medical expert systems is MYCIN, a system for diagnosing a certain class of infectious diseases [3]. The diagnostic success rate achieved by this system is better than that of almost all doctors except those who specialize in this branch of therapy. A general practitioner needs knowledge of many hundreds of branches of medicine like this and cannot possibly be an expert in more than a few. The doctor of the future may carry a case with a screen in the lid for access to medical expert systems. Box 15.1 lists some of the expert systems that are in use.

EXPERT SYSTEMS   Someone who particularly needs help from expert
FOR SYSTEMS   systems is the expert who designs systems. The job
EXPERTS   of the systems analyst is becoming more complex.
                      We want him to build more interesting systems and
to do so much faster by using automated tools—the automation of automation. Systems engineers have to work with more elaborate configurations—distributed computing, distributed data, complex networks, configurations with very small and very large computers, the need for high reliability and availability.

The systems engineer needs guidance in how to minimize the costs and optimize the machine performance. Guidance on using the tools will come from knowledge-based techniques.

Much guidance is needed in the specification of systems. Today there is usually an urge to start programming before the specifications are clear. It is desirable that the specifications should be precise enough to generate the programs automatically. Today this is done with generators such as IBM's

BOX 15.1 Some existing expert systems using knowledge-based technology

- Diagnosis and therapy recommendations for infectious diseases [3]
- Automatic analysis and synthesis in computer-aided design [4]
- Design of complex microelectronics chips
- Diagnosis of faults in the complex equipment of undersea oil rigs
- Interpretation of aerial and satellite photographs
- Intelligent computer-based instruction
- Guidance in complex circuit troubleshooting
- Debugging aids for complex software
- Interactive evaluation of mineral prospecting results
- Assistance in oil-well data interpretations
- Chemical structure analysis from X-ray crystallography and mass-spectral data
- Intelligent user interfaces to complex systems
- Isolation of malfunctions in computer equipment
- Aid to systems engineers in designing DEC VAX configurations
- Monitoring of patients in intensive-care wards
- Analysis and interpretation of sonar reflections
- Analysis of information about potential oil sites
- Aid to operators in diagnosing problems in nuclear power stations
- Assistance in tax minimization
- Instrument data interpretation

ADF or DMS, or more comprehensive specification languages. In the future a much richer family of modules and tools in a library will be available. The analyst will need guidance in what is available and how to use it. The software factory of the future will package its products with a knowledge base to guide its users.

THE HUMAN INTERFACE

Particularly important, knowledge-based inference processing can be used to greatly improve the user friendliness of computers. It can be used in several ways:

- Human language processing so that users can communicate with the machine in English or Japanese
- Assistance in operating the machine
- Assistance in locating data, knowledge, and software (which may be in the machine's library or elsewhere accessible by networks)
- Powerful uses of graphics
- Diagnosis of faults, problems, and operator mistakes
- Assistance in creating specifications from which programs can be automatically generated

It is repeatedly stressed in the goals and budgeting of research for the fifth generation that the human interface must make the systems easy to use by the mass public, not just by trained professionals. The public will have their own friendly accountant, medical diagnostician, and expert on other subjects, who is easy to talk to, who asks questions to establish an understanding of what they want, and who leads them step by step through correct application usage.

INTERNAL KNOWLEDGE BASES

Knowledge-based computers will have internal knowledge bases for their own use. Most important of these will be a human language knowledge base containing the vocabulary and grammatical rules of the language. This will enable the software to communicate with its end users. A systems knowledge base will contain specifications for the system itself and its software. This will give guidance to operators, systems configurators, system engineers, and users. An application-creation knowledge base will guide systems analysts or users in employing application generators.

The Japanese papers say that the fifth generation will contain a "general knowledge base similar to common sense" [1]. Common sense, however, has been a highly elusive attribute of artificial intelligence research so far.

Even the common sense of a dog requires a very wide-ranging set of knowledge. It has been easier to build systems that are "expert" in a limited field than systems that show rudimentary "common sense."

The knowledge-based systems in Box 15.1 all aid the highly skilled expert. As such systems drop in cost and become well understood, they will affect most people in society. There are three aspects of the fifth generation which will cause this to happen: the improvement in human–machine communications; the ability of knowledge-based systems to learn continuously and improve their knowledge; and the power of being able to process over 100 million logical inferences per second. (The human brain might manage 10 per second for certain types of functions, and much less for others.)

The Japanese objectives for their fifth generation put a high emphasis on its aid to human communication. The built-in knowledge base of human languages and "common sense" is part of this. So is the emphasis on speech and picture processing. With these facilities high-level query languages and aids to translation of language will be created.

One of the more extraordinary passages in the Japanese literature is the following [5]:

> An unhonorable reputation for Japan might be contracted to three points as follows:
>
> 1. What Japanese think is not understandable.
>
> 2. Japan does not pay effort to defuse the information of knowhow to be utilized all over the world.
>
> 3. The Japanese is too shy to speak up his idea, thus breaking the atmosphere of a meeting.
>
> The 5th generation computer may work as the machine which is easy to speak and hear foreign languages, and eliminate such language barriers. And foreign people may understand that the Japanese are not people who come from outside space but common beings as they are.

KNOWLEDGE ACQUISITION

A knowledge-based system is designed to constanty *learn* about its area of expertise. When it is asked a question it does not understand, it asks for clarification. It analyzes the results of the clarification, checks them for consistency with what it already knows, and stores them. The knowledge acquisition support system is extremely important to facilitate the growth of knowledge bases.

Knowledge acquisition can be automatic, semiautomatic, or manual. The ultimate goal is to develop fully automatic systems that collect and organize knowledge about a specific domain directly from computer-understandable sources. The literature talks of self-feeding knowledge-based systems. Fully automatic knowledge acquisition is difficult, so to begin with, semiautomatic systems will be built. These allow the experts in a particular subject to interact with the knowledge base. The requirements for such systems are:

- The subject experts need not know how the knowledge is represented in the software. They communicate their knowledge with a language or technique that is natural to them. The system interrogates them in natural language.

- The knowledge-based system automatically checks the consistency of the knowledge it is given.

- The system guides the subject experts to provide valuable and complete knowledge. When it learns about omissions in its knowledge, it asks.

The knowledge acquisition software must be sufficiently user-friendly that experts everywhere who want to immortalize their expertise can do so. Knowledge-based creation and use will become an electronic publishing industry.

Knowledge-based systems will range from very small to very large. Today we have large mainframes, minis, personal computers, and specialized microcomputers hidden in many types of products. The same will be true of knowledge-based systems. There will be large library machines and large corporations will have their own mainframe knowledge bases. Personal knowledge-based computers will sell to business people, hobbyists, and consumers. All manner of machines that today might incorporate microcomputers will use micro-knowledge bases for such functions as diagnostics, preventive maintenance, operator guidance, vision systems, intelligent robot control, and so on.

Knowledge based on specialized topics will be available as time-sharing services accessible via the world's data networks. Large numbers of these will be created, like books in a library. One knowledge-based system will have access to other knowledge-based systems. A user wanting to find a knowledge base on a given topic will sometimes need help from a system that knows where the accessible knowledge bases are. He will use a knowledge base of knowledge bases, which acts as a network switching facility.

CONSUMER SYSTEMS

Some applications of knowledge-based systems will have high consumer appeal, such as expert systems for the minimization of income tax, medical diagnosis, education, investment, stock market advice, and possibly gardening advice, cooking, and hobbies. Much more exotic and educational computer games will become possible. Knowledge bases for the home may be contained on the compact optical discs (digital audio discs, DAD) now coming into use for digital hi-fi. These inexpensive mass-producible consumer-oriented discs have 2 billion bits of storage.

Using videotex-like facilities (home television sets connected to telephone services) a consumer may dial distant knowledge-based systems for applications such as holiday planning, finding minimum airfares, travel-agent services, insurance-agent services, job advice, and so on. Remote medical checks by telephone, on-line to a computer, may become commonplace.

Lifetime education will be increasingly desirable as technology drastically changes the jobs in society. Knowledge-based systems show great potential for computer-based education.

EFFECTS ON THE ECONOMY Economic activity is often categorized into three sectors: *primary industries,* such as agriculture, fishing, mining, and forestry; *secondary industries,* which manufacture goods; and *tertiary industries,* such as legal and professional services, distribution, and government. So far automation has strongly improved the productivity of secondary industries but has had relatively little effect on primary and tertiary industries. It is certain that manufacturing productivity will increase still further with robot-controlled processes and assembly lines.

As this imbalance in productivity continues, social distortions occur. Legal and service costs become increasingly large. Medical, education, and welfare services become far more expensive. The government employs an ever-increasing proportion of the public. Taxes rise unbearably.

In the Japanese view a main reason for needing knowledge-based computers is that they will have a strong effect on productivity in the primary and tertiary spheres. In primary industries better information is needed on mineral prospecting, crop growing, fertilizers, natural resources, fishing, weather, recycling, and so on. Automatically controlled hydroponic farms will grow food. Partially robotized fishing will become possible. Today, Japan is far from self-sufficient in food. Japan has a population density 40 times that of the United States and more than half of Japan is mountainous, where food is not grown. The Fifth Generation papers from Japan state that such computers could make Japan self-sufficient in food.

In tertiary industries the benefits are, perhaps, clearer. Doctors, hospitals, lawyers, accountants, auditors, and government departments could all make excellent use of knowledge-based systems designed to automate and supplement the work of experts. The first experimental knowledge-based systems in medical diagnosis have been spectacularly successful [3].

In the Western world lawyers and government regulations devour an everincreasing part of the gross national product. (This is less of a problem in Japan, which has only 3000 lawyers.) Parts of the U.S. court system are close to breaking down. The Supreme Court has, at the time of writing, almost 6000 cases on its docket and issued only 141 signed opinions last year and 17 in the first half of this year.

Clearly, a knowledge-based system could be a great tool for both lawyers and judges. It could have access to all laws and relevant cases, and could quickly find precedents. Like the existing medical diagnostic systems, it could create judgments. A judge could then check its reasoning. Fifth-generation systems will also have a major effect on the productivity of secondary industry.

The costs of white-collar operations have increased alarmingly in the last 10 years. While the productivity of the factory has improved greatly, office productivity has remained stagnant. The Japanese fifth-generation enthusiasts believe that it will influence office work greatly: "The Japanese, who are capable of adapting themselves flexibly to new environments, will be able to realize sophisticated office automation systems for processing information through various media including images, graphs, speech and the like, and become a world pioneer of office automation" [1].

Knowledge-based systems will help office workers to employ sophisticated tools, trace memos on given subjects, find files, and obtain guidance in procedures. They will assist auditors in their investigations.

The accountant is an expert whose job can be largely automated. The best accounting practices and advice on financial management can be built into knowledge-based systems. Fifth-generation computers can help deal with the incredible complexity of the tax laws so that a corporation can legally minimize its taxes. The computerized accountant and tax expert will be available to small businesses as well as large firms and will be usable by them because the terminals will be easy to communicate with and helpful.

For all types of planning it will be useful to have access to computerized knowledge. The rules that a corporation employs will be fed into the expert system, with that system steadily learning about the organization, asking questions when it needs to. When an executive has a meeting or a salesman has a proposal to prepare, he will use the expert system to help him.

An innovation that will drastically change the office will be the speech-input word processor. A manager or secretary speaks and sees the words appearing on a screen. When the machine misunderstands, the user can manually adjust the words, add proper nouns, and edit the input. There will be little need for many of today's human secretarial functions.

Knowledge-based systems will give guidance in most complex decision making. The tools of operations research are often not used today because most decision makers find them too difficult to use. The fifth generation should make tools involving complex computing easy to use—regression analysis, forecasting techniques, linear programming, nonlinear programming, nonlinear programming, complex scheduling and resource planning, critical path analysis, optimization of flow of work through a job shop, minimization of telecommunication costs, delivery fleet optimization, and so on. Such computers may be instructed to collect experience and analyze it so that more experience is available for decision making.

Computer-aided design and computer-aided engineering will benefit greatly from expert systems that give intelligent help to the designer. Much manufacturing will be done by robot machines. A robot can weld or perform other activities in positions not accessible to human beings. Drastic fabrication changes are needed to take full advantage of robots, and the robots themselves will be changing rapidly.

Today's robots are unintelligent, do not have vision, and use only one arm. Robots of the future will have vision and other senses linked to knowledge-based systems which enable the robot to make sense of what it can see. To have more than one arm is clearly valuable for a robot, as it is for a human worker or a spider, but complex processing is needed to make the arms cooperate and not interfere with one another. The early intelligent robot systems at Stamford Research Institute used knowledge-based software similar to that used in building expert systems.

Robots can be designed to work in places where humans cannot—in high and low temperatures, in vacuum, in high-pressure chambers, in radioactive areas, and so on. This extends the range of manufacturing possibilities. Robots of the future will operate in outer space and under the oceans. They will automate dangerous mining functions. We will need many coal miners in the future, but it will be unthinkable for them to be human beings.

The rice paddies of Southeast Asia will have robots working their way along straight rows of cultivation. They will plant the new rice shoots, tend their growth, and harvest them. A hospital group in France is designing robots to do routine nursing functions. There are many applications of intelligent robots in agriculture, hydroponic food growing, fishing, fish farming, forestry, and other primary industries.

A robot has the most effect on productivity when it can be left unattended. Unattended robots can work 24 hours a day. Factories are already in operation where human beings work one shift and robots work three. The people leave the robots enough work to keep them busy all night. There is much more scope for building unmanned factories when robots are intelligent. Such machines are connected to a central coordinating computer which can monitor the overall production and take intelligent action when needed.

Knowledge-based mechanisms do not have to be large. For many robot applications, intelligence is vitally important, but the knowledge base is small. Small mass-produced units may be built which can be programmed to control a great diversity of intelligent machines.

Similarly with machine maintenance, small knowledge-based units could diagnose faults, give early warning of problems, and ensure that preventive maintenance is correctly done. Such diagnostic and maintenance modules are likely to be built for telephone systems, computers, oil rigs, power stations, farm machinery, and the family car. In the Third World, tractors and other machines are often abandoned due to improper maintenance. Intelligent units in these machines may solve that problem, instructing the human operators when oil or part replacement is needed.

Robot machine tools are already used in a few very small factories.

Intelligent machines will enable a small factory to achieve the high productivity of a large factory. Some factories will be small businesses operated by one person and his robots.

Robots do not make the careless mistakes that a human worker can make. Products made with robots have fewer defects. Knowledge-based robots will have a greater effect on improving the design of products as well as on their overall cost and quality. So far, Japan has been more successful than the rest of the world in introducing robots into industry. The West and its unions have to respond to this challenge; otherwise, their employment will worsen and their wealth will decline. The keynote speech at the initial Japanese conference on its Fifth Generation stated: "The products of our country will be rendered unique and specialized in their respective fields due to their performance, design and knowledge-intensive qualities" [1].

16 ENTREPRENEURS AND GOVERNMENT

If an industrial country falls behind in its research on information technology, this will negatively affect its industrial capacity and balance of payments. The British government, for example, calculated that Great Britain's adverse trade balance in information technology products could reach $1.6 billion by 1990 [1]. Furthermore, it concluded: "Unless our information technology achieves a strong world competitive position, then the efficiency of our other industries in manufacturing and services will suffer" [2]. Many other countries are worse off in new computer developments than Great Britain. The Japanese activities in these areas are a threat to the West which could become economically devastating.

The revenues and employment in the traditional "smokestack" industries are declining in most advanced countries. These industries are slowly migrating to areas of the world such as Southeast Asia and Brazil where labor is cheaper; also, the demand for some of their products is declining. The smokestack industries are partially being replaced by high-technology industries.

Expenditure on electronics and software is growing and will probably reach about 7% of the gross national product of advanced countries in the 1990s. Many countries are simply not carrying out the research necessary to enable them to keep ahead in the computer technologies. Some of the research is highly expensive and needs substantial cooperative effort.

Early in the 1980s various governments and gurus became alarmed by the activities of the Japanese. The Japanese government was heavily funding cooperative efforts between government, industry, and universities in advanced computer technology. The press referred to such cooperative bodies as "Japan Incorporated."

The Japanese government put vast sums, of the order of $100 million on average, into development in each of the following technologies:

- Advanced microchip fabrication
- Pattern information processing systems
- High-speed computers
- Operating systems
- Optoelectronics
- A highly parallel supercomputer

In October 1981, Japan unveiled its dramatic Fifth Generation computer project which was to be still more highly funded by the government. Box 16.1 lists some of the technical targets of the Fifth Generation project for realization by 1990.

BOX 16.1   Targets of the Japanese Fifth Generation project for delivery by 1990 [3]

Mainframe

- A highly parallel machine with 1000 to 10,000 processors.
- 1000 to 10,000 megabytes of solid-state memory.
- 1 to 10 billion instructions per second.

Personal Computer

- 32 parallel processors.
- 10 megabytes of solid-state memory.
- 10 million instructions per second.

Logic Programming Machine

- A machine for processing languages incorporating the predicate logic:
  (a) PROLOG system.
  (b) New language system.
- A mass-produced base machine capable of processing 100,000 lips (logical inferences per second).

BOX 16.1 *(Continued)*

- Personal computers with multiple base machines capable of processing from 100,000 to 1 million lips.

- Mainframes with many base machines capable of processing from 50 million to 1 billion lips.

Numerical Computation Machine

- Mass-produced processor elements capable of 4 million flops (floating-point operations per second).

- A parallel processing system capable of simultaneously operating 1000 such processors, giving an overall performance of about 1 billion flops.

- Development of new higher-speed processor elements capable of 40 to 100 million flops.

- Head-per-track disc of 50 to 60 billion bytes.

- Special-purpose operating systems.

- High-level language compilers.

Relational Data-Base Machine

- Designed to execute relational algebra operations (e.g., search, join, project) with at least 500 to 600 parallel processors.

- Storage capacity for high-speed relational operations: 10 to 100 million bytes.

- Storage capacity for medium- and high-speed relational operations: 100 million to 10 billion bytes.

- Storage capacity for low- and medium-speed relational operations: 10 to 1000 billion bytes.

- Processing throughput with basic transactions: 10,000 transactions per second. (Today's von Neumann machines are capable of up to about 100 transactions per second.)

Knowledge-Based Machine

- Storage and retrieval of 20,000 inferences (rules) and 100 million data items. (One data item requires up to 1000 bytes.)

(Continued)

BOX 16.1 *(Continued)*

Inference Machine

- Capable of processing 100 million to 1 billion logical inferences per second (lips). (One lips means one syllogistic inference per second. This requires 100 to 1000 instructions per second on von Neumann computers. Today's mainframes are therefore capable of about 10,000 to 100,000 lips. Inference machines will achieve a high lips rate by using many parallel processors.)

Picture and Image Terminal

- Screen and tablet with a resolution of 10,000 × 10,000 picture elements.
- Intelligent functions for picture and image processing. Software and hardware to permit smooth user interaction with the computer through picture and image media.

Phonetic Word-Processor System

- Capable of understanding 10,000 spoken words with simultaneous meaning analysis and automatic error correction.
- Generation of whole, comprehensible sentences.

Speech-Responding System

- Capable of understanding 10,000 spoken words.
- Capable of comprehending the meaning of spoken questions; detecting and resolving ambiguities.
- Capable of processing speech input in real time.
- A sophisticated structure to enable natural conversion.
- Capable of handling speech in English and Japanese.

Natural Language Processing

- Parsing of natural language, using a language knowledge base with 10,000 words and 2000 rules.
- Semantic analysis.
- Ambiguity detection and resolution.
- Discourse analysis.
- Sentence construction and speech synthesis.
- Elimination of the language gap between a computer and user.

THE ALVEY REPORT The vision began to grow in Europe of the years ahead being a high-technology shoot-out between the United States and Japan with Europe slipping far behind. The British government reaction is contained in the Alvey report [2]. It concludes: "Urgent steps are needed to improve our general competitiveness in Information Technology. . . . Unless our Information Technology industry achieves a strong world competitive position, then the efficiency of our other industries in manufacturing and services will suffer." The report points out that the major objective of the Japanese program is to apply advanced systems to those areas of society where increases in efficiency and productivity would be most beneficial.

It concludes that based on current trends, Great Britain's share of the market will decline. "The issue before us is stark. We can either seek to be at the leading edge of these technologies; or we can aim to rely upon imported technology; or we can opt out of the race. The latter we do not regard as a valid option. Nor is reliance on imported technology practical as a general strategy, though we cannot be completely self sufficient either" [2].

The Alvey Committee concluded that Great Britain should have a national program for advanced information technology (AIT) costing £350 million ($560 million) over five years. Government should contribute two-thirds of this and industry one-third. (In Japan the government contributes 100% of the research funding.) The program should be a collaborative effort among industry, the academic sector, and government. The results should be disseminated fully to the British information technology industry, including firms that did not contribute to the program.

The program covers "precompetitive" activities. The closer one gets to marketing products, the more difficult collaboration becomes. The program rules out the participation of foreign multinational corporations except where they can contribute a particular asset vital to the program, and where it is guaranteed that technical information will not leak from Great Britain.

Various other countries have, or are considering, a broadly similar type of government program. The EEC government has proposed a European program called ESPRIT. In the United States a consortium of computer firms have combined to form a collaborative research organization.

FOUR ENABLING TECHNOLOGIES The program covers four key *enabling* technologies: that is, technologies which are an essential basis for diverse product development. These technologies are:

1. Software Engineering

- The development of the tools and techniques for creating reliable software, with high productivity.

- The development of "Information System Factories" which provide integrated hardware and software tools, libraries, data bases, and communications networks, for software development.
- The change from ad hoc design and programming to fully engineered software building as automated as possible.

2. Human–Machine Interface

- Research on input/output devices to improve human–computer communication.
- Speech processing.
- Image processing.
- Work on terminal dialogue design.
- Work on cognitive compatibility between users and systems and how symbiosis can be improved.
- Analyze human problem-solving behavior and create systems that are compatible with human reasoning.

3. Intelligent Knowledge-Based Systems

- Work on all aspects of knowledge-based systems, as described in Chapter 15.
- Create demonstrator projects.
- Develop widespread education in this area, which is now largely unknown.

4. VLSI

- Develop the capability to specify, design, make, and test chips 1 centimeter square containing approximately 1 million logic gates each capable of switching delays down to 1 nanosecond.
- Create tools for computer-aided design of bug-free complex chips.
- Create special chips for new areas such as speech recognition, picture processing, and knowledge-based systems.
- Research new chip fabrication processes.

EXCITEMENT   Government technology projects which have changed the world are those which have set startlingly ambitious targets—targets that almost certainly would not have been achieved by single corporations—the moon shot, the Voyager space probes to Jupiter and Saturn, and Project Manhattan. Sometimes such projects have been economic disasters, such as the building and operation of the Concorde, because the checks and balances of business managers, who can go bust if they are stupid, have been missing. Sometimes government projects exist to fill an urgent perceived need, such as the U.S. Department of Defense's creation of very high speed chips (VHSIC) for future defense systems.

The projects with startlingly ambitious goals often succeed because they generate a sense of excitement and urgency among the participants which causes them to work feverishly hard. The human spirit can stretch itself to amazing achievements when extreme motivations exist. Young people dare to charge at seemingly impossible goals and succeed.

The Japanese Fifth Generation project appears to be an example of this. Japan is a country that venerates old age. Elderly executives populate the boards of directors. The Fifth Generation project breaks the pattern in that almost all of its managers and engineers are below 30. This young group is fired with excitement, told to wrest world leadership in computing away from the West, and is given extremely tough tasks and schedules to meet. All the excitement of the moon shot pervades the project. Most government projects, by comparison, are a big yawn, with people on a mediocre salary coming to work from 9 to 5.

ENTREPRENEURS   A high proportion of the ideas that have changed the high-technology world have come not from giant organization but from small firms with very bright individuals.

A 1981 study from the U.S. National Science Foundation showed that small firms produce about 24 times as many innovations per research-and-development dollar as large firms do. Government departments are *much* more expensive than even large firms in their innovation costs. Another survey reports that research efficiency goes down where there are more than seven researchers.

In the world's biggest research and development organizations, every time you open a broom closet a Ph.D. falls out. The talented staff are underemployed, underpaid, and have often passed from excitement, to frustration, to lethargy. Their pet ideas and projects have not been implemented. They sit around debating with each other intellectually. They criticze the organization. They dream about leaving and forming their own company but never do. In the end they settle for a comfortable if unproductive life.

If the same individuals work in a small company around Boston or Santa Clara, they have a piece of the action and challenging tasks that might make them rich if they create something that the marketplace really needs. They work 70 hours a week and take technical papers to bed at night. Their brilliance is needed and challenged. Their inspirations are put to work. They have a dream and are determined to make it reality. There is a pot of gold at the end of the rainbow. Life is an adventure.

Where government wants to direct innovation, as sometimes it must, the best way to do it is often to find the most brilliant small firms and give them tough contracts. As in the marketplace, they should be paid for success. Many of the items that are ingredients of a government's overall plan can be farmed out to aggressive small corporations. Government innovation in the United States often does this, but the pattern is rare in Europe. This support of entrepreneurial corporations has the advantage that it helps to build the corporations that will become a major growth force in a country's high-technology industry in the future.

SKUNK WORKS   Two McKinsey executives, Peters and Waterman, studied 62 large companies that have been highly successful, for their book *In Search of Excellence* [4]. They contrasted them with an anonymous sample of companies that were in trouble. The latter firms usually had endless task forces, mostly with full-time staff, and filing cabinets full of market analyses. The successful firms typically had small bands of 5 to 10 people, sometimes 5 to 25, who behaved like entrepreneurial groups. They are sometimes called venture teams, sometimes bureaucracy busters; in Texas they are called "skunk works." The authors said that at the top of their list of big successful companies (such companies as 3M and Hewlett-Packard) "the entire institution is designed as a wholesale collection of ten-person skunk-works."

In one of the world's richest oilfields, the oil company with the best geologists, the most planning, and the most accurate surveys had a 20% chance of striking oil when it drilled a hole. The wildcatters with no detailed surveys and planning struck oil in only 10% of the holes drilled [5]. So surely the planning paid off? No! The wildcatters dug 12 times as many holes per dollar spent, and so obtained six times as much oil per dollar.

Peters and Waterman described the typical innovation policy of big firms going bust as "allow 250 engineers and marketers to work on a new product in isolation for 15 months." The world of big-money technology is filled with horror stories of large projects that failed. These projects are often secret, hushed up, too embarrassing to mention, and quickly forgotten. At least in industry the management can cut their losses. In government it is more difficult to do so. The project is too visible. The supporters of the project do not want to lose face. They pump more money in, as with the Concorde, until the thing finally flies. Every Concorde now flying an average of about 50 passengers across the Atlantic costs the taxpayers effectively about half a billion dollars.

The Alvey Committee report, like most such government reports, does not mention the word "entrepreneur." It seems to have no idea how the U.S. venture capital industry works.

In software engineering the improvements in techniques that are having the most effect on real installations are application generators and data-base languages such as FOCUS, RAMIS, NATURAL, MANTIS, Cullinet products, EASYTRIEVE, NOMAD, LINC, ADMINS, VISICALC, LOTUS 1-2-3, EXPRESS, SAS; program design techniques from Jackson and Yourdon; the HOS tools for creating provable correct specifications and generating code; and information engineering methodologies and tools. All of these came from entrepreneurs who set out to find the best solutions to real customer problems. The Alvey Committee report mentions none of them and contains no understanding of the types of techniques they use.

The best recent examples of improvements in human–machine dialogues come from the world of personal computers—the TV games, Visicalc, business graphics packages, LISA, Wang's word processing, and numerous application packages. Again, all of these are from relatively small corporations. The growth of Silicon Valley is a history of entrepreneurial success.

WHAT SHOULD BE GOVERNMENT'S ROLE?

In view of this, what role should government play? The aspect of the information technology industry most lacking outside the United States is entrepreneurial growth. The United States has a large number of *foreign* entrepreneurs who believe that they have a better chance of succeeding here than in the countries they left. The U.S. venture-capital industry has much *foreign* capital in pursuit of entrepreneurs, believing that this is one of the best investment opportunities of our age.

The Alvey report says that its program will help to halt or even reverse the brain drain of some of the country's best researchers. It completely fails to mention the entrepreneur drain, which is greater in numbers and *much* greater in financial consequences than the researcher drain. If a government wants to develop its own equivalent of Silicon Valley, it needs to educate, encourage, and cultivate its potential entrepreneurs. It needs a U.S.-style venture-capital industry.

Entrepreneurs in Canada, Australia, New Zealand, and Great Britain are leaving in droves. One meets them everywhere in the global village of computing. There are no clear government statistics on the entrepreneur drain as there are on the researcher drain. Entrepreneurs leave because of high taxes, bureaucratic harassment, and a lack of venture capital. The U.S. venture-capital industry provides not only money, but also management and marketing help. It judges what types of people are needed to make the fledgling company succeed. It helps to move key executives into place to build up to the marketing capability and the financial control. Venture capitalists sit on the boards of directors of the companies they invest in to protect their investment and make it grow. They are business managers with experience and a sharp intuition about what makes companies succeed. In some countries this activity is almost entirely absent. To develop "enabling" technologies without entrepreneurs and venture capitalists is like developing warfare systems without soldiers and generals.

RESEARCH INAPPROPRIATE FOR PRIVATE INDUSTRY

There are, however, some types of important research which entrepreneurs will not do and venture capitalists will not invest in. They are types of research that take too long, are too expensive, or are uncertain in their payoff but nevertheless are thought to be needed for the national well-being. This is the area where it makes sense for government, industry, and universities to cooperate. Universities alone do not have the money. Universities and government combined do not have the commercial sense. (There is also much academic research that ought to be done to expand the theoretical frontiers but which has no payoff in the next 20 years.)

Cooperation of government, universities, and industry can make good sense for long-term research, but only if the following conditions apply:

1. The government-funded program avoids areas that an entrepreneurial corporation ought to find lucrative on its own.

If a target activity *could* be done by a small corporation but is not being done in practice, that means that either there is something wrong with the target activity or there is something wrong with the country's entrepreneurship. If the latter is the problem, it should be dealt with directly.

2. Research or projects are selected which are likely to contribute greatly to the national wealth or well-being but which are too long-term to be attractive to private industry working alone.

The development of knowledge-based technology might be an example.

3. Wherever possible, lengthy projects are broken into short projects which themselves can be market tested.

The Japanese Fifth Generation, for example, can be subdivided into many small projects, mostly marketable in their own right. Consider the building of a future large computer which combines many powerful small processors operating in parallel. This can be broken into several projects:

- The powerful small processors can be built and marketed separately.
- The parallel architecture can be built with a small number of existing processors, possibly as a personal computer.
- The architecture can be expanded to the final configuration but with existing processors.
- The new processors can be substituted for the existing processors.

Each of these steps may produce a marketable result on its own. If the corporation that creates it succeeds in marketing it, a worthwhile goal has been achieved. If not, there may be something wrong.

4. Prototypes for real-world testing are built wherever possible.

Many pilot products fail when they are market tested. To go for a long time without such tests is dangerous. Most researchers believe that their project will succeed spectacularly in the marketplace; most are wrong. Early feedback is vital.

5. Components of a project are farmed out to entrepreneur corporations, not done in big government development laboratories.

This takes advantage of the lower research and development cost in small corporations. It helps to grow the new corporations which will become the country's technical strength in the future.

A vigorous economy is like an orchard. It is necessary to cut out the dead wood and plant new trees. The new trees need to be vigorously fertilized. Even so, some will fail.

CONCLUSION   If a country wants a healthy information technology industry, which will effect the productivity of other industries, it needs vigorous growth among its small high-technology companies. It needs the maximum support and encouragement of its entrepreneurs. It needs an active, healthy, U.S.-style, venture-capital industry. However, to stay ahead of the Japanese it needs well-funded research in areas too long-term for entrepreneurs. This research is probably best conducted as a cooperative effort between industry, universities, and government. The research should be directed so that entrepreneurs can utilize pieces of it wherever possible. Where it involves complex projects, contracts for portions of those projects should be assigned to aggressive, capable, small companies.

Direction of the long-term research needs an understanding of the forces at work which are changing computing—a much better understanding than that demonstrated in the Alvey report. The long-term projects should be broken into short-term steps wherever possible and constantly tested against the marketplace.

17 CHAIN REACTION

THE AUTOMATION OF AUTOMATION The automation of automation is the beginning of a chain reaction. Historians of future centuries will look back at the growth of computing as one of the most important factors in the fate of humankind. Computerization began, they will say, with crude machines and manual techniques. But just as the Industrial Revolution, two centuries before, was to bootstrap itself from primitive beginnings, so was the computer revolution.

The Industrial Revolution led to machines with immensely greater *physical* muscle than man; the computer revolution led to machines with immensely greater *mental* muscle than man. Awesome libraries of programmed knowledge and functions circled the earth, available everywhere via computer networks. The screens in almost every home and office became windows to logic power vastly beyond the comprehension of any one individual. New social contracts had to evolve to establish peoples' roles in a world where cybernetic tools outstripped human brains as much as a jumbo-jet outstrips a butterfly.

The steam engine introduced a new phase into the ascent of machines, giving the first power source that could be installed anywhere. An equivalent phase in the ascent of computers was the *automation* of the methods of systems analysis and programming.

As long as systems analysis and programming used *manual* methods, the methodologies were restricted to those with which a humble human being could cope. More powerful methodologies were suggested, but they were too tedious to be practical for our error-prone brains. The powerful methodologies needed automation. It was a shock for the early systems analysts and programmers to realize that they must automate their own jobs. But only when that was done could computing take off beyond the confines of the human being sitting at a pad of paper.

Museum curators of the future will look back like doting Egyptologists at their specimens of programs handcrafted in languages crudely designed for human beings, such as COBOL, FORTRAN, and Ada. Complex programs were undebuggable and the computer world accommodated itself to software that was not quite trustworthy. Operating systems exhibited mysterious behavior, and maintenance was a nightmare. Large numbers of analysts and programmers were trained in various "structured techniques," but these were still designed for use with pencil and paper and so did little to improve the situation. Corporate data bases were filled with jumbles of redundant data that often defied the extraction of information needed by management. Dijkstra [1] lectured on mathematical techniques but applied them to programs too small to be useful. Fred Brooks [2] cynically compared building complex software to prehistoric animals struggling in the tar pits that existed on earth 100 million years ago. The fiercer the dinosaurs struggled, the more entangling was the tar.

New automated technique can get us out of the tar pit. We can assemble larger and larger building blocks that are bug-free and interlink them without interface errors. When modifications are made in complex systems, we are not sucked into the tar. We can immediately see on a graphics screen the consequences of our modification.

The techniques used would be too tedious for pencil-and-paper design. They require computerized tools. The tools must *automatically* generate the programs because we cannot expect human beings to do so. With such techniques the software factories of the future will be built.

Only with this rigorously based automation can the chain reaction occur which allows explosive growth of complex software. No doubt we shall see various very powerful new methodologies now that we have the capability to automate them. The automation of automation is vital.

Norbert Wiener, the great pioneer of computers, wrote a book the title of which will long be remembered: *The Human Use of Human Beings* [3]. His view was that jobs which are inhuman because of drudgery should be done by machines, not people. Among these jobs he did not include that of the programmer! In a sense the programmer's job is inhuman because we require him to write a large amount of complex code without errors. But his animal-like brain cannot handle the meticulous detail and the vast numbers of combinatorial paths. Furthermore, if we want 1000 lines of code produced per day, not 10, then the job is even more inhuman. It is a job for machines, not people. Only recently have we understood how to make machines do it.

Once we have the capability to make machines create error-free code, the whole evolution of computers must change. The era of ad hoc hand coding is a temporary aberration in the history of computing.

PYRAMIDING
High-level *control structures* can be built out of primitive control structures. Still-higher-level ones can be built out of these, and so on. Essential in this is the rigor of the mechanism that enforces correct interfacing among the modules. It is this rigor that allows pyramiding of modules.

The same technique can be applied to hardware design. Like software, hardware designs are plunging into great complexity. We will build microelectronics wafers with many millions of logic circuits. Provably correct design is needed. We will build highly parallel computers out of hundreds or thousands of microcomputers, which need control mechanisms of great logical complexity. Integrated hardware–software designs are needed that are provably correct.

As the pyramids build we will reach very high-level constructs. High-level design languages will allow fast, very complex design. Millions of computers on worldwide data networks will interchange libraries and data bases. Knowledge-based systems will acquire ever more inferences and become self-feeding. Intelligent network directories will allow machines and users to find the resources they need.

Vitally important is the design of the human interface so that ordinary people everywhere can use and instruct the computer. There are numerous different ways to make the computer user-friendly. Many of them need *highly* complex software under the covers for processing the human–machine interaction.

CHANGING THE COMPUTER INDUSTRY
Conversion of the computer industry to rigorous design will obviously not happen overnight. The investment tied up in existing hardware, software, and techniques is gigantic. The insularity of the major computer corporations is immense and so is their resistance to methods that they do not originate internally.

Let us hope that the software for the dramatically complex fifth-generation hardware will not again be the undebuggable mess that has characterized large-computer operating systems in the past. C. A. R. Hoare described manufacturers' software as "the worst engineered products of the computer age," of unnecessary and still increasing complexity "which totally beggars the comprehension of both user and designer" [4].

Much Japanese software had been atrocious and this failing of the Japanese has to some extent protected the West from an onslaught of Japanese computers. If the Japanese started using HOS tools to develop their software, the West might have cause for concern. At the time of announcing their Fifth Generation, they appeared not to have heard of the technique; they wrote: "Supposing a specification is clearly given, if a correct and efficient program in accordance with it could be automatically synthesized, this would be ideal. However, realization of this ideal is *still far away in the future*" [5].

THE KNOWLEDGE-BASED CHAIN REACTION

The chain reaction from automating programming will supplement what might be a far more dramatic chain reaction: the spread and interlinking of knowledge-based computers.

The knowledge of experts, once captured in a knowledge-base, can be made available to everybody like books in a library. One knowledge-based computer will be able to find other knowledge bases via intelligent (knowledge-based) directories.

We sometimes think of "artificial intelligence" as residing in a large mainframe in one location. That is clearly wrong. We will have millions of artificial intelligence machines all interconnectable via the world's data networks and satellites. Knowledge bases will be embedded in mass-produced micros, personal computers, large mainframes, and library systems.

With fifth-generation computers, vast numbers of people will become involved in creating both software and knowledge bases. Software will be built with automated techniques. Knowledge bases will be built by experts, teachers, entrepreneurs, and university staff. We will have the tools to build on top of what already exists, building to ever more powerful structures. Mechanisms added to software libraries will be defined in terms of mechanisms already in those libraries. Knowledge-based systems will become *self-feeding,* acquiring more knowledge either by automatic input of various types, or by the system asking questions when it detects that it needs more knowledge.

A knowledge-based system is initially like a baby. The mechanism is there for learning. The more it learns, the more it is capable of learning. The child expands its knowledge until reaching its mental capacity. We may then organize networks of knowledge bases with different machines specializing in different areas, interchanging their knowledge.

When knowledge-based networks are self-feeding, how fast will they feed? Probably at an exponentially increasing rate. The terminals in every manager's office and the television terminals in the home will have access to an army of automated consultants and often it will be very difficult to argue with their advice.

The systems we build today are limited in their complexity by the capability of human beings to operate them correctly and make decisions about them. The short-term memory of our brain typically handles only about seven chunks of information at once [6]. Fifth-generation mainframes are planned to process 100 million to 1 billion inferences per second. If they can be made reliable (through parallelism) they will be able to control much more complex systems than are currently possible or imaginable.

Some of today's systems have exceeded the ability of their operators to handle complexity. This was true for the human operator errors which partially caused the disaster at the Three Mile Island nuclear power station, for example. Even a simple knowledge-based system aiding in the operation of that power station would have prevented the catastrophe.

In war, events rapidly pass beyond the ability of human beings to know all they need to, and make good decisions. A knowledge-based component seems necessary for defending warships, controlling aerial battles, or building command and control systems.

As we learn to trust our friendly new systems which are superintelligent in a narrow field, we will no doubt build systems and control mechanisms far beyond the ability of human beings to control. Automated verification techniques will help us to handle the complexity. It is certain that fifth-generation computers will trigger the realization of developments and phenomena which are today undreamed of.

COMPLEXITY

The Japanese, in what must be their most optimistic projection for their Fifth Generation, state that one of society's worst problems will be solved—the growth of government bureaucracy [7]. Certainly, much of what civil servants do today would be done with expert systems. Better knowledge could be accumulated for the running of society and made available to everyone who needs it.

The danger of automation of government regulations is that bureaucrats will be tempted to create still more regulations and make them still more complex. There is a law of bureaucracy which Northcote Parkinson ought to remember for his next book: *Complexity expands to fill the available computer power.*

It seems likely that we will continue increasing the complexity of society until only computers can cope with it. Human beings will be increasingly dependent on their friendly electronic servants.

SOCIAL EFFECTS

The social effects of fifth-generation computers will be great. The Japanese list numerous benefits. Robot factories will greatly increase manufacturing productivity, but to increase overall productivity across society, various bottlenecks will have to be improved:

- The office
- Education
- Agriculture and fishery
- Engineering design
- Medicine
- Public service
- Government

Knowledge-based systems will have a strong effect on all of these.

A factor that remains uncertain, however, is employment. What will people do if we have robot factories, automated offices, no need for secretaries, and expert systems replacing bureaucrats? Almost all jobs, physical and mental, which are boring, repetitive, routine, dangerous, or done in unpleasant conditions can potentially be automated. Jobs that are in some way uniquely human will be left.

Many people react by saying: "Slow down. Don't automate because it will cause unemployment." However, the most technological societies will solve their own employment problems by exporting them, as Japan has done for the last 10 years. They will flood the world with products at lower prices than can be achieved by countries with less automation. Union members who prevent automation will ultimately endanger their own jobs, as they did in Detroit when Japan was robotizing its production lines.

It is very dangerous to run the risk of falling behind in technology. It will result in a worsening standard of living, and unless make-work jobs are created (which further worsens national productivity), it will ultimately be likely to *cause* unemployment.

AUTOMATION OF WORK

Box 17.1 lists aspects of work that will be automated and those that will not. Many jobs encompass aspects from each side, so they will be partially automated, making the individual more powerful or productive.

Robot systems are now being built which will automate nursing tasks in hospitals, but the love and compassion of the nurse will still be needed. Education will change dramatically with intelligent, computer-aided videodiscs capturing on interactive television the world's best teaching, but the inspiration, originality, and motivation powers of the human teacher will still be needed. The entrepreneur will have much better information and decision support, but his human creativity and leadership will be indispensa-

BOX 17.1

Aspects of Work That Will Be Automated	Aspects of Work That Will *Not* Be Automated
● Simple tasks ⎫ Physical ● Routine tasks ⎬ and ● Reproducible tasks ⎭ mental ● Tasks requiring complex logic or calculation ● Expertise that can be reduced to rules ● Tasks requiring vast knowledge	● Originality ● Intuition ● Inspiration ● Art ● Leadership ● Salesmanship ● Humor ● Love ● Friendship

ble. In fact, the nurse, the teacher, the entrepreneur, and other people with creative or compassionate jobs will be able to spend much more time on those aspects of their job which are the truly human ones.

However, if we assume that 10 or 20 years from now most of the tasks on the left of Box 17.1 are automated, that will clearly play havoc with society. The rate of change in the next 20 years will be fierce.

For society to function adequately, every individual in it, except the pathological, must be able to feel that he has a worthwhile role to play. If we build a society in which a substantial proportion feel they have no part to play, even though a welfare system supports them, they will feel alienated and hostile. Sociologists tell us that this will lead to a high level of social violence. Welfare alone is not an appropriate solution.

TECHNOLOGY POTENTIAL/ HUMAN POTENTIAL

One of the most important aspects of the introduction of high technology is that it needs to go hand in hand with higher levels of human interaction, care, love, teaching, leadership, and creativity. As we expand technology potential we must expand human potential along with it. Perhaps a slogan should be TP/HP—Technology Potential/Human

Potential. If hospitals automate the chores of nurses, the nurses should use their human healing skills more deeply. Computer-based training has immense potential, but it needs far more skilled course creators and teachers who pay more attention to the human needs of the student. If television has hundreds of channels, it needs higher-quality programs. Robots in factories should be linked to increased use of quality circles. If we work fewer hours because of automation we need to be better equipped for a rich set of leisure activities.

Advanced countries are losing their smoke-stack industries. In the 1950s the United States made half of the world's steel; now it makes 11%. At one time the majority of the United States work force was engaged in manufacturing; now only 13% is. *Newsweek* estimates that up to 75% of the remaining factory workers could be displaced by robots by the year 2000. Third World countries are rapidly increasing their manufacturing capability.

Meanwhile the number of knowledge workers is growing by leaps and bounds. In 1950 only 17% of Americans worked in information jobs; now more than 60% do. However, simple white-collar jobs are being displaced by automation. A French Government report predicted that France would lose 30% of its banking and insurance workers in the next ten years.

Advanced countries are moving rapidly into an *intellect-intensive society*. Daniel Bell called it a *post-industrial society*. John Naisbitt ("Mega-trends") called it an *information society*. Neither of these terms describes it well because industry will remain and be vital, and many intellect workers will not be information workers. An *intellect-intensive society* seems to be a better term—a society in which routine or simple jobs will be automated.

Not everyone in society is intellectual. So the intellect-intensive jobs must be mixed with jobs involving human warmth, craftsmanship, and creativity. As technology potential grows explosively, human potential needs to be expanded across a broad front involving all of the aspects on the right-hand side of Box 17.1.

We are unlocking great riches in the technology we now know is possible. It gives us the tools to put an end to most human drudgery. Industrial progress has brought us masses of consumer products. These will become better, more intelligent, and cheaper. The television set will become a wall-sized screen linked to libraries of the best programs made. The house and garden can be tended by robots manufactured by other robots. We can feed the inflated world population with hydroponics, high-rise greenhouses, shrimp farms, fish farms, and the like, all controlled by intelligent machines.

Perhaps the finest organ ever built is that in the Sydney Opera House. It is a thundering magnificent organ with 10,500 pipes, which shake the bones in your chest. But it is computer controlled. When the world's best organists go to Australia to play it, their music can be recorded digitally, and when they have left the performance can be repeated. If we wanted we could build organs like this everywhere, and capture the playing of the greatest performers.

The question becomes: How do we want to spend the riches we are unlocking? And how do we achieve the transformation to living in a world of intelligent machines? In industrial societies today there are more electric motors than people; soon there will be more intelligent computers than people. What will people do? What will be the mix of jobs?

Only the aspects of work on the right-hand side of Box 17.1 are a truly human use of human beings. The rest can be done by machines. We need to create a vision of a society where everyone contributes, and is brought up from childhood to contribute, those talents that *every* human being has in some form or other.

A most urgent question for people who can understand technology today is

What sort of a world do you want your children to live in?

Appendix

HOW TO IMPROVE DP PRODUCTIVITY

Higher Levels of Automation

- Avoid conventional programming wherever possible.
- Recognize that all systems can be built without conventional programming and that the price of the new methods should be evaluated.
- Automate the system design process wherever possible.
- Seek out the highest productivity tools and techniques.
- Introduce a thorough education program for the new development methodologies.
- Recognize that the new methods totally change the traditional development life cycle.

Application Creation Software

- Acquire comprehensive understanding of the software for application development without traditional programmers:
  - Query and update languages
  - Report generators
  - Application generators
  - Fourth-generation languages
  - Generators of provably correct code
- Understand that these new software packages are not a panacea. High technical skill is needed in selecting and designing their use.

(Continued)

- Encourage end users to employ fully the new user-friendly languages and tools—but with appropriate management controls.
- Use the most flexible information retrieval and data management facilities (e.g., relational data bases).

Application Packages

- Use application packages where appropriate.
- Recognize the dangers in packages.
- Evaluate how well the package fits with corporate data structures.
- Evaluate carefully the cost and difficulties of future modifications to any package. Assess the maintainability of the package.
- Use a sound contract for package maintenance. (Most software contracts do not help the user enough.)
- Understand the balance between application packages and generators.

User-Driven Computing

- Recognize the difference between prespecified computing and dynamically changeable user-driven computing.
- Set up a separate management to encourage, spread, support, and ensure quality in user-driven computing.
- Establish information centers with sound technical management.
- Motivate and train end users to obtain the information they need with query languages and report generators.
- Carefully select the most user-friendly facilities for end users.
- Use thorough education for information center skills.
- Use salesmanship to sell the information center capabilities throughout the enterprise.

Changes in DP Management Organization

- Establish an advanced development group as well as information centers to use and improve skills with the new development methods and software.
- Link these new channels of development firmly into information engineering management with top-level data administration.
- Develop high technical expertise with nonprocedural languages.
- Measure the productivity of the advanced development and move application development to this channel as fast as appropriate.

Sound Data Design Techniques

- Understand the importance of sound data analysis.
- Automate the data modeling process.
- Use stability analysis to make data bases give minimum future maintenance costs.
- Employ enterprise-wide strategic data planning to prevent the spread of incompatible data.
- Use the most powerful software for data-base application creation.
- Use structured methodologies designed for use with data models and fourth-generation languages.
- Ensure that a data administrator responsible for the data-base techniques listed above reports at a high enough level.
- Endorse the principles of information engineering and involve top management in it.

Improved Systems Analysis Methods

- Seek out tools that automate the systems analysis process as fully as possible.
- Avoid hand-drawn charts of excessive complexity. Replace these with computer-drawn charts.
- Use systems analysis tools that result in automatic generation of code.
- Link systems analysis fully to the data administration process.
- Avoid systems analysis techniques that are nonrigorous and lead to ambiguity.
- Avoid, where possible, systems analysis techniques that are slow and laborious (detailed English specifications, flowcharts, unnecessary data flow diagramming). These can be replaced partially or completely with direct prototyping linked to data models.
- Use self-documenting software and techniques.
- Make the analysts interact continuously with the end user and generate either a prototype or the final result (to avoid the high proportion of bugs that are in requirements and design specifications).
- Use structured techniques that are
  - As user-friendly as possible so that users can check the design
  - Rigorous, with automated verification checks
  - Oriented to sound data administration
  - Oriented to fourth-generation languages and generators

(Continued)

Prototyping

- Build prototypes that end users employ before any expensive lengthy development.
- Provide multiple versions of prototypes if needed.
- Develop expertise on prototyping tools and languages.
- Convert the prototype directly to the final application, where adequate machine performance can be attained.

Lessening of Maintenance Costs

- Use techniques that make maintenance easier, faster, and cheaper. These often relate to the design phase and tools.
- Convert systems with expensive maintenance using techniques that drastically reduce maintenance costs (e.g., generators, sound data-base facilities, fourth-generation languages).
- Use tools that make all variables and logic traceable.
- Use data-base management systems selected to minimize future maintenance costs (e.g., with field sensitivity).
- Use data models designed to be as stable as possible.

Avoidance of Debugging Problems

- Use techniques to discover errors as early as possible in the development life cycle. This is best done with rigorous specification-language tools.
- Use tools that provide automated verification of design wherever possible.
- Use software that generates bug-free code.
- Avoid the need for dynamic testing and saturation testing wherever possible with appropriate generator software.
- Use techniques that prevent interface problems with separately developed modules or systems.

Better Programming Tools and Techniques

- Where a conventional programming (COBOL, Pascal, Ada, etc.) *must* be used, seek out the highest-productivity design, coding, debugging, and management tools.
- Use structured design, structured coding, and data-base techniques.
- Employ programmers' workbench tools.

- Generate all program data structures (e.g., Data Division of COBOL, IMS PSB's, etc.) automatically from a data dictionary.
- Use high-level debugging tools, code analyzers, compilers with good diagnostics, cross-reference lists, etc.
- Employ preprogrammed standard routines (e.g., file access, input/output) where possible.
- Use building block generators, like IBM's ELIAS.
- Use good library support for standard routines.
- Avoid unnecessary duplication of program logic.
- Use preprocessors (e.g., which generate COBOL) where applicable.
- Use nonprocedural code in programs where applicable (e.g., SQL).
- Use structured walk-throughs and management checkpoints.

Decision Support Systems

- Distinguish clearly between decision-support systems and routine processing systems.
- Seek out the best decision-support software and hardware.
- Plan that the requisite data are available for decision-support systems.
- Plan appropriate data extractors for providing data to personal computers and information center systems.

Avoidance of Systems Software Programming

- Do not modify complex systems software. This puts you in a severe maintenance trap.
- Do not write systems software (e.g., data-base management or networking software).
- Avoid hardware–software configurations that will require expensive conversion or modification later.
- Select equipment so as to avoid expensive systems programming where possible.

Personnel Selection and Motivation

- Seek out the highest-quality staff (top quality programmers obtain 10 times the results of average programmers).
- Use techniques for achieving high team morale.
- Employ thorough training, especially of the best staff. Train them in high-productivity techniques.

(Continued)

- Use modularization, data modeling, and very-high-level languages to achieve one-person projects. Select, excite, and reward the one-person developers well.

- Use techniques for high motivation of staff.

- Use techniques for high motivation of end users to participate fully in development and employ end-user software.

Strategic Planning

- Use information engineering techniques to achieve a common stable data infrastructure, and the most effective data-base techniques.

- Use strategic planning of systems to minimize redundant application development.

- Use strategic planning to maximize return on investment of DP effort.

- Identify strategic information resources.

- Use network and data planning to achieve interoperability of systems and avoid expensive incompatibilities.

- Plan hardware, network, and software resources to facilitate the fastest creation of results.

Changing the Development Life Cycle

- Understand the difference between second-generation, third-generation, and fourth-generation development methodologies.

- Avoid obsolete methodologies (recognizing that these are often in the DP standards manuals and externally purchased "methodologies").

- Recognize that the traditional development life cycle is thoroughly changed by application generators, data modeling, prototyping, information centers, user-driven computing, provably correct code techniques, nonprocedural languages, information engineering, data-base tools, and decision-support software. Look for the fastest life-cycle methods.

- Upgrade the DP standards manual to thoroughly encompass fourth-generation methodologies and the life-cycle changes they require.

Seminars

- Ensure that *all* staff members understand the techniques on this chart and that all cooperate to obtain the best information systems.

- Send *all* staff members involved with computers to the James Martin seminars periodically.

Appendix

 MANIFESTOS

**APPENDIX II-A:
MANIFESTO FOR
SENIOR
MANAGEMENT**

Understand how your organization ought to change as it becomes a fully electronic enterprise. Electronics are changing products, services, fabrication techniques, selling techniques, decision making, flows of information, mechanisms of control, and management structures.

Understand that a revolution is taking place in DP but that many DP departments are not moving fast enough to the higher-productivity techniques. There is often psychological or political resistance to the new methods, which management needs to overcome. Ensure that *your* organization is migrating away from slow methods and can respond rapidly to information needs by using fourth-generation languages, information center techniques, flexible data bases, and the maximum automation of the DP function as described in this book.

Ensure that decision makers at all levels have the tools they need for making the best possible decisions. Ensure the necessary information resources are available to them. To achieve this, ensure that information engineering has been done throughout the enterprise.

Information engineering needs top-down management of information resources, thorough data modeling, and strategic planning of networks. These essential aspects of managing a computerized corporation have often failed because of organizational and political factors. They have been managed at too low a level. Top management must understand the need for them and ensure that an appropriate information infrastructure is built.

**APPENDIX II-B:
MANIFESTO FOR
END USERS**

Become literate with computers. *Invent* ways in which on-line data bases can improve your procedures. *Learn* the skills needed to extract and manipulate data from workstations. *Understand* how end-user computer languages are replacing much conventional programming.

Insist that information centers are built to give fast reaction to your information needs. Understand the importance of information engineering with shared data models and give full support to the data administrator.

Learn how computing can help in decision-making processes. Use and become fully familiar with at least one decision-support tool on a personal computer. Insist that appropriate computerized information and decision support are provided to you.

APPENDIX II-C: MANIFESTO FOR DP EXECUTIVES

Distinguish clearly between second-, third-, and fourth-generation methodologies. Swing your organization as rapidly as possible to fourth-generation techniques, including fourth-generation languages, application generators, prototyping, information engineering, flexible data bases, nonprocedural data-base languages, fourth-generation networks, low-maintenance software, support of user-driven computing, support of single-user computers, and powerful decision-support systems.

Establish information centers to encourage, support, and assure quality in user computing. Establish an advanced development group to become skilled with software and techniques for faster application building. Wind down the conventional programming team until it does little more than maintenance. Rebuild systems that are expensive to maintain using software that gives low-cost maintenance. Encourage systems analysts to become expert with software with which they can build a complete application, not pass specifications to programmers. Use techniques that give one-person projects wherever possible. Ensure that thorough information engineering is done with computerized tools, and that sound data models are the basis for all future development. Build the capability to provide executive decision-support systems as fast as possible.

Hire the best-quality developers, pay them well for excellence, and build high team morale. Motivate and reward developers highly for high-speed, high-quality completion of projects.

Ensure that strategic planning is done to ensure interoperability between systems, and ensure that users or information centers can extract and manipulate required information quickly using the networks and data bases.

Provide services so that users can obtain the information they need (text and data) by themselves as much as possible, and can manipulate data without help from traditional programmers.

Understand that the traditional development life cycle needs fundamental changing for many end-user requirements. The old standards and procedures are crippling for these requirements. You need a manual of DP development encompassing the new techniques.

APPENDIX II-D: MANIFESTO FOR SYSTEM ANALYSTS

Make yourself completely skilled with at least one fourth-generation language. Acquire the ability to build an application rather than writing specifications for someone else to build it. Use this application building skill to exercise maximum creativity.

Build prototypes and adjust them fully to the users' needs. Learn everything you can about good human factoring of systems.

Learn human communication skills. Learn to understand the end users' real problems and solve them. Become fully skilled with a report generator.

Learn the principles of data analysis (canonical data modeling). Ensure that soundly modeled data are used for all applications. Understand the role of information engineering and help the data administrator.

Understand the benefits and limitations of the different structured techniques. Understand techniques that can generate bug-free code. Learn the significance of specification languages and seek out those from which code can be generated automatically. Learn those tools that automate as fully as possible the design and development process.

As you rise to management, build a team that understands information engineering and employs the most automated tools.

**APPENDIX II-E:
MANIFESTO FOR
PROGRAMMERS**
Make yourself as valuable as possible by becoming skilled with tools more powerful than third-generation languages. Learn rigorous techniques that lead to error-free code. Learn fourth-generation and nonprocedural languages. Gain experience with workbench tools. Acquire the ability to obtain bug-free results 10 times faster than with languages such as COBOL, FORTRAN, PL/1, or Pascal.

Determine whether your career path is to be:

1. in program design and coding.

2. in using specification languages and code generators, working more as an analyst.

3. in an information center environment working with end users.

Plan how you can achieve higher salaries and promotions by making yourself more powerful with more automated tools.

**APPENDIX II-F:
MANIFESTO FOR
COMPUTING
PROFESSORS**

There is a gigantic gulf between the most useful new directions of commercial data processing and what is being taught in most universities. Much university research relates to problems of the past rather than the urgent new needs. There are endless research opportunities in the new DP directions, such as nonprocedural languages, specification languages, decision-support systems, CAD/CAM, user-driven computing, generation of provably correct code, new hardware–software architectures, high-productivity application generators, relational engines, knowledge-based system components, languages and techniques for expert systems, ultraparallel machines, natural language interfaces, and the evolution from ad hoc methods to engineering discipline.

Orient the teaching to future real-world needs. Teach students languages such as FOCUS, SQL, and PROLOG, not BASIC. Teach them about the constructs needed in fourth-generation languages, nonprocedural languages, and languages for expert systems. Teach them how to create very high-level languages that are very well human-engineered. Teach them information engineering, decision-support techniques, problem-solving techniques, and human communications skills. Stop research oriented to third-generation languages and focus it on the immensely exciting future possibilities of computers, and extend the foundation principles of computing.

Forge links with industry so that professors consult on current problems and so that the money available for research is greatly expanded.

**APPENDIX II-G:
MANIFESTO FOR
SOFTWARE HOUSES**

Create, sell, and utilize software that gives the maximum automation of automation.

Teach all developers what is meant by, and techniques for achieving, user-seductive software.

Understand the techniques of generating provably correct code. Understand specification languages from which code can be generated automatically. Build a team that utilizes these as fast and effectively as possible.

Select techniques that give the fastest and easiest maintenance of software.

Create the best possible training courses on your products and write manuals that are as easy to understand as possible. Package very user-friendly training and HELP facilities into your products.

**APPENDIX II-H:
MANIFESTO FOR
COMPUTER
MANUFACTURERS**

Change the hardware to give the maximum machine efficiency with nonprocedural languages. Support the most effective non-von-Neumann languages with non-von-Neumann hardware.

Create a product line that *integrates* office automation, transaction processing, and the most effective decision-support systems. Build distributed resources with powerful single-user computers, excellent business and design graphics, personal electronic filing systems, highly flexible data-base systems, local area networks, and fourth-generation networks.

Build highly flexible data-base machines that use parallel processors to perform high-speed searches and relational operations, and possibly later, knowledge-based operations.

Build architectures that utilize future powerful mass-produced micro-computers in highly parallel configurations to minimize the cost of mass computing power, and provide no-fail systems.

Build systems that enable users to locate and extract the information they need quickly and manipulate it with powerful decision-support facilities, often down-line loading data via high bandwidth networks in a personal computer.

Put the maximum emphasis on human factoring to make systems as user-seductive and natural to use as possible. Understand that much of the software that is called user-friendly is inadequate and poor in its human factoring. Most analysts and programmers still fail to understand excellent human factoring.

Explore all possible ramifications of the Japanese Fifth Generation, inference processing engines, expert systems, knowledge bases, and artificial intelligence in general. Build expert systems for systems analysis and design, debugging, microchip production and other internal functions, so that expert system technology is better understood. Build a personal computer for expert systems using the most practical of the Fifth Generation ideas.

APPENDIX II-I:
MANIFESTO FOR
ENTREPRENEURS

The information system revolution described in this book presents great business opportunities. New software and software–hardware combinations will make old, established languages and architectures appear clumsy and disastrous. Some old computer vendors are trapped with obsolete architectures for computers, operating systems, and data-base systems.

New software companies will grow rapidly by providing fast solutions to computer users' needs. The ideal fourth-generation language is yet to be created.

Much money will be made by building and utilizing expert systems and knowledge bases.

It seems likely that the fastest-growing commercial computer company is yet to emerge by creating a software–hardware combination aimed at the automation of automation. It will build hardware to execute nonprocedural languages with data-base engines, designed to take maximum advantage of future mass-produced microprocessors. Keys to success will be the best possible design of user-friendly interfaces, elegant graphics, and concentration on users being able to create fast decision-making assistance.

REFERENCES

Chapter 1

1. R. B. Rosenberger, "The Information Center," SHARE 56, *Proceedings,* Session M372, Share, Inc., New York, 1981.

2. J. Martin and C. McClure, *Maintenance of Computer Programming,* Prentice–Hall Inc., Englewood Cliffs, NJ, 1983.

3. "Business is Turning Data into a Potent Strategic Weapon," *Business Week,* August 22, 1983.

4. J. W. Johnson, "Implementation of Computer-Assisted Underwriting," *Interfaces,* Vol. 6, No. 2, February 1976, The Institute of Management Sciences, New York, NY.

Chapter 2

1. T. C. Jones, "The Limits to Programming Productivity," Guide and Share Application Development Symposium, *Proceedings,* Share, Inc., New York, 1979. (T. C. Jones' meticulous research has resulted in software for estimating programmer productivity, project times and costs, number of errors, etc.)

2. G. W. Willett et al., *TSO Productivity Study,* American Telephone and Telegraph Long Lines, Kansas City, April 1973.

3. P. Freeman and A. I. Wasserman, *Tutorial on Software Design Techniques,* IEEE Computer Society, Catalog No. 76CH1145-2, 1977.

4. C. V. Ramamoorthy and H. H. So, "Survey of Principles and Techniques of Software Requirements and Specifications," *Software Engineering Techniques 2,* invited papers, Infotech International Ltd., Nicholson House, Maidenhead, Berkshire, UK, 1977, pp. 265–318.

5. M. E. Fagan, "Design and Code Inspections to Reduce Errors in Program Development," *IBM Systems Journal,* Vol. 15, No. 3, 1976 (Reprint Order No. G321-5033).

6. J. Fox, *Software Management,* Prentice-Hall, Inc., Englewood Cliffs, NJ, 1981.

7. J. Martin, *Application Development Without Programmers,* Prentice-Hall, Inc., Englewood Cliffs, NJ, 1982.

8. Further information and manuals on FOCUS can be obtained from Information Builders, 1250 Broadway, New York, NY 10001.

9. Further information and manuals on RAMIS can be obtained from Mathematica Incorporated, P.O. Box 2392, Princeton, NJ 08540.

10. Further information and manuals on NOMAD can be obtained from National C.S.S. Ltd., 187 Danbury Road, Wilton, CT 06897.

11. Further information and manuals on MANTIS can be obtained from Cincom Systems, 2300 Mantanna Avenue, Cincinnati, OH 45211.

12. Further information and manuals on NATURAL can be obtained from Software A.G. of North America, Reston International Center, 11800 Sunrise Valley Drive, Reston, VA 20915.

13. Further information and manuals on IDEAL can be obtained from Applied Data Research (A.D.R.), Route 206 and Orchard Road, CN-8, Princeton, NJ 08540.

14. Further information and manuals on SAS can be obtained from SAS Institute Inc., SAS Circle, Box 8000, Cary, NC 27511.

15. James Martin, *Fourth-Generation Languages,* Savant Research Institute, 2 New Street, Carnforth, Lancs, LA6 9BX, UK.

16. C. A. R. Hoare, "The Engineering of Software: A Startling Contradiction," *Computer Bulletin,* British Computer Society, December 1975.

Chapter 3

1. U.S. Department of Defense, *Management of Computer Resources in Major Defense Systems,* Directive 5000.29.

2. J. Martin, *Application Development Without Programmers,* Prentice-Hall, Inc., Englewood Cliffs, NJ, 1982.

3. Advanced Technology Library, Deltak Inc., Naperville, Ill. This contains videotapes, multimedia, and computer-assisted courses on end user products and information center techniques.

Chapter 4

1. T. de Marco, *Structured Analysis and System Specifications,* Yourdon, I c., New York, 1978.

2. J. Fox, *Managing Software,* Prentice-Hall, Inc., Englewood Cliffs, NJ, 1981.

3. *Hearings on Cost Escalations in Defense Procurements,* Department of Defense Authorization for Appropriation for Fiscal Year 1975, Committee on Armed Services, U.S. House of Representatives, 93rd Congress, 1974.

4. *Hearings Before the Subcommittee on Federal Spending Practices, Efficiency, and Open Government,* Committee on Government Operations, U.S. Senate, 94th Congress, 1st session, June–July 1975.

5. *Hearings on Military Posture and H.R. 5068:* Department of Defense Authorization for Appropriations for Fiscal Year 1978, Committee on Armed Services, U.S. House of Representatives, 95th Congress, 1st session, February–March 1977.

6. These diagramming techniques are explained in James Martin and Carma McClure, *Structured Techniques for Computing,* Volume I, Savant Research Studies, Carnforth, Lancs, LA6 9BX, UK, 1984.

7. Richard Hamming suggested this in a review of the author's report, *Program Design Which Is Provably Correct,* Savant Technical Report 28, Savant Institute, Carnforth, Lancashire, UK, 1982.

Chapter 5

1. D. Ross, "Structured Analysis (SA): A Language for Communicating Ideas," *IEEE Transactions on Software Engineering,* Vol. SE-3, No. 1, 1977.

2. M. Alford, "A Requirements Engineering Methodology for Real-Time Processing Requirements," *IEEE Transactions on Software Engineering,* Vol. SE-3, No. 1, 1977.

3. T. de Marco, *Structured Analysis and System Specification,* Yourdon, Inc., New York, 1978.

4. *HIPO—A Design Aid and Documentation Technique,* IBM Manual Ref. GC20-1851.

5. D. Teichroew and E. A. Hershey III, "PSL/PSA: A Computer-Aided Technique for Structured Documentation and Analysis of Information Processing Systems," *IEEE Transactions on Software Engineering,* Vol. SE-3, No. 1, 1977.

6. SofTech. Inc., *Architect's Manual: ICAM Definition Method*, IDEF Version 0, 1978; Version 1, 1978, Waltham, MA.

7. J. Martin, *Application Development Without Programmers*, Prentice-Hall, Inc., Englewood Cliffs, NJ, 1981.

8. J. Martin, *Strategic Data-Planning Methodologies*, Prentice-Hall, Inc., Englewood Cliffs, NJ, 1982.

9. J. Martin, *Managing the Data Base Environment*, Prentice–Hall Inc., Englewood Cliffs, NJ, 1983.

10. W. L. Trainer, "Software—From Satan to Saviour," NAECON Conference, *Proceedings*, May 1973.

11. M. Hamilton and S. Zeldin, *Integrated Software Development System/ Higher Order Software Conceptual Description*, Research and Development Technical Report ECOM-76-0329F, U.S. Army Electronics command, Fort Monmouth, NJ, 1976.

12. Diagram adapted from one by A. M. Davis, "The Design of a Family of Application-Oriented Requirements Languages," *Computer*, May 1982.

13. S. H. Caine and E. K. Gordon, "PDL—A Tool for Software Design," AFIPS Conference, *Proceedings*, Vol. 44, 1975 NCC, AFIPS Press, Montvale, NJ.

14. B. E. Casey and B. J. Taylor, "Writing Requirements in English: A Natural Alternative," IEEE Workshop on Software Engineering Standards, San Francisco, CA, August 1981.

15. R. Balzer et al., "Informality in Program Specifications," *IEEE Transactions on Software Engineering*, Vol. SE-4, No. 2, March 1978.

16. C. R. Everhart, "A Unified Approach to Software System Engineering," Compsac '80, *Proceedings*, IEEE Computer Society, Los Alamitos, CA, October 1980.

17. J. Martin, *Architectures for Distributed Processing*, Savant Technical Report 6, Savant Institute, Carnforth, Lancashire, UK, 1979, Chapter 2.

18. CCITT, *SDL User Guidelines*, Study Group XI, Working Papers 3-1, 3-4.

19. M. W. Alford, "A Requirements Engineering Methodology for Real-Time Processing Requirements," *IEEE Transactions on Software Engineering*, Vol. SE-3, No. 1, January 1977.

20. A. M. Davies, "Automating the Requirements Phase: Benefits to Later Phases of the Software Life-Cycle," Compsac '80, *Proceedings*, IEEE Computer Society, Los Alamitos, CA, October 1980.

21. The COSS-RL language designed for the definition of central office switching systems at GTE Laboratories, Waltham, MA.

Chapter 6

1. J. Martin, *Strategic Data-Planning Methodologies,* Prentice-Hall, Inc., Englewood Cliffs, NJ, 1982.

2. J. Martin, *Managing the Data Base Environment,* Prentice–Hall, Inc., Englewood Cliffs, NJ, 1983.

3. For example, Data Designer, from Database Design Inc., Ann Arbor, MI.

4. J. Martin, *Application Development Without Programmers,* Prentice-Hall, Inc., Englewood Cliffs, NJ, 1982.

5. J. Martin, *LAMS and DADS,* Savant Technical Report 29, Savant Institute, Carnforth, Lancashire, UK, 1982.

6. J. Martin and C. Finkelstein, *Information Engineering,* 2 vols., Savant Institute, Carnforth, Lancashire, UK, 1981.

Chapter 7

1. R. B. Rosenberger, "The Information Center," SHARE 56, *Proceedings,* Session M372, Share, Inc., New York, 1981.

2. Conference on Information Centers and Fourth Generation Languages, Database Design Inc., and the University of Michigan, Ann Arbor, MI, April 1983.

3. Interview on a Deltak video course in the Deltak Advanced Technology Library developed with James Martin.

4. Information from Jim Johnson, Operations Engineering Department, Equitable Insurance Co., New York.

5. Information from P. J. Entwistle, Chief Manager (Data Processing), Lloyds Bank Ltd., London.

Chapter 8

1. James Martin, *Fourth-Generation Languages,* Savant Institute, Carnforth, Lancashire, UK, 1984.

2. James Martin and Carma McClure, *Structured Techniques for Computing,* Vol. I, Savant Institute, Carnforth, Lancashire, UK, 1984.

3. K. Winter, Database Design Inc., Ann Arbor, MI.

4. J. Martin, *Managing the Data Base Environment,* Prentice–Hall Inc., Englewood Cliffs, NJ, 1983.

5. J. Martin, *Program Design Which Is Provably Correct,* Savant Technical Report 28, Savant Institute, Carnforth, Lancashire, UK, 1982, Chapter 13.

Chapter 9

1. H. K. Berg, W. E. Boebert, W. R. Franta, and T. G. Moher, *Formal Methods of Program Verification and Specification,* Prentice-Hall, Inc., Englewood Cliffs, NJ, 1982.

2. J. von Neumann, *Collected Works,* Vol. 5, A. H. Taub. ed., Pergamon Press, Oxford, 1963, pp. 91–99.

3. R. W. Floyd, "Assigning Meanings to Programs," Symposium on Applied Mathematics, *Proceedings,* American Mathematical Society, Vol. 19, 1967.

4. J. E. Stoy, *Denotational Semantics: The Scott–Strachey Approach to Programming Language Theory,* The MIT Press, Cambridge, MA, 1977.

5. B. W. Boehm, R. K. McClean, and D. B. Urfreg, "Some Experience with Automated Aids to the Design of Large Scale Reliable Software," *IEEE Transactions on Software Engineering,* Vol. SE-1, No. 1, 1975.

6. R. J. Rubey, J. A. Dana, and P. W. Biche, "Quantitative Aspects of Software Validation," *IEEE Transactions on Software Engineering,* Vol. SE-1, No. 2, 1975.

7. R. Milner, "An Algebraic Definition of Simulation Between Programs," 2nd International Joint Conference on Artificial Intelligence, *Proceedings,* London, 1971.

8. A. Blikle and A. Mazurkiewicz, *An Algebraic Approach to the Theory of Programs, Algorithms, Languages and Recursiveness,* Mathematical Foundations of Computer Science, Warsaw, Poland, 1972.

9. A. Church, *The Calculi of Lambda-Conversion,* Annals of Mathematical Studies, Vol. 6, Princeton University Press, Princeton, NJ, 1951.

10. W. E. Howden, "Methodology for Generation of Program Test Data," *IEEE Transactions on Software Engineering,* Vol. SE-2, No. 3, 1976.

11. J. A. Darringer and J. C. King, "Application of Symbolic Execution to Program Testing," *Computer,* Vol. 11, No. 4, 1978.

12. Z. Manna, "The Correctness of Programs," *Journal of Computer and System Sciences,* Vol. 3, No. 2, 1969.

13. C. A. R. Hoare, "An Axiomatic Approach to Computer Programming," *Communications of the ACM,* Vol. 12, No. 10, 1969.

14. D. Gries, "An Introduction to Current Ideas on the Derivation of Correctness Proofs and Correct Programs," *IEEE Transactions on Software Engineering,* Vol. SE-2, No. 4, 1976.

15. E. W. Dijkstra, *A Discipline of Programming,* Prentice-Hall, Inc., Englewood Cliffs, NJ, 1976.

16. B. Wegbreit, "Constructive Methods in Program Verification," *IEEE Transactions on Software Engineering,* Vol. SE-3, No. 2, 1977.

17. S. Owicki, "Axiomatic Proof Techniques for Parallel Programs," Ph.D. thesis, Department of Computer Science, Cornell University, 1975.

18. S. Owicki and D. Gries, "Verifying Properties of Parallel Programs: An Axiomatic Approach," *Communications of the ACM,* Vol. 19, No. 5, 1976.

19. L. Flon, "On the Design and Verification of Operating Systems," Ph.D. thesis, Department of Computer Science, Carnegie-Mellon University, 1977.

20. E. W. Dijkstra, "The Humble Programmer," *Communications of the ACM,* Vol. 15, October 1972.

21. M. Hamilton and S. Zeldin, "The Relationship Between Design and Verification," *Journal of Systems and Software,* Vol. 1, 1979.

22. M. Hamilton and S. Zeldin, "The Manager as an Abstract Systems Engineer," *Digest of Papers.* Fall COMPSON 77, Washington, D.C., IEEE Computer Society Cat. No. 77CH1258-3C, September 1977.

23. M. Hamilton and S. Zeldin, *AXES Syntax Description,* TR-4, Higher Order Software, Inc., Cambridge, MA, December 1976.

24. M. Hamilton and S. Zeldin, *The Foundations of AXES: A Specification Language Based on Completeness of Control,* Doc. R-964, Charles Stark Draper Laboratory, Inc., Cambridge, MA, March 1976.

25. M. Hamilton and S. Zeldin, *Integrated Software Development System/ Higher Order Software Conceptual Description,* TR-3, Higher Order Software, Inc., Cambridge, MA, November 1976.

26. M. Hamilton and S. Zeldin, "Higher Order Software—A Methodology for Defining Software," *IEEE Transactions on Software Engineering,* Vol. SE-2, No. 1, 1976.

27. M. Hamilton and S. Zeldin, "Reliability in Terms of Predictability," Compsac '78, *Proceedings,* Chicago, IEEE Computer Society Cat. No. 78CH1338-3C, November 1978.

28. Higher Order Software, Inc., P. O. Box 531, 806 Massachusetts Avenue, Cambridge, MA 02139.

29. J. Martin, *LAMS and DADS,* Savant Technical Report 29, Savant Institute, Carnforth, Lancashire, UK, 1982.

30. *Introduction to the Application of HOS to Hardware Design: The CORDIC Algorithm,* IDA Study of Hardware Description Languages, National Academy of Sciences, Woods Hole, MA, 1981. Prepared by HOS, Inc., Cambridge, MA.

31. *Specifying Ada Semantics in HOS,* Technical Report 34, Higher Order Software, Inc., Cambridge, MA, May 1982.

32. M. Hamilton, "The Ada Environment as a System," ADA Environment Workshop, *Proceedings,* sponsored by Dod High Order Language Working Group, Harbor Island, San Diego, CA, November 1979.

33. F. P. Brooks, Jr., *The Mythical Man-Month: Essays on Software Engineering,* Addison-Wesley Publishing Co., Inc., Reading, MA, 1974.

Chapter 10

1. *MIS Week,* February 10, 1982, p. 1, Fairchild Business Newspaper.

2. M. Hamilton and S. Zeldin, "The Relationship Between Design and Verification," *Journal of Systems and Software,* Vol. 1, 1979.

3. J. Martin, *Application Development Without Programmers,* Prentice-Hall, Inc., Englewood Cliffs, NJ, 1982.

4. D. K. Lloyd and M. Lipow, *Reliability: Management Methods and Mathematics,* Prentice-Hall, Inc., Englewood Cliffs, NJ, 1972.

5. G. W. Willett et al., *TSO Productivity Study,* American Telephone and Telegraph Long Lines, Kansas City, April 1973.

6. T. C. Jones, "Optimizing Program Quality and Programmer Productivity," Guide 45, *Proceedings,* Atlanta, GA, November 1977.

7. T. C. Jones, "A Survey of Programming Design and Specification Techniques," IEEE Symposium on Specifications of Reliable Software, April 1979 (IEEE Order No. 79 CH1401-9C).

8. J. Martin, *Managing the Data Base Environment,* Prentice–Hall, Inc., Englewood Cliffs, NJ, 1983.

9. M. Hamilton and S. Zeldin, "Higher Order Software—A Methodology for Defining Software," *IEEE Transactions on Software Engineering,* Vol. SE-2, No. 1, March 1976.

Chapter 11

1. R. Hackler, *An HOS View of ASAS,* Technique Report 32, Higher Order Software, Inc., December 1981.

2. M. Alford, "A Requirements Engineering Methodology for Real-Time Processing Requirements," *IEEE Transactions on Software Engineering,* Vol. SE-3, No. 1, 1977.

3. SofTech, Inc., *Integrated Computer Aided Manufacturing* (ICAM), Waltham, MA, 1978.

4. SofTech, Inc., *Architect's Manual: ICAM Definition Method (Version 0 and Version 1)* (IDEF), Waltham, MA, 1979.

5. *Computable IDEF,* a series of reports prepared for the Air Force Systems Command, Wright-Patterson Air Force Base, Ohio, by Higher Order Software, Inc., Cambridge, MA 1978–1982.

6. *Computable IDEF Preliminary Design,* Higher Order Software, Inc., Cambridge, MA, 1982.

7. J. Martin, *Strategic Data-Planning Methodologies,* Prentice-Hall, Inc., Englewood Cliffs, NJ, 1982.

8. F. P. Brooks, Jr., *The Mythical Man-Month; Essays on Software Engineering,* Addison-Wesley Publishing Co., Inc., Reading, MA, 1974.

Chapter 12

1. Headquarters, Department of the Army, USA (HQDA), letter DAMO-RQ, November 3, 1977, subject: "Interface Requirements."

2. Headquarters, Department of the Army, USA (HQDA), requirements definition for an "Army Battlefield Interface Concept" (ABIC), November 1977.

3. J. Martin, *Design and Strategy for Distributed Processing,* Prentice-Hall, Inc., Englewood Cliffs, NJ, 1981.

4. J. Martin, *Computer Networks and Distributed Processing: Software, Techniques, and Architecture,* Prentice-Hall, Inc., Englewood Cliffs, NJ, 1981.

Chapter 14

1. The author is indebted to John Hope, who works with James Martin Associates, for this word. Hope is a world authority on development divorced from reality and how to prevent it.

2. H. Kahn, *World Economic Development,* Westview Press, Inc., Boulder, CO, 1979.

Chapter 15

1. K. Fuchi, "Aiming for Knowledge Information Processing Systems," in *Fifth Generation Computer Systems* (Proceedings of the International Conference, Tokyo), North-Holland Publishing Company, Amsterdam, 1982.

2. T. Moto-Oka et al., Keynote Speech, in *Fifth Generation Computer Systems* (Proceedings of the International Conference, Tokyo), North-Holland Publishing Company, Amsterdam, 1982.

3. E. H. Shortliffe, *Computer-Based Medical Consultations: MYCIN,* American Elsevier Publishing Company, Inc., New York, 1976.

4. M. Dincbus, "A Knowledge-Based Expert System for Automatic Analysis and Synthesis in CAD," IFIP Congress 80, *Proceedings,* 1980.

5. H. Karatsu, "What Is Required for the Fifth Generation Computer—Social Needs and Its Impact," in *Fifth Generation Computer Systems* (Proceedings of the International Conference, Tokyo), North-Holland Publishing Company, Amsterdam, 1982.

Chapter 16

1. *A Strategy for Information Technology,* report to the British National Enterprise Board by PACTEL, 1981.

2. *A Programme for Advanced Information Technology,* The Report of the Alvey Committee, Her Majesty's Stationery Office, London, 1982.

3. T. Moto-Oka et al., Keynote Speech, in *Fifth Generation Computer Systems* (Proceedings of the International Conference, Tokyo), North-Holland Publishing Company, Amsterdam, 1982.

4. T. Peters and R. Waterman, *In Search of Excellence,* Harper & Row Publishers, New York, 1982.

5. "Five Ways to Go Bust," *The Economist,* January 8, 1982.

Chapter 17

1. E. W. Dijkstra, *A Discipline of Programming,* Prentice-Hall, Inc., Englewood Cliffs, NJ, 1976.

2. F. P. Brooks, Jr., *The Mythical Man-Month: Essays on Software Engineering,* Addison-Wesley Publishing Co., Inc., Reading, MA, 1974.

3. N. Wiener, *The Human Use of Human Beings,* The MIT Press, Cambridge, MA, 1950.

4. C. A. R. Hoare, "The Engineering of Software: A Startling Contradiction," *Computer Bulletin,* British Computer Society, December 1975.

5. K. Fuchi, "Aiming for Knowledge Information Processing Systems," in *Fifth Generation Computer Systems* (Proceedings of the International Conference, Tokyo), North-Holland Publishing Company, Amsterdam, 1982.

6. G. A. Miller, "The Magical Number Seven, Plus or Minus Two: Some Limits on Our Capacity for Information Processing," *Psychological Review,* Vol. 63, No. 2, March 1956.

7. T. Moto-Oka et al., Keynote Speech, in *Fifth Generation Computer Systems* (Proceedings of the International Conference, Tokyo), North-Holland Publishing Company, Amsterdam, 1982.

INDEX